DON'T CALL ME PRINCESS

ALSO BY PEGGY ORENSTEIN

Girls & Sex: Navigating the Complicated New Landscape

Cinderella Ate My Daughter: Dispatches from the Front Lines of the New Girlie-Girl Culture

Waiting for Daisy: A Tale of Two Continents, Three Religions, Five Infertility Doctors, an Oscar, an Atomic Bomb, a Romantic Night, and One Woman's Quest to Become a Mother

Flux: Women on Sex, Work, Love, Kids, and Life in a Half-Changed World

Schoolgirls: Young Women, Self Esteem, and the Confidence Gap

DON'T CALL ME PRINCESS

ESSAYS ON GIRLS, WOMEN, SEX, AND LIFE

PEGGY ORENSTEIN

HARPER

An Imprint of HarperCollinsPublishers

HarperCollins books may be purchased for educational, business, or sales promotional use. For information, please email the Special Markets Department at SPsales@harpercollins.com.

FIRST EDITION

Designed by Jamie Lynn Kerner

Library of Congress Cataloging-in-Publication Data has been applied for.

ISBN 978-0-06-268890-3 (pbk.)

ISBN 978-0-06-283405-8 (library edition)

18 19 20 21 22 LSC 10 9 8 7 6 5 4 3 2 1

For Steven, a prince of a guy

CONTENTS

PART 3: NOT YOUR MAMA'S MOTHERHOOD

PART 4: GIRLS! GIRLS! GIRLS! (AND ONE ABOUT BOYS)

INTRODUCTION: TWO GIRLS IN A ROOM

WHEN I WAS SEVENTEEN YEARS OLD, A SENIOR AT ST. LOUIS Park High School in Minnesota, I was summoned to the counselor's office. Ms. Peckham, a middle-aged woman with bronze-tinted hair and thick, plastic-rimmed glasses, was, to me, the essence of clueless adulthood. So I was shocked when she asked me to write a story for the school newspaper on students who were teen mothers. It never occurred to me that one of my peers might have a baby, though given that there were twenty-eight hundred of us, maybe it should have. Truthfully, I didn't even know kids my age were having sex.

A couple of days later, I met with another twelfth grader, a girl I'd never seen before, in an empty classroom. She told me about life with her two-year-old daughter, the secrecy, hardship, and shame. Her mom babysat during the day while the girl was at school or working at a minimum wage job. She didn't go to parties. She didn't go on dates. She didn't have many friends. Hardly anyone knew about her double life. It was brave of her to trust me with her story: I promised I wouldn't use her real name in the article, and, what's more, I'd never reveal it to anyone, not ever.

When we were finished, she thanked me for listening. "But if you see me around," she added, still smiling, "please don't say hi. There's no reason that someone like you would know someone like me. And I don't want anyone to ask questions." Then she left the room, disappearing into the crowded hallway.

This wasn't, I realized, simply a cautionary tale about the perils of teenage sex. It was the story of the two of us, girls who, through choice or chance, were on very different paths. Even more, it was about how class, status, and stigma limited the new opportunities of girlhood, about how far women had come, and how far we still had to go.

That was, I think, the moment I became a writer: the moment I recognized the power of individuals' stories to illuminate something universal, something essential about our time. Nearly forty years later, the stories I'm most drawn to telling are still about women. I came of age in the turbulent wake of feminism's second wave; education, work, relationships, parenting, sexuality—all had been abruptly transformed. What could be more compelling than documenting the impact of that? When I'm honest, though, I have to admit that I was pushed into my subject matter as much as pulled toward it, that constraint played as much a role as interest. I graduated college eight years before Anita Hill would bring sexual harassment out of the shadows—over three decades before allegations against producer Harvey Weinstein would set off a tsunami of #metoo activism. So, when during an interview for my first job, as a typist at *Esquire* magazine, I was told that one editor had a penchant for rubbing up against young female staffers, and asked could I "handle" that, of course I assured them I could. I kept at least six feet away from the guy for the next three years, but there were also editors there, men as well as women, who championed me, mentored me, and encouraged me to stop typing other writers' manuscripts and get to work on my own.

With a few exceptions, female writers at the time (not to mention the entire category of women's magazines) were tacitly, and sometimes explicitly, considered lesser than the guys—less talented, less prestigious, and, of course, lower paid. Writing about women, particularly for publications that weren't specifically geared toward them, meant I avoided direct competition with men while creating a distinctive niche, if one that was sometimes seen as token. And it was a pretty sweet beat: after all, women are nearly fifty-one percent of the world's population. Since we tend to be seen as female first—*women* directors, *women* executives, *women* politicians—I gained entree into worlds I might otherwise never have seen.

Being a feminist writer, though, does not just involve *whom* I write about. It's about *how* I write: my stance relative to the reader, a skepticism about hierarchy and expertise. I generally reject authority in authorship, positioning myself as the readers' companion rather than superior: asking questions, expressing doubts, working my ideas out on the page. I want to share the journey, not just present tidy conclusions. Similarly, I decided early on that if I was willing to hold other women's lives and decisions up to scrutiny I had better be willing to do the same with my own: if every woman's life tells a story, mine would, too. Reviewers have sometimes referred to my first-person work as "honest," especially my essays on infertility and cancer. I'm pretty sure that's meant to be a compliment, but I sometimes suspect it may be code for TMI. The truth is, I don't know how to write any other way. Observing my own experience, documenting my successes and missteps as a modern mother, wife, woman, worker, human, is how I make meaning for myself and, ideally, for others; it is also how I hope to galvanize change and progress.

I'm a little stunned to find I have a body of work to look back on: time seems to have skittered by while I focused on the day-to-day stuff of working; falling in love; building a marriage; struggling to have a child and then raising her. Yet, I don't feel ever so far from the girl reporter at the high school newspaper.

I'm not sure how far the world has come, either. Progress seems more a spiral than a straight line, though I have faith that it moves mainly, if not consistently, in a positive direction. If I didn't, I wouldn't bother writing. Nonetheless, I'm struck by how many stories from years ago resonate now, at this moment when women's political, social, economic, and reproductive rights are newly under threat.

I don't know how these latest battles will resolve, but I do know this: telling our stories is more important than ever. Not the endless churn of "content" featuring trumped-up princesses and pop stars and famous-for-being-famous social media creations, but *real* stories about *real* women, including women of color, queer women, immigrants, the poor, the very old, and the very young. There can never be enough stories.

As for the teen mother I wrote about so long ago: I don't know what happened to her. I no longer remember her name. I've even lost the article I wrote, left it behind in some old apartment in some other city. But I still think of her courage regularly, with gratitude; and I have never forgotten what she taught me.

—Peggy Orenstein, August 2017

PART 1

STARLETS, SCIENTISTS, ARTISTS, ACTIVISTS
& OTHER NOTEWORTHY WOMEN

ATSUKO CHIBA: THE NONCONFORMIST

I was twenty-six years old, living in New York City mostly writing pithy pieces on shopping or Hollywood gossip when Betsy Carter, the editor of New York Woman magazine, called me into her office. She handed me Atsuko Chiba's New York Times obituary and said, "I want you to write a posthumous profile of this woman." I knew nothing about Chiba, nothing about her illness, nothing about Japan. I had never even written a magazine feature: I have no idea why Carter thought I should write this one.

And yet, I'm amazed (and a little freaked out) by the way this piece, which came out in March 1989, predicts the themes of my own life: I had moved to California by the time it was published, where I would soon meet and marry my husband, who is Japanese American; I would end up spending extensive time in Japan, and eventually, inspired by my own medical crisis there, write a taboo-breaking piece about women's health—in my case, on miscarriage; like Chiba, I, too, would develop breast cancer at an unusually young age, turning to my work,

*much as she did, as a source of solace, understanding,
and activism.*

Atsuko Chiba came to New York to die. It was 1983, and
the cancer that had taken her left breast two years
earlier—the cancer that had made her notorious as the first
Japanese journalist to write candidly about the disease—had
settled in a lymph node at the base of her neck. Ever since her
stint as a Nieman Fellow at Harvard University in 1968, Chiba
had dreamed of returning to the States to try her hand as a
freelancer. But more to the point was this: "No matter what
happens," she said to her friends, "I don't want to die in Japan."

Death in Japan is no more ignominious than in other
countries, but dying of cancer is. Cancer has long been a taboo topic in Japan; patients are rarely given details about their
treatment, and doctors often avoid the terminally ill. So Chiba
sold her furniture, donated her books to a library, packed up a
favorite silk dress from childhood and the one being she was
dependent upon—a Siamese cat named Be-be—and headed for
a new life at One Astor Place.

From the moment her plane landed at JFK until July 1987,
when she died at the age of forty-six, Chiba devoted herself to
encouraging change in her native country. In two weekly columns, "Preparing for Death" and "Living with Cancer," and
in thirteen books written over the course of three years, she
offered a running commentary on the American and Japanese
medical establishments. She wrote every day, even when her
life was reduced to a three-week cycle of chemotherapy. Some
days she wrote while vomiting continually into a paper bag.
She wrote of life in New York, of the theater, of politics and

soirees. Mostly she wrote of herself: "Not once have I shed tears in connection with my sickness," she wrote. "I have no time to be immersed in sentiments; I am only thinking about how to use the time left meaningfully. . . . I don't see my cancer as a particularly tragic event. My life up to now, although there have been tough times too, is filled with wonderful memories."

There is an aphorism in Japan: "The nail that sticks out gets hammered down." Atsuko Chiba stuck out. She stuck way out and waved her arms. In a society where individuality—especially in women—is squelched early on, Chiba flaunted her mind, her body, and her spirit. She challenged the relegation of female journalists to newspapers' society pages and became the first female economics reporter for a major Japanese newspaper. She took the victory with grace and irony: sure, she would cover the stock market as well as anyone, but she'd do it in a short, tight dress.

Chiba was, in a way, the epitome of an American career woman carried to the extreme. Her work was her compulsion: two days before she died, while passing out from pain, she was cabling the *Asahi Shimbun* in Tokyo, assuring her editors she'd meet her deadline. Yet there were those see-through blouses she wore to press conferences at the Ministry of Finance. Provocative clothes on the job aren't exactly commonplace in Japanese society. Neither is sexual freedom. Mutsuko Murakami, Atsuko's closest Japanese friend, says she was shocked when, during the two journalists' first evening together, Chiba pulled out a magazine clip that quoted her as saying, "I believe in freedom in sexual relations and am carrying out my beliefs." Murakami remembers that Chiba thought, "one boyfriend should not last more than three months."

Chiba's reaction, on Christmas Eve 1980, when she found a lump in her left breast that she correctly sensed was malignant, was, as her friends say, "typically Atsuko-like." That very evening she began jotting down ideas for a book. "I thought of this as an assignment," she said. "To lose a part of my body and to write about it as objectively as possible."

In late January, a day or two before she entered the hospital for a mastectomy, Chiba had snapshots taken of her nude from the waist up. The pictures show a beautifully formed woman with sharp, unflinching eyes, pointing to a barely visible malignancy. In those eyes you can read the phrase that became the title of her book: *Breast Cancer Can't Defeat Me.* Seventeen days later, when she left the hospital, the book was nearly completed. Chiba discovered that she was the only woman on her ward who had even been told that she had cancer, and only then because she forced the issue. Doctors hid the truth, concerned that if a patient knew she had cancer she'd stop fighting or, worse yet, use it as an excuse to commit unethical acts.

Breast Cancer Can't Defeat Me eventually included controversial chapters on how Chiba's lovers dealt with her mastectomy. Even more scandalous was her choice for the cover: one of her topless snapshots. To advertise the book her publisher blew the cover up to poster size and plastered it all over the Tokyo subways. An American colleague, then *Wall Street Journal* Tokyo bureau chief Mike Tharp, saw one of the posters on his way to meet Chiba and ripped it down. When he asked her for an autograph, she smiled and signed proudly. "It was pretty dramatic, that cover, but that was just the way Atsuko was," Tharp remembers. "She believed in it, and she knew she had to take the heat as well as any of the glamour."

Her ability to suffer for the strength of her convictions

may well have been a legacy from her parents. Chiba was born in Shanghai in 1941, the eldest of four sisters. Her father was a Communist activist jailed in his youth up to eight years at a time, but Chiba had little knowledge of his past until her junior year at college, when she learned about it in his eulogy. Her mother was also an activist, whom Atsuko would invoke during her own ordeal: "In 1932, at the age of seventeen, my mother was tortured by two police officers . . ." Chiba wrote. "She was stripped naked and hung upside down while the police pulled her legs. Just by imagining the scene, I realize that my present suffering is nothing compared with what my mother went through."

Chiba seems never to have questioned why her parents hid their activism from her or why they neither encouraged their daughters to lead a traditional life nor discouraged them from becoming enchanted with Western ways. After her father's death, as she became increasingly worldly and independent, Chiba distanced herself from her more traditional mother and sisters. She hated falling prey to anyone's expectations. She chose an unlikely major—economics—at Gakushuin University, one of Japan's top schools.

Although Chiba knew she was just as capable as the men in her classes, when it came time to parade her credentials before prospective employers, she was bitterly disappointed. No one in Tokyo would hire her. Eventually she landed a job as a society reporter for *Tokyo Shimbun*. She soon muscled her way onto the economics beat, where she was given the toughest assignments—like covering the rice market—in the hope that she would become discouraged and quit. In the end she did quit, but not for the reasons her bosses had hoped: she left to take the prestigious Nieman Fellowship.

By the mid-seventies, Chiba was firmly entrenched as a freelancer, snagging stories for the Asian *Wall Street Journal*, *Forbes*, and *Institutional Investor*. Even so, being taken seriously on a turf so heavily dominated by men was a constant struggle. In a piece eulogizing her, Gilbert E. Kaplan, editor in chief of *Institutional Investor*, remembers Chiba's first encounter with a particular source. "She joined me for a breakfast with the head of a major corporation," Kaplan wrote. "He spoke only to me, bragging about his firm, and never once included her in the conversation. Finally Chiba chimed in with a technical question about why one of his financial ratios had been down three years in a row. From that point on, she was an integral part of the discussion, and the executive also became one of her best sources."

In Tokyo, Chiba became famous during her off-hours for her weekly parties: she hosted a revolving salon of novelists, artists, bankers, bureaucrats, and radical feminists. "She would throw us together in this small physical situation and let us mix and mingle," Tharp recalls. "One of the neatest things was the way the Japanese men dealt with her. It was not unusual, for example, to see the director of the Economic Planning Agency get all the plates when people were finished eating and do the dishes."

When dawn broke and the inevitable Scrabble game ended, Chiba preferred to spend time alone. The three-month rule, the freelance lifestyle, the increasing distance from her family—these were marks of a person whose greatest luxury was solitude. "Because I have been living on my own," she explained, "I . . . would work and play at my own pace and have the kind of relationships with men best suited to me." The esteem in which she held independence allowed her to leave her home, her friends, and her family to take a chance on moving 14,500 miles to an uncertain future in New York.

During her four years in New York, Chiba fought hard to stay productive and independent. "She was like a little general," says a friend. She refused, even when dangerously ill, to accept unsolicited help. Her studio on Astor Place had a loft bed. One day Dolores Langone, Chiba's closest friend in the city, asked her why she continued to make the climb each night. "She got really angry," Langone remembers. "She said, 'Don't you ever ask me that again. That is the way I want to do it. And I *can* do it.'"

The sicker Chiba got, the more prolific she became: columns on cancer, a newsletter for Japanese career women, and, of course, the amazing number of books that rolled out of her word processor. One volume detailed life in New York: "I am not feeling very well, but I decided to go to the Museum of Modern Art, which was having a press preview of the Paul Klee exhibit. I was taken by an acute sense of joy the minute I entered the exhibit hall." Another volume was on the idiosyncracies of the Japanese; a third was an advice manual, *New Woman*, offering helpful hints for the emerging Japanese career woman, tempered with Chiba's penchant for organization. "When I buy a skirt," she wrote, "I go straight to the hosiery department and buy about six [pairs of] stockings in the same color."

Organization is a corollary of control, and as Chiba's days became more uncertain, control became an all-important issue—not just in determining how and with whom she would spend her time, but in her fight to triumph over her disease. When she had to start a course of chemotherapy, she marched into a barbershop and had her head shaved.

"Why did you do that, Atsuko?" Langone asked. "It's going to fall out anyway."

"Yes," Chiba answered, "but this way I control it."

Despite the strength of her will, Chiba could not staunch the flow of her illness, and certain losses were difficult to bear. In November 1986, her voice became a husky rasp. "I had lost one breast from a mastectomy and at one point lost all my hair from anti-cancer drugs," she wrote in that week's "Preparing for Death" installment. "However, those losses were nothing compared to the loss of my voice. My voice, my manner of speech, my vocabulary, my intonation—these were all-important means to express who I am. . . . I imagine that I will experience one kind of death after another and that the accumulation of deaths will eventually lead me to the final death. I must mourn each death to my heart's content, for behind each death is the preceding bright life that existed."

For the first time she seemed to come to terms with her family, with whom she'd fought both in person and in print. Her mother had battled stomach cancer for fifteen years, experimenting with any treatment she came across—much to Chiba's dismay. But despite their differences, Atsuko admired her mother: "[She] thinks it's most natural for me to be working, even if I am seriously ill," wrote Chiba. "The truth is that I am still upset about my loss and am encouraged by my mother's positive attitude. . . . I told my mother that there was no longer a . . . cure for me. She started, 'I know you will get upset, but in Osaka, a patient who'd been told that there was no hope had . . .' I had to intervene with the little voice left to me. I cannot tolerate . . . illogical arguments. Fortunately we did not have to hang up in a quarrel. The truth is that I love my mother deeply and trust her completely."

There was never a weakening of her spirit. Chiba seemed invulnerable. Part of that was simply a matter of the barriers she had put up. She continued to see many people—Norman Pearlstine (good friend and managing editor for the *Wall Street Journal*), Langone, Angela Santoro (her first roommate in New York), Fred Jaffe (her neighbor on Astor Place)—but confided in none of them. Jaffe was surprised to find out that he'd made a number of appearances in her column. "She never said she had written about me," he says. "I had no idea that any of our encounters were that important to her."

Some of Chiba's apparent invulnerability may have stemmed from a fear of slowing down. She bought books she would never read and tickets to events she might never see, planned trips she would never take. "If I don't make plans," she wrote, "that's . . . the same as dying." Chiba seriously looked into moving to Moscow to try her hand as a correspondent there. She was always hopeful a drug might be found that would offer reprieve. But the miracle didn't happen; in the last few months, as the pain became all-encompassing and the good days began to dwindle, a sense of discouragement began to invade Chiba's columns. "I wonder if I have not reached the end of my endurance," she wrote in April 1987. "Is there still a meaning to keep on living under such pain? If it would ease the pain, I feel I am almost ready to make a declaration of surrender. If I stop the treatment now, the cancer that has become smaller will once again grow. But now I do not even have one day of relief from this pain. . . . If I were given one comfortable day where there would be no pain and nausea . . . I would like to walk around the city and have three delicious meals, and I would be content to die that night."

It was Langone who commanded her to enter the hospital on July 7. She was in terrible pain, and Langone sat with her in her apartment, rubbing her back. Afterward, Chiba sat up, and as Langone walked away, she caught a glimpse of Chiba's body going down. Langone grabbed her before she hit the ground. "Atsuko," Langone said, "I'm not asking you anything from now on; I'm taking over. Do you know what just happened?"

"No," Chiba replied. "What happened?"

"You passed out, and I don't want to be here if you're going to pass out forever. I'm calling an ambulance." Chiba argued, saying she could walk downstairs and take a taxi, but Langone held firm. When Chiba started to faint again, Langone called the paramedics. Atsuko Chiba died two days later, on July 9, 1987.

Langone wonders if Chiba simply decided that she'd had enough. The doctors had not expected her to die for quite some time. Maybe Chiba won her battle with the disease by choosing to throw in the towel. Her last night in the hospital she began talking about death with Langone's husband. "John asked her very directly if she was scared," Langone remembers, "and Atsuko said, 'No, I am not afraid. I've done everything that I've ever wanted to do.' He was a basket case, crying at her bedside, and she said, 'Relax, John, everything's going to be all right.'"

The Tokyo newspapers ran front-page obituaries, which made Mutsuko Murakami both angry and proud. "I resented that if the newspapers were willing to give this kind of space for her, they could have given her a lot of opportunity while she was alive," she says. Sales of Chiba's books increased, and Murakami is somewhat bitter about that, too. But every yen the books bring in will go toward Chiba's last request: an annual award for excellence in reporting by a non-Japanese

Asian journalist. ("The Japanese have enough money," Chiba once explained.)

Chiba further stipulated that no funeral be held for her. Instead, Murakami and a few other friends organized "A Meeting to Think About Death and Life in Memory of Atsuko Chiba" (to take place in the same Tokyo auditorium where, a year earlier, in a voice rattling with disease, Chiba had given her final public lecture: "Dying Well Is Living Well"). The auditorium had a capacity of eight hundred, and Murakami worried that it was too large. She notified the publications in which Chiba's columns appeared and sent out a general media alert in hopes of reaching those who had followed Chiba's journey through her books and columns.

When the day finally came, a thousand people packed the hall, overflowing into the aisles, out the doors, sitting two to a seat: friends, family, other journalists, young women for whom Chiba had been a model, cancer patients who—thanks to Chiba—had the courage to demand more from their doctors. They listened to speakers on death and dying, to a tape of Chiba's last speech, to messages from her friends in New York. And they listened to Fumiko Chiba, Atsuko's mother, speak in a high, thin voice about outliving her forty-six-year-old daughter. "People say, 'You must be very depressed that Atsuko passed away,'" she said. "I am not only sad but feeling very satisfied because Atsuko completed her life the way she wanted to and the way her mother could be proud of her."

That was why the thousand came together. To mourn perhaps, but more to celebrate a woman who resolutely lived the life she desired and who, finally, died as she chose—deliberately, without fear, and as she once said she hoped: "writing . . . until the end."

GLORIA STEINEM AND ROBIN MORGAN: *MS.* FIGHTS FOR ITS LIFE

I first met Gloria Steinem and Robin Morgan my junior year of college while working as an intern at Ms. Revisiting this piece, I feel I was a little impatient with them, perhaps in the way that the younger generation can be when rebelling against its elders. In truth, I deeply admire both women: for their work as well as their personal generosity toward me. This piece, which was published in November 1990, also offers a glimpse into the economics and the sexism of the traditional magazine industry, both of which, for better and for worse, have been challenged by the rise of the internet. Magazines have struggled in the new era; feminism has thrived, though so has its inverse. Finally, as my first foray into writing about girlhood this story would lead me, a year later, to begin my book Schoolgirls.

WAS ELEVEN WHEN TIBETHA SHAW SHOWED ME MY FIRST COPY OF *Ms.* magazine. Tibetha had untamed orange hair and was the only girl in the sixth grade of Minneapolis's John Burroughs Elementary School who wore black all the time. Her mother, unlike the mothers of the rest of my friends, worked outside the home and had an apron emblazoned diagonally with three-inch-high white capital letters that said HOUSE-WORK IS BULLSHIT, which Tibetha proudly showed me the first time she invited me over to play. I don't think I ever met the exotic woman who probably would have insisted on being called Ms. Shaw. And I don't recall hearing anything about Tibetha's father. In retrospect, I imagine her parents may have been divorced. At that time, in our idyllic Midwestern community, separation was still something you did to remove the yolks from the whites of eggs; it would be a good two or three years before my classmates' families would begin exploding around us.

My own mother subscribed to *Redbook*, *Good Housekeeping*, and *Ladies' Home Journal*. She welcomed me home from school each day with freshly baked treats and milk. At Tibetha's, there was no adult supervision. There was dust on the furniture. There was *Ms.* We ate Oreos and pored over the magazine, not quite understanding the anger, but grooving on the energy.

Ms. had resurrected Wonder Woman, the Amazon Princess from Paradise Island, aka Themyscira, who parried bullets with her steel bracelets and brought pernicious forces of evil to their knees with her magic golden lasso. Inspired by her, we fastened towels around our necks with clothespins and climbed onto the roof of the Shaws' garage. The houses on Lyndale Avenue were close together, and the distance between the pointed garage roofs was slightly longer than a leggy eleven-year-old's stride. Yet we took deep breaths and leapt—screaming, "Wonder Woman! Wonder Woman!"—flying from roof to roof and back again, towel capes streaming out behind us, buoyed up by exhilaration, discovery, and danger.

In the dead center of Times Square, there is a building wrapped by the world-famous news zipper, a building suspended over endless subway catacombs and topped by the glowing ball that drops on New Year's Eve to the strains of Guy Lombardo. As I walk in to the ground floor, a young, female Bible-thumper looks me dead in the eyes and screams that I'm going straight to hell for unbridled forn-i-cation and for murdering babies through abortion. When I ride up to the eighteenth floor and enter the soothing pink and mauve décor of the Ms. offices, Gloria Steinem is waiting, with a different kind of damnation on her mind.

"I read thirty women's magazines recently and it was very depressing how little they'd changed," she says, in her ever-modulated, always polite tone of voice. "There was the occasional piece on domestic violence—unillustrated—or a survey of readers' opinions on abortion, which is carefully equivocal. . . . Today a writer called me because she was doing a serious article about what women think of the fact that a lot of women are allowing their bra straps to show out on the street. I told her to please quote me exactly and said, 'I think women should be able to wear anything they fucking well please.'"

That was precisely the attitude that led to the founding of Ms.

The story of Ms.'s first issue, launched as a supplement to 1971's year-end issue of New York magazine, is the stuff of Andy Hardy movies: A group of women meeting in living rooms around New York City wanted to create a publication in which readers could find information on the women's movement without joining any organization. Someone suggested a newsletter. "No, no," said Brenda Feigen, an officer of NOW. "Let's start a magazine!"

The women envisioned a publication that would be both slick and beautiful, one that would appeal to newsstand browsers who didn't necessarily identify themselves as feminists. But when a group led by the already famous Steinem went looking for backers, everyone they approached laughed.

"We had the impossible condition that women control the magazine," says Steinem. "There are still no women controlling women's magazines financially. It was only because Clay Felker, for whom I'd been working as a political columnist, needed a theme for his year-end double issue that it happened. He wouldn't pay our salaries, but he said he'd pay for the costs of producing one sample magazine if he could pick from it whatever he wanted for his own magazine."

Three hundred thousand copies of the first bona fide issue of *Ms.* shipped to newsstands in January 1972. Steinem began a cross-country promotional tour, but in every city, she encountered complaining crowds. "People came up to her and said they couldn't find the magazine anywhere," says Joanne Edgar, the magazine's de facto managing editor from the pilot issue until the spring of 1989. "She'd call Clay and say, 'It's not here! Get on the distributors!' It turned out that all three hundred thousand copies sold out in ten days. We got thirty thousand subscribers from that one issue."

Steinem went trolling for backers again, and this time no one snickered. She raised a million dollars, which *Ms.* needed to begin monthly publication, from Warner Communications.

During those early years, the pages of *Ms.* were consumed by revelation, by the simple act of naming: pay equity, maternity leave, wife battering, date rape, sexual harassment. If contributors to *Ms.* found an exuberant power in diagnosis, the magazine's readers found strength—and relief—in being diagnosed. The letters section of *Ms.*, significantly longer than those of other magazines, showed the publication's effect most directly (and voyeuristically). Readers talked to each other in the pages of *Ms.*: chords were struck, confessions proffered, anger vented. By the end of 1973, the magazine received two hundred personal letters a day, most of them as powerful as this one, written anonymously, in December of that year:

I am writing this on a day when I could not possibly feel any greater depression, alienation or isolation. I am writing to you because I have no one, male or female, to talk to who will not try to push, cajole, threaten, even beg me into accepting my "proper" role and "duties" as a housewife and mother. . . . I had been losing courage and had started to believe there was really something wrong with me, until I began to receive your magazine. It has been literally a "lifesaver."

The feverish new swirl of ad hoc political groups also took *Ms.*'s politics personally. Feminist activists dropped by the Lexington Avenue offices to offer up advice and critique what they viewed as their magazine. "Housewives came and said we weren't doing enough on homemaker issues," says writer and editor Letty Cottin Pogrebin. "Lesbians came by, younger women, women of color. In those days, people really made their feelings known. And we heard them out."

As the seventies rolled on, though, the myriad concerns of the women's movement became difficult to contain in a one-hundred-page magazine. Women channeled their energies into specific issues—reproductive rights, lesbian rights, crisis intervention—and they bumped against their differences. Antiporn and pro-sex feminists squared off, women of color felt shunted aside by white feminists, rural women were bulldozed by urban professionals. Diagnosis was no longer enough. *Ms.* had to change with the political culture, to try to address the diversity of its constituents as well as their sophistication and occasional disillusionment.

"In the early seventies, we were riding on this rainbow of enthusiasm," says Edgar. "We thought if you just explained the injustice of discrimination, it would go away, because everyone would see it's not nice to discriminate against women. We were naive, to say the least."

AS STUDENTS IN ONE OF THE MOST LIBERAL OF LIBERAL-ARTS COLleges in the early eighties, concerned about sexism in the classroom and the curriculum, militant about Taking Back the Night, and obsessed with the quest for better access to contraception and abortion, my friends and I had numerous dinner-table disputes over whether to call ourselves "feminists." We weren't interested in labels of any kind, we said, let alone one that an older generation had already freighted with such finger-wagging, beleaguered connotations.

We weren't alone in our ambivalence. Ten years after *Ms.* began, Ronald Reagan had been elected president and the country seemed to be hurtling backward. Membership in the National Organization for Women began a descent, which was to last until the decade's end. For us as young women, the early successes of the women's movement—particularly in employment and discrimination battles—made it less likely that we would rebel in the same way as our elders. Instead of feeling indebted to or proud of feminism, we saw in it the threat of permanent marginalization (Would we have successful relationships with individual men if we hated them as a group? Was the commitment to feminism irrevocable and intractable?). In a sense, the women's movement had provided us with the luxury of inaction, of splitting hairs over semantics.

Feeling assured, however naively, of success and equal treatment in the "real world," I was impatient with *Ms.*'s Horatio Alger–like tales of (women's) triumphs against all (male) odds. With fewer real victories to report, and an acute fear of revealing divisions within the movement to a voraciously hostile outside world, *Ms.* fell into a pattern: it continued to remind its readers that the same old inequities were still the same old inequities, and it found smaller, individual victories to exult in, victories that often seemed sugar-coated.

"My husband used to leaf through *Ms.* and say, 'This is a cheering squad for women,'" says feminist writer and occasional *Ms.* contributor Katha Pollitt. "'They'd write a positive article about any woman who was doing anything, regardless of whether it was interesting.' And I'd say, 'Well, there's a place for that. It's like how our grandparents were always thrilled when a Jew did things.' Part of it is opening new roles.

"But it's true that they didn't like to run unfavorable book reviews. And they bought into this women-are-better line. I remember when Sandra Day O'Connor was appointed—they ran this piece about how she was going to be better because, as a woman, she'd be more this and less that. Maybe she's not as bad as Rehnquist, but she's pretty much a standard Reaganite figure who has not done great things for women. They were a little gullible because they wanted to be optimistic."

"I remember feeling, when we were celebrating women coal miners, that we were celebrating black lung and we should think about that," says Pogrebin. "Just because you got a piece of the pie doesn't mean the pie wasn't full of worms. But the counterargument was that women wanted these jobs and they're proud of themselves and if they want to take this chance, they have a right to take it. As much as it bothers me, it's a point of view. You can't be a purist in support of women."

MS. MAY HAVE BEEN FLAWED, BUT IT WAS THE ONLY WOMEN'S MAGAzine that showcased intelligence, placed some premium on substance over style, and tried consistently to push independent voices into the mass market. I wanted to be one of those voices. So I leapt at the chance in 1982 to leave the flatlands of Ohio to take an internship at *Ms.*, working for then–contributing editor Robin Morgan on *Sisterhood Is Global*, an anthology of women's writings worldwide.

When I arrived in New York, the magazine was financially imperiled. Paper and postage costs (the most expensive aspects of magazine production) had skyrocketed. In desperation, Steinem and publisher Pat Carbine had turned *Ms.* into a tax-exempt, nonprofit organization in 1979. Although the move prevented *Ms.* from continuing to rate and endorse political candidates, the postage break alone saved hundreds of thousands of dollars a year, and under the auspices of the Ms. Foundation for Education and Communication, Steinem could raise funds more aggressively.

I spent nine months hovering on the periphery of the

magazine, doing part-time fact-checking work to support myself while I plumbed statistics on policies and practices of eighty countries on contraception, abortion, violence against women, family law, labor law, suffrage, and women's history, in research for Morgan's book. The editors, for the most part, were warm and friendly; I admired the genuine financial and emotional sacrifices they'd made to keep their magazine and movement alive. I was starstruck by conversations in which Andrea Dworkin apprised Gloria Steinem of her encounters with William F. Buckley Jr., while, nearby, Robin Morgan chatted on the phone with Kate Millett. But because of the enormous injustice I was uncovering in my research, I was also going through a process of discovery, a politicization that I felt these women were well beyond.

When I returned to college, I read Mary Daly, Susan Brownmiller, Susan Griffin, Kathleen Barry, Audre Lorde, and Nawal El Saadawi. I read everything I could get my hands on. But I still only skimmed *Ms.* for an occasional news flash, even though I wanted badly to return to the magazine after graduation. Now an ardent feminist committed to the idea of writing about women in a political way, I couldn't imagine where else I would work. *Redbook? Vogue?* Middle-class, middle-management slicks like *Savvy* and *Working Woman?* I began to understand why most of the editors of *Ms.* had remained entrenched there for ten years; *Ms.* was a beachhead in a war to change cultural patterns, but the invading army still hadn't gotten past the sand.

Unable to find a niche at *Ms.*, where every would-be feminist journalist in America applied for a job each year, and unwilling to give up the dream of working at a glossy magazine, I called Robin Morgan that summer and told her I'd taken a job at *Esquire.*

"*Esquire?*" she said. "Oh, Peggy, how could you?"

I answered flatly, "I didn't have a choice."

As a young editor at *Esquire*, I quickly learned that the magazine industry is among the most cutthroat and sexist industries in the country, primarily paid for—and often dictated to—by advertisers. In spite of spiraling production costs, there were about 650 more publications on the newsstands in the mid-eighties than the mid-seventies. Most mass-market publications cut subscription rates so low that they actually lost money on them, under the assumption that the extra body count would lure advertisers in this extremely competitive market.

Many magazines weren't above promising a little extra incentive to curry advertising favor. When I was editing *Esquire*'s semiannual travel section, the magazine's advertising department regularly provided me with a list of vacation spots to cover. Readers, of course, were none the wiser. A few years later, *Vanity Fair* stood accused of running adulatory profiles of designers Ralph Lauren and Calvin Klein—two of the publication's bigger advertisers. And, according to the *Columbia Journalism Review*, *The New Yorker*, once the home of Rachel Carson and Jonathan Schell, recently toned down a piece on the history of environmentalism by former Sierra Club Books editor John G. Mitchell to satisfy the needs of a toothless Earth Day advertorial section.

These pressures are doubly fierce for magazines perceived as "political" or, in industry parlance, as "hostile editorial environments." Nothing scares off advertisers like controversy, and nothing spells controversy like politics. *Mother Jones, The Nation, Harper's,* and *The Atlantic* all rely on big-money donors or wealthy owners to supply hundreds of thousands of dollars in deficit spending each year. Without such a deep pocket, *Ms.* was increasingly at the mercy of advertisers. And advertisers rarely showed much mercy.

Steinem virtually stopped editing after the pilot issue; she and publisher Pat Carbine devoted themselves full-time to finagling more than $2 million worth of ads a year. "Some advertisers would spit on the magazine," Steinem remembers. "There was a food advertiser in California who made us take him to the world's most expensive dinner, which we could ill afford. After the meal, he threw the magazine on the table and said, 'I wouldn't advertise in this fucking piece of shit if it were the last magazine on earth.' People loved to have us make presentations with the purpose of humiliating us."

"[Prospective advertisers] took us personally," says Pogrebin. "They didn't want to buy an ad in *Ms.* because it was the reason their wives left them, or because their product showed motherhood as Madonna and child and we'd show pictures of bloody, natural birth."

Without the promise of editorial obeisance, *Ms.* didn't stand a chance of tapping into the gold mine of cosmetic and fashion ads (the fact that shilling those products in the magazine would have been somewhat antithetical to the *Ms.* message is, perhaps, a contradiction best pondered by the financially solvent). Instead, the magazine looked like it was produced for fast-driving cross-addicts: its ad pages were almost exclusively the province of cigarettes, hard liquor, and cars.

Those advertisers also had their unspoken demands. Mary

Thom, an editor of *Ms.* since its first issue, admits that the magazine went light on its coverage of women and smoking: "We tried to cover those issues when there was news—when research on fetal alcohol syndrome came out, that kind of thing. But to do a major job on addiction or on cross-addiction meant that those advertisers couldn't be in the book. So we didn't cover it in an in-depth, ongoing way."

And Steinem remembers nearly coming to blows over an offensive portrayal of Volkswagen. "There was a piece about Nazi Germany by Andrea Dworkin in which she had used 'Porsche' [which is distributed by Volkswagen]," she says. "Volkswagen doesn't interfere at all; they don't ask anything of you, unlike women's products. Except they don't want to be in a piece about Nazi Germany. It was too late to change the fact that the ad was in the issue and Porsche was in the piece. So I changed Porsche to 'expensive car.' Andrea was furious. Really, really, seriously furious. It really jeopardized our friendship. And I felt really victimized. I said, 'Andrea, you don't understand this.' I tried to explain. Now I realize she was right. But at the time, in the context—some of us weren't making salaries; we didn't know if we could meet the printing costs; we were making ends meet with contributions. This was one of the few advertisers who wouldn't interfere. . . ."

Finally, the pressure of running at a constant deficit, reducing or going without salaries, and never knowing if the next issue would be the last became too much. The Ms. Foundation began hunting for someone to buy its major asset in late 1986. "I can't even begin to express what the pressures were like," Steinem says with despair in her voice. "It was giving us all ulcers and sweaty palms. We knew that if we closed our doors, that we could wrongly be seen as damaging the women's movement. Like losing the Equal Rights Amendment. I can't tell you how terrible that feels."

Anne Summers, an Australian feminist who served for three years as chief advisor on women's issues to Australian Prime Minister Bob Hawke, had been spinning her wheels as the U.S. political correspondent for a John Fairfax, Ltd., newspaper when she heard *Ms.* was for sale. Together with Sandra Yates, who had come Stateside to launch a smart-talking publication for teenage girls, she convinced Fairfax to bid for *Ms.* The girls' magazine, they reasoned, could become the cash cow that would keep its older, prestigious sister afloat.

"Fairfax was clearly a better choice than Hearst or Condé Nast, who would've turned it into a totally conventional magazine," says Steinem now. "We would've liked to have the money to go on ourselves, but we never thought we were the only people who could do this." When the deal closed in October 1987, Summers—who, with her platinum hair and black, thick-framed, round glasses has a look as singular as Steinem's—was named editor of *Ms.*; Yates was named publisher.

And nothing worked out as they planned.

In some ways, what Anne Summers was trying to do was to resurrect the initial vision of *Ms.*, but to do it eighties and nineties style: "People my age and a bit younger would tell me, 'I used to read *Ms.*, but then it stopped doing anything for me and I haven't read it since the early eighties,'" she told me one morning in her Upper West Side condominium. "I think a lot of women, as they started to get good jobs, started having kids, saw themselves developing in all kinds of ways the magazine wasn't keeping up with. I thought there was a constituency out there that I could claim."

Under Summers, who took the magazine back to a for-profit status, *Ms.* could rate political candidates for the first time in ten years. The magazine showed new edge during the 1988 presidential campaign, when it offered updates on candidates' positions on child care, abortion, and women's employment issues. But Summers wanted to be a player on Madison Avenue as well as Capitol Hill. To create a "conducive" editorial environment, she introduced a column about gardening to the magazine. She also launched a controversial—and embarrassing—attempt at a fashion section: "Personal Appearances," which featured the everyday wardrobe secrets of prominent feminists, ran for seven issues. "That was a disaster," Summers says now. "It just put advertisers off because women were wearing their own clothes, which weren't necessarily fashionable. And readers said that they'd rather hear about a woman's ideas."

Summers never had a chance to find out if her new ideas for *Ms.* would work. Six months after buying the magazine, Fairfax fell into hard times and began scaling back operations, starting with its new U.S. holdings. Frantic to keep control of both *Ms.* and *Sassy*, Summers and Yates formed Matilda Publications, and raised $20 million—enough to buy the two magazines and infuse them with capital. But Citicorp Venture Capital, Inc., one of Matilda's biggest backers, took a particularly active interest in its investment. Matilda agreed to ambitious quarterly performance goals, which relied on everything going right. There was no room for slippage of any kind. Two weeks later, in mid-July 1988, things didn't just slip, they crashed: six major advertisers pulled out of *Sassy*.

From its first issue in March 1988, *Sassy* had been a smash. Falling somewhere between the prom-queen primness of *Seventeen* and the tackiness of *Teen*, it tried to speak to what was really going on with teenage girls. Talking in an occasionally grating teen argot (like, you know, pointing out when the Red Hot Chili Peppers acted like total dags), it ran articles on previously taboo subjects: drawn in by promises of lipstick lessons and dish on Johnny Depp, the fourteen- to nineteen-year-old audience was also instructed on how to protest the antichoice parental-notification rule, offered a condom update, introduced to gay teens, and educated about AIDS. In fact, with its younger and less judgmental readers, the early *Sassy* seemed to have found that delicate balance between frivolity and feminism, which often eluded *Ms.* Within seven issues, it matched its éminence grise, with four hundred fifty thousand subscribers.

Then, after the magazine caught the attention of a couple of reactionary moms from Wabash, Indiana, two fundamentalist Christian groups launched a letter-writing zap against the magazine. Six of *Sassy*'s biggest advertisers (including Revlon, Maybelline, Noxell, Gillette, and the ostensibly progressive Reebok) pulled their ads.

"We didn't realize initially how serious it was or how long it would go on," says Summers. "We thought advertisers would be back in a few months. But *Sassy* had become controversial. Big advertisers who said they'd come in after the second year, like Procter & Gamble and Bristol-Myers, backed off. Small advertisers got nervous. The impact was catastrophic. Some months in early 1989, *Ms.* had more ads than *Sassy*; then we really knew we were in trouble."

Major advertisers pulled out of *Ms.*, too. While the number of ad pages went up slightly, to 503 in 1987 (still down from the old *Ms.*'s 555 in 1985), by the next year that figure had dropped to 343. "It became very clear that we'd become a marginal buy," says Mary Thom. "When ads began to go down in the industry, we were the first to be cut off the schedule."

Summers became painfully aware of stories that would insult advertisers. As with Steinem, her breaking point came when she perceived a threat to the magazine's much-needed car advertising. When columnist Barbara Ehrenreich proposed an acid satire about fast cars, Summers balked and asked her to write something else (the column eventually appeared in *Mother Jones*). "I felt shocked to be running into that kind of censorship at *Ms.*," says Ehrenreich. "And if it was any other place, as I told Anne, I would've quit right there. But because it was *Ms.* and I was trying to be understanding about the difficulties of surviving, I shrugged and did something else for them."

Finally, even the magazine's covers fell under advertisers' scrutiny. "The worst thing I ever did was change the cover because of advertisers," Summers admits. "We made the mistake of telling them once that Hedda Nussbaum [the abused partner of Joel Steinberg, a New York City lawyer who murdered his six-year-old daughter in 1987] was going to be on the cover. She'd been on *Newsweek*, and it was a legitimate news photo and an issue that *Ms.* readers were interested in. But that kind of cover is not tolerated in women's magazines. They want nice covers. We lost seven advertisers, but four came back when we promised to change it. We had two days to put together a new cover. It was a naked woman, a grainy picture that said, 'Dangerous Liaisons: Women & Estrogen, Hedda & Joel, The Supreme Court & Abortion.'"

Citicorp waltzed in to end Matilda's misery just as the July 1989 issue was about to ship. The company went back on the block, its attractiveness enhanced by the slowly recovering *Sassy*. Summers had tried desperately to find a partner who would allow her to keep the magazine going, but even sympathetic prospects, like multimillionaire media heiress Sallie Bingham, turned her down. "*Ms.* had been around for seventeen years," Summers says, "and every deep pocket was exhausted. The usual suspects had already been approached in the past and either had given money or didn't want to give."

In August 1989, Dale Lang, who owns *Working Woman*, *Working Mother*, and once owned *McCall's*, signed a letter of intent to buy *Ms.* and 70 percent of *Sassy* (Citicorp retained the other 30 percent). Lang promptly left for a motorcycling holiday in Europe, without announcing his plans for either publication, but the word on the street was that he was not interested in *Ms.*

"He started running the publication about two months before he officially owned it," one publishing insider told me. "He was trying to sell ads in trios—*Sassy*, *Working Woman*, *Working Mother*, but not *Ms.* He made no statement supporting *Ms.*, so ads naturally evaporated. To Madison Avenue, it looked like not even the white knight was supporting the publication, that he was actually trying to undermine it. Finally, there was an issue on the boards ready to go with only seven pages of ads. And he refused to print it."

On October 13, 1989, Summers turned full control of

Matilda Publications over to Lang, and *Ms.*, the publication founded on the principle of female self-determination, became the domain of a man. He immediately suspended publication. Editors were allowed to stay on, but the ad staff was fired. Some learned their fate from that morning's *Wall Street Journal*.

Summers still broods over the failure of her mass-circulation *Ms.* "I've thought a lot about what I'd do differently," she says. "We should've taken some stronger stands on some issues. I think I was treading softly, very conscious of potential criticism for tampering with this American institution. That was a mistake. I should've done savage profiles. We were too soft.

"But in the two years we were there, there wasn't even a quarter where we were free of significant business worries that impacted on Madison Avenue and which were used as an excuse or reason not to advertise in the magazine. Maybe we could've made it. Maybe. But never under those conditions."

According to *Ms.* staffers, Lang assured Summers that she would be editor of any new version of *Ms.* that was in the offing—a promise he did not keep. Instead, Summers was named editor-at-large for Lang publications. And when the new bimonthly, ad-free publication *Ms.: The World of Women* was announced in December of last year, the name topping the masthead came as something of a surprise. My old boss Robin Morgan, child actress and radio personality, founder of the Redstockings, organizer of anti–Miss America protests, international activist, antiporn crusader, prolific writer (most recently of *The Demon Lover: On the Sexuality of Terrorism*), had been anointed. Her name and high historical profile clearly signaled the latest direction *Ms.* would take, the language it would speak, and the women it would speak to.

"IN THIS *Ms.*, THERE WILL BE NO SLICK PAGES AND NO SLICK THINK-ing," Robin Morgan announces in her ringing voice. She stands at about five feet and is waving one of the cigarettes she's forever trying to give up. "It was amazing what the magazine tried to accomplish in its pre-Australian period, considering all the tightropes that it walked. But the sheer effort of trying to be everything to everybody meant reaching a lowest common denominator to some degree."

It is May 1990 in the offices of the new *Ms.*, and I have left Steinem to her rounds of meetings, interviews, and phone calls. It has been seven years since my last phone conversation with Morgan, during which time I navigated my way through several magazine jobs—leaving one when the editor resigned after refusing to pander to advertisers, and another just before the owner pulled the plug, citing lack of advertiser enthusiasm—before moving west to work at *Mother Jones*. Morgan and I have just had lunch. We have caught up. I have been held out to younger staff members as a shining example of where a *Ms.* internship will get you. Now she is walking me through the new magazine.

"I'm trying to put together a magazine that's lively, fair, beautiful, funny, and moving," she tells me. "A magazine that will get people to act." As she begins to run down the list of articles in the first issues, though, I hear a litany of familiar, venerable names—Adrienne Rich, Lily Tomlin, Andrea Dworkin, Alice Walker, Marilyn French—and predictable topics that make me uneasy. This sounds like a narrowly focused *Ms.*, a magazine that will appeal overwhelmingly, perhaps exclusively, to its original constituency.

To its credit, and especially to Morgan's credit, the new *Ms.* places a particular emphasis on features and news briefs about women around the world. But the rest of the magazine seems designed not just for women who identify themselves as feminists, but for women who define feminism in a specific way, who want the best and the worst of their worldview confirmed rather than challenged. There is a "Feminist Theory" section on the centrality of ageism to the patriarchy; "Inner Space," on the angry face of the goddess; Bella Abzug on widowhood; an arts section featuring an essay hailing last year's release of *Camille Claudel*.

"The Accidental Activist," which spotlights ordinary people who were made political by circumstance (such as Karen Bell, whose daughter died from an illegal abortion and who was also featured in a recent issue of *People*), is the only nod to the uninitiated. There's even a section in the new magazine called "Instant Classics," which will reprint what Morgan calls "basic clicks that are hard to get ahold of." The first one is Judy Brady's "Why I Want a Wife," which appeared in the first issue of the old *Ms.* (It also appeared in the December 1979 issue, and its companion piece, "The Housewife's Moment of Truth," appeared in the October 1980 issue.)

I ask Morgan what she is doing for young feminists and for could-be feminists. She squints at me as if I've hit a sore spot, and lights another cigarette before responding. "There aren't as many young feminist voices in the magazine as I want," she says. "But I think they'll begin coming in. We're going to have a piece on frat gang rape in the second issue, and a young feminists' dialogue in the third issue. . . . But I'm not going to search out younger women—thirty and under—to the degree I abandon baby boomers, people forty-five to fifty-five."

Steinem had told me that she always saw *Ms.* as an "intake mechanism" for the feminist movement. "We've never been like *Commentary*, where you grow old right along with Norman Podhoretz," she said. But that seems to be exactly what the new *Ms.* is doing, and, in the process, it may be giving up the last shred of hope of reaching beyond its natural grasp. Neither Steinem nor Morgan sees reaching younger, more casually feminist women as the critical focus it was back in 1972. Steinem says that there are now other intake mechanisms for the feminist movement, like women's-studies courses (*Ms.* is attempting to market itself to colleges as a text in women's-studies departments), but those certainly aren't comparable to a mass-market glossy magazine. When I persist in raising questions about this shift, Morgan finally says, exasperated: "Look, this is me you're talking to. I'm not going to go in for that either we're this or we're that. Reaching you women of whatever age is one function. But another and, quite frankly, more basic one is to speak to our own constituency, which has been ignored by everybody. Some of the feminist media, in trying to do outreach, has ignored the long-distance runners. We deserve some sustenance, too."

Since Lang now refuses to talk to the press, it's hard to say what his real intentions and plans for *Ms.* are; but a look at his business plan—in which the ad-free publication runs solely on its forty-dollars-a-head subscription revenue (with only a few targeted mailings to lure subscribers) and newsstand sales—leads one to suspect that the new *Ms.* may really be a step toward no *Ms.* In fact, fewer than one hundred thousand subscribers have signed on for the new *Ms.*, less than half of the original estimate.

When his business plan was originally unveiled, Lang told *Newsday* that magazines such as *The Nation*, *New Republic*, and *Commentary* have long thrived on subscription revenue—which isn't true. *The Nation* runs at a deficit, made up by owner Arthur Carter. According to publisher David Parker, the publication also takes in $350,000 worth of ads each year. "There's no reason not to take some advertising, for products the readers might really want to see, except as a marketing ploy," says Parker. "Not that they were getting ads anyway. It's sort of like saying, 'I would never marry Princess Caroline of Monaco.' Well, she never asked." In reality, the most prominent of the few American newsstand magazines that survive without advertising revenue are *Consumer Reports* and *MAD*.

The fact is, Americans are used to magazines that are heavily subsidized by advertisers; we aren't accustomed to paying production costs of the media we read and watch. "There's no way *Ms.* is going to get away with charging three or four times more than other magazines," says Rick MacArthur, publisher of *Harper's*. "It would be great if they succeed, because I'd be happy to imitate them. But we know from experience that readers won't do it. There's an immediate impact if you raise your rates."

Neither Steinem nor Morgan is a likely mark for the false promises of a male corporate executive, and each seems fully confident of Lang's integrity. "He may be discovering it feels good to feel good," Morgan says. "He was amazed by the mail when he suspended publication, by the real-life stories. Part of it is probably a sense of pride—he's big enough to own *Ms.*"

Still, there was the little matter of the letter. When the new

Ms. was announced, subscribers received an exuberant pink-and-purple mailing from Steinem and publisher Ruth Bower, offering them the chance to "vote" with their dollar: since they had already paid fifteen dollars for the old *Ms.*, they could cast their "ballot" for the first year of the "editorially free" *Ms.* for a mere twenty-five dollars.

The trouble was, not all subscribers got that letter. An unspecified number received a more subdued note on official stationery, informing them that *Ms.* had ceased publication and offering to fill the subscription with *Ms.*'s "sister publication" *Working Woman.* If that proved unsatisfactory, loyal subscribers could switch instead to *Working Mother*, "another sister publication to *Ms.*" Far down at the bottom of the letter was a little PS: "Should a newly formatted version of *Ms.* emerge in the future, please let us know if you wish to be contacted."

Morgan says the second letter was a mistake; it was composed in October, when *Ms.* was in limbo, and should never have been mailed. "It was fuckups within fuckups. There was an error in circulation, one in fulfillment, one in the mailing place. It seems to not have been a mistake of venality, but of different layers of incompetence."

"The coincidence in timing is pretty strange," counters a Lang Communications insider. "No one knows how many people got it or how they were chosen. The truth is, *Working Woman* has a rate-base problem. They need to guarantee a million readers to advertisers and they can't. So they gave a certain number of people the second letter, then the next week dumped five months of back issues in their mailboxes." Magazine insiders took the episode to mean that *Ms.* was hanging by a thread, dependent on the whims of Dale Lang.

In that transfer of readers from *Ms.*—even a flawed *Ms.*—to *Working Woman*, something tragic occurs. *Ms.* has been on the ropes for a number of reasons: a decade-long backlash against the women's movement; mistakes made by its editors in an atmosphere where no mistakes could occur, in an industry where the ephemeral eclipses the enduring, in a culture where a magazine dedicated to selling women's ideas instead of their bodies is unacceptable; and finally—and perhaps most tellingly—because of the sheer gutlessness among advertisers whose influence over publishing has effectively narrowed the scope of voices on the newsstand.

But without *Ms.*, or something like it, what is going to convince today's eleven-year-old girls that they can fly? I imagine Tibetha Shaw, still flame-haired and rebellious, barreling defiantly down some city street in a pro-choice demonstration, clad in her regulation black. Or perhaps she decided feminism was her mother's trip, and joined the flocks seeking happiness through the great and powerful god, MBA. Either way, part of whoever she has become, and who I am, is due to *Ms.* We donned those towel capes because we saw, for the first time, that little girls could become not just women, but wonder women, women who could participate in the full scope of public and private life. *Ms.* was dedicated to that possibility, and no other mass-market magazine has taken up that torch since, or is likely to do so.

Magazines such as *Working Woman*, *Savvy*, *New York Woman*, and *Mirabella* may have poached some of the *Ms.* terrain, but they've manipulated the message, reflecting change but not inciting it. *Ms.* was the only magazine on the newsstand to take as its mission reaching out across lines of class, race, age, and experience to guard the interests of all women. And the potential for a magazine to do that now—when we need it as much as ever—died with a mass-market *Ms.*

At press time, Morgan and Steinem appeared confident that *Ms.* would survive. Although the first run of the magazine sold out at the newsstands, publisher Ruth Bower would not reveal the number of copies printed. Perhaps that's because, according to sources, the total was only about a tenth of the three hundred thousand copies that flew off the stands during the magazine's initial debut in 1972. "I haven't felt depressed about losing the old *Ms.*," Steinem mused in our final conversation. "I feel something healthier, which is anger. I feel angry—and we all ought to feel angry—that a magazine like *Vanity Fair* can waste fifty million dollars on fewer subscribers than we used to have. Or that Time, Inc., can spend more money than *Ms.* has ever had on testing a magazine that they never even published. I feel angry about that when I walk by the newsstand. And I'll never stop feeling angry."

PHOEBE GLOECKNER: A GRAPHIC LIFE

I originally intended this piece to be about a group of female cartoonists—including Julie Doucet and Debbie Dreschler—who were making radical, authentic work on girls' sexuality and on sexual victimization. Narratively, though, it worked better to focus solely on Gloeckner. I was (and remain) a huge fangirl, obsessed with A Child's Life and Other Stories. *The piece was published in August 2001, and I'm struck by how girls' sexuality and their sexual objectification seem to have become both more openly discussed, yet no easier to navigate. Maybe that's why the release of the film version of* Diary of a Teenage Girl *in 2016 still felt so relevant. Personally, I loved the movie—almost as much as the book.*

Bob's diner on Polk Street is just two blocks up from where tourists catch the cable car for a joy ride to downtown San Francisco and just beyond where the hustlers and junkies stroll. Plastic grapes festoon the walls above cracked gray vinyl booths. The chow is strictly short order. In the center of

the restaurant, her tweed coat slipping onto the speckled lino-
leum, a forty-year-old woman sketches in a notebook. When
she looks up, time bends. Phoebe Gloeckner has expectant hazel eyes and brown hair shot through with red highlights. She
wears round antique spectacles over a small Band-Aid where
her two-year-old accidentally jammed them into the bridge of
her nose. She may be an established medical illustrator and
mother of two married to a chemistry professor, but she also,
quite startlingly, has the face of her fifteen-year-old alter ego,
Minnie, the subject of Gloeckner's semiautobiographical cartoons. Minnie, who was booted from some of the finest Bay
Area private schools. Minnie, who was sexually involved with
her mother's boyfriend. Minnie, whose best friend dosed her
with quaaludes then traded Minnie's body for more drugs. In
fact, if you set the Way Back machine to a quarter-century ago,
you could find the teenage Phoebe sitting in this very spot,
scribbling in her diary, bearing witness to her life. Bob's was
her refuge; safely above the street scene's DMZ, she wasn't
likely to run into anyone here who would question what she
was writing or why.

Now, in 2001, Gloeckner is only visiting her former
stomping grounds. She lives on Long Island these days, where
she is finishing *Diary of a Teenage Girl*, a hybrid between a conventional and graphic novel based on the very journals she
penned in this diner. The book mines the same territory as
A Child's Life and Other Stories, Gloeckner's first book, a story
collection in cartoon form that R. Crumb says includes "one
of the comic book masterpieces of all time." Like Crumb's,
Gloeckner's work is challenging stuff, graphic in every sense
of the word. But while the images are similarly explicit—and
have raised comparable charges of obscenity—the context

could not be more different. The Minnie stories describe an adolescence that is at once traumatic and picaresque. They explore the power a girl feels in her emerging sexuality as well as the damage inflicted by those who prey upon it. In the process, they raise unsettling questions about vulnerability, desire, and the nature of a young woman's victimization. "Phoebe looks square in the face of extremely disturbing subject matter," says Kim Thompson, copublisher of Fantagraphics Books, the largest publisher of alternative comics. "But she has this illustrative style that's so beautiful. It's like going to a movie that looks like Merchant Ivory but turns out to have a Charles Bukowski story."

Confessional comics are an intriguing, surprisingly supple medium in which to tell young women's stories. Gloeckner is arguably the brightest light among a small cadre of semi-autobiographical cartoonists—including Debbie Drechsler and Julie Doucet—who are creating some of the edgiest work about young women's lives in any medium. The narratives are often presented as diaries, that quintessential literary form of female adolescence. (There is virtually no tradition of diarists among teenage boys.) Perversely, even their marginalization—as cartoonists, as literary cartoonists, as female literary cartoonists—works in these artists' favor. Free from the pressures of the marketplace, they can explore taboo aspects of girls' lives with the illusion of safety; since their work is usually hidden behind racks of X-Men in shops that smell like a sweat sock, few people are likely to stumble across it. "They're like what independent films were before they stopped really being independent," says

Drechsler, whose collection *Summer of Love* will be released this month. "You have total freedom. Nobody cares what you're doing because nobody's going to make money off of it."

That's how it has been for Gloeckner for years. Some call her a "cartoonist's cartoonist," a backhanded compliment that both acknowledges her exacting skill as an artist and the fact that even for comics, her work has not sold especially well. "Phoebe is one of the most accomplished artists in terms of mastery of the medium," says Bill Griffith, the creator of *Zippy the Pinhead*. Griffith was among the first to publish Gloeckner's work, when she was in her late teens. "Her drawing conveys a lot of the underlying feeling of what's going on in the same way a movie can have a shot without dialogue that's a major turning point or a major insight into a character. It's a delicate balancing act. The pictures have to propel the story without overtaking it. That balance—it's almost a tension—occurs when a cartoonist is equally good as a writer and artist, and it's very rare."

Richard Grossinger, publisher of North Atlantic Books/ Frog Ltd., which put out *A Child's Life*, says: "In a perfect world, she would have as large an audience as R. Crumb or Art Spiegelman. She's that good. But we haven't been successful in letting that world know about it."

Diary of a Teenage Girl, which will be published next spring, could change that. Inspired by, among other things, the illustrated novels of the Victorian period, it takes the form a step further. Instead of a fully illustrated graphic novel, like Spiegelman's *Maus* or Daniel Clowes's *Ghost World*, Gloeckner's book is largely text that periodically bursts into comics the way a musical bursts into song: with no warning whatsoever, as if it's normal. Because its raunchier themes are explored through prose rather than through images, *Diary* has a better shot at being picked up by conventional bookstores than *A Child's Life* did. Gloeckner is the first to admit that's an exciting opportunity. She's also the first to question whether it's one she wants.

In conversation about her work, Phoebe Gloeckner shifts arbitrarily between referring to "Minnie" and "me." "I was so needy," she remembers of herself as a teenager, followed immediately by, "In that sense, there was nothing particularly remarkable about Minnie." Because of the permeable boundary between fact and fiction in Gloeckner's life, I find myself, at times, picking peculiar arguments with her. "One of the things that interests me about Minnie," I say, "is that she is very pretty. We talk a lot about the damage done to girls by unrealistic standards of beauty but not about the vulnerability that comes when you actually meet them."

Gloeckner replies: "I don't think Minnie was beautiful. I honestly don't."

"Well," I say, "I think she probably was. She turns heads wherever she goes." We both laugh awkwardly at the perversity of speaking in the third person.

Gloeckner considers this for a moment. "I always hoped people would think I was pretty, but I always felt painfully ugly," she says slowly. "Painfully. Whether that was the reality or not. I know a lot of girls feel that way. I could not deal with my appearance or my sexuality. I just wanted someone to see who I was for real and love me for it. So I would talk to anybody, go anyplace with anybody in the hope that they would see me and help me." She shakes her head. "And I can't even say how I meant that."

Gloeckner is the daughter of a librarian from a blue-collar family (her mother) and an unemployed artist from a blue-nosed one (her dad). Her parents divorced when she was four. Eight years later, her mother remarried and moved the family from Philadelphia to San Francisco. The early Minnie stories portray a stepfather who was arbitrarily cruel and who leered at Minnie and dropped sexual innuendos. In real life, the marriage quickly deteriorated, and to shield her from the tension, Phoebe was shipped off to an elite boarding school. By the time she returned home at fifteen, her mother was dating again.

There is an image that Gloeckner returns to in her work that acts as a kind of pivot point, a defining moment both in her own life and her character's. She drew it in one of her first comics at sixteen. It appears again, in writing this time, in *Diary of a Teenage Girl*. It is not one of the more lurid images in her repertoire, but it may be the most chilling: it shows one of her mother's boyfriends, someone Minnie trusted and admired, running a casual finger across her bare midriff. It is his first tentative crossing of a line, quite literally sending out a feeler to gauge the girl's vulnerability. "When he first made those advances, my initial thought was, 'This is not right,'" she says. "But then I thought, Maybe it is and I don't know. Minnie had been bombarded with adults who had no boundaries and were overtly sexual with children. You get used to that, and at a certain point you think of yourself and value yourself solely as a sexual being."

Whatever tenuous stability Minnie had felt at home crumbled as that initial touch turned into an affair. In "Minnie's

3rd Love, or Nightmare on Polk Street," a story in *A Child's Life*, Gloeckner's alter ego is seen on her knees in the laundry room of her apartment building. Next to her is a Hello Kitty diary. Minnie looks tearfully up at her lover/surrogate father, on whom she is about to perform fellatio, begging him to tell her he loves her. In her right hand, she clutches a bottle whose label reads, "The kind of good, cheap California wine that makes girls cry and give blow jobs to jerks." To escape both her shame and her obsession with her mother's boyfriend, Minnie runs away to Polk Street with another girl, a teenage junkie with whom she falls in love. She takes whatever drugs come her way, then is pimped by the girlfriend for more. "I was in a lot of pain, so I would do anything," Gloeckner says about her own life at that time. "If someone said, 'Shoot up this' or 'Take this pill,' I'd do it. I guess I didn't really care."

Though Frog Ltd. was eager to publish *A Child's Life*, its printers balked. One refused outright, the other agreed, but backed off after staff members objected to the graphic imagery in "Minnie's 3rd Love." Eventually, the second company did print the book after work hours. Gloeckner had caused controversy before: in 1995, British customs officials seized an anthology of comics that included an earlier version of the same story, claiming the laundry-room panel was child pornography. "There's resistance to something that's drawn that wouldn't exist if it were written," says Frog's Grossinger. "If you're talking about child sexual abuse, *Bastard out of Carolina* is in many ways harsher than Phoebe's work. If you drew that, you'd be marginalized."

A British judge eventually ruled in favor of the book's distributor, but last year, when *A Child's Life* was confiscated at the French border, there was no such reversal: the book never was allowed into the country (although, interestingly, R. Crumb's comics depicting his sometimes violent sexual fantasies are readily available). "Some people think what I draw is pornography," Gloeckner says. "But there are children who experience this, who have this penis in front of their faces. They see it, so why can't I show it to make the impact clear?"

It's a question she hasn't fully answered herself. Gloeckner describes her creative process as a wrestling match between the compulsive demands of her own vision and a fear of those who might label it "dirty." There's the voice of her publisher, who has—no pressure—mentioned that without the images of erect penises, her books would be easier to market. There's the voice of her mother, who has "not been pleased" with the Minnie stories. There's the voice of herself as a mother, fretful over what her daughters will think when they are old enough to see her work. There's the voice of her own shame. "I'm constantly fighting with it," she says, "but if I censor myself, it makes me feel sick. Actually physically ill."

Ultimately, Gloeckner says, she has no choice but rigorous honesty, including this: Gloeckner doesn't flinch from the blurry lines between experimentation and exploitation. A panel in *A Child's Life* shows Minnie reading *Lolita*. In *Diary*, Minnie describes her excitement at provoking desire in adult men in a bar (as well as her revulsion when they respond). She confides the thrill of picking up strangers in Golden Gate Park. And she admits to actively participating in the affair with her mother's boyfriend after he made the first move. Even at her most debased, Minnie sometimes seems to be having fun. As Gloeckner's fellow cartoonist Clowes says: "Phoebe doesn't paint herself as either a hero or as a victim or say that this guy is evil and this guy is good. She's just there in the world as she should be, and you have to interpret the events she depicts." Minnie's complicity doesn't change the fact of her abuse, but it does provide insight into its dynamics. It's a daring subtheme, and it is part of what makes Gloeckner's work ring true, what makes it transcend the genre of most child-abuse memoirs.

In a way, the European border patrol was onto something—Gloeckner's cartoons may be devastating, but they can be arousing as well, because that, too, is part of Minnie's experience. The most explicit images threaten to implicate the reader, transforming a sympathetic eye into a voyeuristic one. That quality may be what offends censors and raises red flags among the bookstore buyers who won't carry her work. "Maybe it is titillating," Gloeckner admits. "It can be titillating for the child in a way. But it's also confusing, destructive and horrifying and can be rape and everything else. So to draw things as either black or white is a lie. Because that titillation is in you. I'm not saying it's good, but it's there."

Even so, Gloeckner remains ambivalent, veering in our conversations between self-righteousness and embarrassment, between dreaming of a larger audience and hoping no one she knows will ever see her books. When asked what her suburban neighbors think of her comics, she laughs. "I just tell them I'm a medical illustrator," Gloeckner says. "I don't think they would let their children play with my children if they knew what I drew."

Of course, she's telling this to a reporter from the *New York Times*, which has a substantial circulation on Long Island. Chances are, she's about to be outed. "I know, I know," she groans. "But I haven't lived there that long and I don't know anyone really well. . . ." She trails off for a moment, snared in her own loopy logic. "Well, I don't know how many people will recognize my name," she concludes, weakly. "So I think it's not going to be that bad."

There was no great epiphany, no moment of being scared straight, no hitting bottom, despite how low she sank. Hers was an incremental awakening. At seventeen, Gloeckner was still prowling Polk Street, shoplifting on the side. She remembers thinking that in another year, if she were caught, she could be jailed, and that scared her. Then there was her grandmother, a doctor back in Philadelphia, whom Gloeckner admired and wanted to emulate. Instead, she seemed to be taking after her father, who had become irretrievably lost in drug and alcohol addiction. And Gloeckner knew she had a gift; even at her lowest ebb, she drew comics on paper bags or in her diary. "They weren't very good, but they sustained me," she says. "I felt good about that part of myself—and only that part of myself—but it was something I could feel good about. It made me feel there was some hope that I could do something if I tried."

She managed to squeak through what she describes as a "school for incorrigibles" and did well enough on her SATs to enroll at San Francisco State. "I don't know exactly how I made that leap back to normal life," she says. "I wish I did. I suppose that even though I got kicked out of all those private schools, they had given me a sense that there was something else to strive for. Other kids I knew didn't have that."

Eventually, Gloeckner studied art and medicine, earning a master's in medical illustration. It's a career that suits an artist as meticulous as she. ("It's really hard for me not to fill up every space with crosshatching," she jokes.) But more than that, it's the perfect day job for a person compelled to make the hidden visible, then present it for public display. "I was always aware that the interior was as much a part of my body as the exterior," she says. "I've always done things like try to imagine what it looks like inside when I'm swallowing. Or what it looks like inside when you have sex. So I wanted to understand the interior better. I guess interior life in general."

THERE IS A TRIPTYCH OF MINNIE IN *A CHILD'S LIFE*. IN THE FIRST drawing, she is eating candy dots, those bits of colored sugar peeled from strips of paper, while gazing up at a chevron of migrating birds. In the next, which faces it, she holds a Tootsie Pop. Both are archetypal images of childhood. But turn the page and "Little Minnie" is about to kiss a grown woman, her mouth wet and open, her eyes glazed in anticipation. Is Minnie a child or an adult? Innocent or carnal? "That adult woman is me," Gloeckner says. "I was having a hard time doing the book. I was really nervous about it. So I thought: 'How do I feel about this little girl? Well, I like her, and I want to tell this story for her sake. And I just have to look at it that way and not worry about what people will say.' So that picture is supposed to be me as an adult kissing Minnie. In a sense, it's myself kissing myself. And there is something sexual about it because we're blending in my brain. So I could see that people would interpret it differently." She shrugs. "But that's okay."

It may be that you have to be forty before you can reconcile with fourteen, before you can reach back in time and offer a consoling embrace. Gloeckner imagines teenage girls would be the natural audience for her work if it were more readily available in conventional bookstores. But for the most part, it doesn't cross their paths. Even so, the dedication of *Diary of a Teenage Girl* reads, "For the girls after they've grown."

"Although I was exposed to all those things when I was a kid, I don't think everyone should be, even through a book," she says. "So the dedication is hopeful in that sense. It is for girls, but let them stay as ignorant as they can be of these things until they're stronger or know more. Unless, of course, they're forced to grow up too soon."

CAITLIN MORAN: THEY DON'T MAKE FEMINISTS THIS OUTRAGEOUS ANYMORE

I love Caitlin Moran. She is seriously funny and comically serious. This piece ran in July 2012. I still see Moran from time to time—and I will never, ever let her forget about those espresso martinis she spilled on my head!

NOT LONG AGO, A GROUP OF PROMINENT BRITISH JOURNALISTS, all female, went out for an evening to get drunk on gin. *Very* drunk on gin. One of them walked headlong into a door. Another confessed to having been caught in flagrante delicto at a funeral. Eventually, they settled into one of their favorite pastimes: bemoaning—increasingly loudly—the sorry state of contemporary feminism. How had a movement that had once been so incendiary, so vibrant, and so effective become so . . . *tedious*? How had it been hijacked not only by stodgy academics but by *Sex and the City* divas: women who, as Caitlin Moran, a columnist at the London *Times* (and, as it happens, the woman who banged into the door), said, would have us believe that "if we have fabulous underwear we'll be somehow above the terrifying statistic that only one percent of the world's wealth is owned by women."

Was it any wonder recent polls had found that 52 percent of British women and 71 percent of American women didn't identify as feminists? The assembled ladies pounded their fists on the table. They tossed back more gin. Finally, someone—it's unclear who—said that one of them needed to write a book: something raucous and real about why feminism still mattered. A taking-stock of womanhood in an age of unprecedented freedoms and nagging contradictions.

And Caitlin Moran responded: "Okay, I'll race you!"

FIVE MONTHS LATER MORAN FINISHED HER MEMOIR-SLASH-manifesto, *How to Be a Woman*. The book, which will be released this week in the United States, spent nearly a year on the top 10 list in England. It has been published in eighteen countries (when we met it was being translated into Portuguese, leaving Moran, who spends several pages fulminating over the rise of pubic deforestation, wondering what Brazilians call a "Brazilian"). She has amassed nearly two hundred forty thousand Twitter followers (the modern metric of success) as well as a dedicated fan blog, *fuckyeahcaitlinmoran*, based on the viral meme popularized by Ryan Gosling enthusiasts. The photo from the book's cover—Moran with her distinctive skunk-striped bouff of a hairdo and winged liquid eyeliner—was acquired by London's National Portrait Gallery, tucked in among other superstars of the realm: King Henry VIII, Queen Elizabeth I, Sir Paul McCartney.

Moran typically describes *How to Be a Woman* as "an update of Germaine Greer's *The Female Eunuch* written from a barstool." The books actually have little in common, but the sound bite rightly places her on a continuum of liberationist bad girls stretching from Greer in the 1970s (notorious for urging women to empower themselves by tasting their menstrual blood) to the riot grrrl rockers of the 1990s ("I *loved* riot grrrl," she said. "Not only was it a punk rock revolution, but it meant you could get dressed for a night out for less than two pounds!").

But funny. Like Greer, Moran's feminism is as much attitude as analysis. She is, in equal measure, intellectual, rebel, and goofball: that's part of her "let's all be feminists at the pub" charm and why I both enjoyed her book (for which I provided a blurb) and wanted to meet her. She is a woman who has incorrectly pronounced her first name for nearly twenty-five years (née Catherine, she rechristened herself *Cat*-lin at age thirteen after a character in a racy novel whose name she'd misread). A thirty-seven-year-old who set a fire in her sink while trying to suavely light a cigarette in front of a guest. A woman who tripped while gawking at an aging pop star in a posh London club ("I can't believe it! *Kevin fucking Rowland!*") and dumped an entire tray of espresso martinis on my head.

How to Be a Woman follows its antiheroine from her thirteenth birthday (182 pounds, friendless, fleeing from gravel-flinging yobs) onward, with stops along the way to praise masturbation, argue both for and against motherhood, celebrate her abortion, and more. Each self-deprecating chapter ("I Start Bleeding!" "I Become Furry!" "I Don't Know What to Call My Breasts!") is an occasion to explore how, from puberty through senescence, the modern female body has become a series of problems to be solved—usually at great expense to its inhabitant. There is, for instance, the upkeep of that new presumed depilation ("I can't believe we've got to a point where it's basically costing us *money* to have a vagina"); the tyranny of stratospheric heels ("The minimum I ask for my footwear: to be able to dance in it and that it not get me murdered"); ever-teenier underpants ("How can 52 percent of the population expect to win the war on terror if they can't even sit down without wincing?").

Moran is all about sweating the small stuff. She justifies that choice by invoking the "broken windows" theory of criminology—the idea that ignoring one broken pane of glass in an empty building leads to increasing acts of vandalism. Similarly, minor slights against women—dismissing politically powerful women as "ugly" or using "you're fat" as the ultimate trump card in an argument—make possible more brazen attacks, a takeover of rights by metaphoric squatters. Consider the male legislator in Michigan who, last month, had a female colleague banned from the House floor for using the word "vagina" during a debate over one of the most restrictive antiabortion bills ever proposed. The bill passed twenty minutes later. First you can't speak the word for part of a woman's anatomy; next you lose control of it.

"If every woman in that room stood up and said 'vagina!,' what could they do?" Moran said. "Or, for total rock 'n' roll, if every woman who'd had an abortion stood up and said, 'I have had an abortion, and I would not be here now if this legislation had been passed back then.' If every woman who's had an abortion took tomorrow off in protest, America would grind to a halt. And that would be symbolic: because women grind to a halt if they are not in control of their fertility."

Like ex-Mayor Rudolph Giuliani, who based his crime policy on the "broken windows" theory, Moran calls for "zero tolerance" of "all the patriarchal bullshit": a colleague's crude "joke," Disney princesses, Botox. To all those women who recoil from the word "feminist," she asks, "What part of 'liberation for women' is not for you? Is it freedom to vote? The right not to be owned by the man you marry? 'Vogue' by Madonna? Jeans? Did all that good shit *get on your nerves*? Or were you just *drunk at the time of the survey*?"

It was after midnight at the Groucho, a private social club in London's Soho neighborhood, and the next round was on Caitlin Moran. "Feminism is paying for these drinks!" she shouted, waving a cigarette.

"The Grouch" as it is affectionately known, caters to those in the media and entertainment industries. Founded as an alternative to stuffier establishments, it was named for the old Groucho Marx quip that he would never join a club that would have him as a member. Moran reconciled that particular paradox by straddling it: ejected from the club twice in her youth for property destruction and public lasciviousness, she was in 2011 named its "Maverick of the Year" and awarded a free membership for life.

Sitting outside on a rooftop deck Moran presided over a revolving scrum of actors, writers, and musicians. And fans. Her admirers came up in a steady stream, spanning the gamut of age, stylishness, sex, and sexual preference. It was as if she'd made feminism itself—the ultimate club that no one wanted to join—the hottest room in town. A woman with a graying topknot caught sight of Moran and genuflected; a gay man pumped his fist, shouting, *"Fat! Fat! Fat!"* Another man, with short-cropped hair and hipster sideburns, asked to take a photo with her. A tipsy woman in a black bubble minidress with a plunging neckline brandished a Cosmo and called out, "Zizi!," the French word she favors for her own nether parts. "Drunk women love me," Moran crowed. "I have cornered the market in wasted chicks who talk about their vag!"

Regardless of how many people demanded her attention, Moran's good humor never flagged. At one point, a friend and colleague from the London *Times* turned to me remarking, "You have to remember, Caitlin is someone who had no friends until she was sixteen. *No friends.* Can you imagine that? I think she still can't believe people like her. The way she grew up . . . she always says she made it through because she is ebullient. That's the word she uses. *Ebullient.*"

Moran talks about her childhood almost as if she were part of a cult. She was the eldest of eight; her mother loved having babies but, once they were toddlers, much of their care fell to Caitlin. Her father had some early success as a drummer in a psychedelic rock band. He believed—the entire family believed—it was only a matter of time until he hit it big again. "We'd watch Live Aid," Moran recalled, "and think, Once Dad makes it we'll be friends with Bob Geldof's kids. I'd think, This time next year . . ."

Meanwhile, the family lived in subsidized housing in the grim, industrial town of Wolverhampton, subsisting on public assistance. There were few clothes—Caitlin wore her mother's patched skirts or her father's cast-off thermal underwear. Occasionally, they had no food; the rest of the time, they binged. As a result the Moran siblings were obese. They were allowed little contact with the outside world: no friends, no birthday parties. And no classrooms. Moran's description of herself as "homeschooled" is a bit misleading: Her parents yanked her from formal education at age eleven because she was bullied. That also gave her more time to help out at home.

Through it all, Moran was an insatiable reader and avid diarist. Before our evening at the Groucho, she read me excerpts that she'd transcribed onto her computer. "Here's a typical one from when I'm eleven," she said. "'Woke up. Jam sandwich for breakfast. Went to supermarket with Dad then doctor with Mum. Ate some candy and coleslaw for lunch. I'm making pasta bolognaise for tea. Thoroughly tidied. Washed walls. Hoovered floors. Disposed of cobwebs in Eddie's room. Washed the landing and Eddie's room's windows and frames. Put up a curtain rods [sic] and curtains. Finished my Agatha Christie book. Made new place to put shoes—a cardboard box under the sink! Mom says I'm very good. The dog's missing.'"

She glanced at me over the screen. "To have been raised like that and then to have gotten out of it . . . I sometimes get dizzy with it. The odds were just not good."

By thirteen, Moran realized the family's fortunes would never change. Plagued by the fear that they'd lose their meager government allowance, she decided to rescue them in proper Jo March fashion: by writing a novel. It wasn't very good, she admits now, but it did get published and the gimmick of her backstory—along with genuine talent and a drive forged of massive anxiety—launched her career. She began writing for a music magazine at sixteen. By seventeen, she was hosting a pop music show on national TV. Suddenly, the teenager who had rarely spoken to anyone beyond her immediate family was interviewing the likes of Björk and the band Oasis.

This was the early 1990s, when the grunge-infused riot grrrl movement was on the rise. "riot grrrl was absolutely the university I went to," Moran recalled. Overtly feminist, blisteringly angry, and utterly subversive, the movement rejected market-driven images of femininity: it was the word "slut" scrawled across the belly of a fleshy, shaven-headed young woman in a miniskirt and combat boots who was passing out hand-printed copies of her zine about incest. And it was the perfect fit for a girl who didn't fit in. "When Courtney Love came along I was fifteen, and fat, and talked too much, and drank too much," Moran recalled. "And what I really needed— and what I am eternally grateful to her for being—was a woman who just *didn't give a shit*." A year later Moran cheered when Donita Sparks, the lead singer of the all-female grunge band L7, tossed her used tampon into the crowd at the Reading Music Festival. "By comparison," she observed now, "writing a chapter about wanking is small-fry."

The riot grrrls eventually disintegrated, replaced by the more palatable—and profitable—Spice Girls. "I say it jokingly, but I really think it's true," Moran said, "it all went wrong with the Spice Girls: obviously, the appropriating of the phrase 'girl power,' which to them meant nothing apart from being friends with your girlfriends. Aren't you *supposed* to be friends with your friends?"

Caitlin Moran, meanwhile, turned eighteen, became a newspaper columnist, and eventually, to her relief, joined the middle class. Yet, even today, with a husband, two children, a house, and a flourishing career, she can't relax, can't trust that her success is real. She is prone to panic attacks, which are only relieved by either "lying very still in bed with my husband watching really shit television while he strokes my head" or writing.

"Writing saved me," Moran told me. "Writing *still* saves me." She ran a hand across the edge of her laptop. "This is where I live. Twitter means all my friends are in my computer. All my ideas are in my computer. I can do whatever I want in there, I'm kind of . . . bionic."

Moran talks faster than most mortals can listen, her references ranging—seemingly in one long spume—from the benefits of dry shampoo, to the work of Alain de Botton, to the original meaning of "Jubilee," to the site of the world's first public television broadcast, which is visible from the living room of her North London home.

She greeted me there one day, dressed in jeans, sneakers, and a T-shirt that read, my feminist marxist dialectic brings all the boys to the yard. Walking past rooms lined floor to ceiling with books and vinyl albums, she paused at the kitchen doorway to point out a Post-it note that had been slipped to her by a fifteen-year-old fan in Holland. It read, "too bad you're not a lesbian," punctuated with a smiley face.

Next to that was a photo of Moran and her husband, a music critic and radio documentarian, taken on a windy beach shortly after they met. She was only seventeen then; her face round, her smile wide and genuine. They married when Moran was twenty-four; by the time she was twenty-eight, they had their two daughters. Such traditional choices seemed surprising for such a wild child. "It's always seen as this binary thing with women," Moran explained. "You're either going to be rock 'n' roll or you're going to be a housewife. It's either cupcakes or crack. I wanted both. And I got it." She paused. "Well, not the crack," then added jokingly, "I quite liked crystal meth, though. . . ."

Moran's oldest daughter, whom she calls Lizzie in her writing, is eleven, nearly the age Moran was in the opening scene of *How to Be a Woman*. She clamored into the kitchen, dressed in a school uniform of a gray skirt, white blouse, and maroon sweater, searching for her copy of *The Hunger Games*. "I'll tell you," Moran said after the girl left, "the greatest luxury is to not make your kids as worried as you were. I would rather my daughters be unexceptional but happy. Though the thing is, that they are exceptional *and* happy."

They are also feminists. As toddlers, Moran taught them to shout, "Thanks for that, the patriarchy!" whenever they scraped a knee. At age eight, when Lizzie questioned Barbie's improbable curves, Moran had her draw pictures of what the doll *ought* to look like. ("An outline that was kind of representative," Moran said. "Feet big enough to stand on and a monobrow because Lizzie has a monobrow. Hair on her legs. And she made one breast slightly larger than the other, so I was like, Thanks.") For Halloween last year, the girls dressed as suffragettes.

Figuring out how to introduce them to her beloved pop music has proved trickier. "I didn't want them to reject pop," Moran said. "But the best stuff that's being made at the minute is by women who aren't wearing many clothes." It's not sexiness that bothers her—rock 'n' roll is supposed to be hot—it's the lack of variety, the soul-numbing repetition of one, wildly unrealistic porn-inflected ideal for women. "Adele is the only woman for years who's been allowed to get to number one wearing sleeves," Moran said. For a while her politics bumped uncomfortably up against her passions. Then she found the funny. "What I finally came down to is that we would *pity* Rihanna," she said. "I told my girls, 'Look at Rihanna: She's one of the biggest pop stars in the world. She's really famous, really powerful, really rich. Yet in every single video she can only wear panties. *Poor* Rihanna! We'll know when she is properly powerful and successful when we see her in a lovely cardigan.'"

So many waves of feminism have washed up on America's shores. Moran's hopes for her own impact initially come off, like her book itself, as deceptively personal, the dreams of an awkward girl turned celebrity journalist. "I just want Tina Fey to be my best friend," she said. "And Lena Dunham. And Oprah, too. I just want those three chicks to read it and say, 'You did good.' Just those three." She paused. "And Roseanne Barr. Four. I only really want to sell four copies in America. If I can sell it to those four chicks . . . and Hillary. Okay, five. And Michelle Obama. Okay, six. If I could get those six women to read it . . ."

Each of those women has publicly struggled with the complexities of "how to be a woman" and, in doing so, expanded the possibilities. And that, in the end, is all—and everything—Moran wants: for women to be able to truly define themselves, to author their own fates. "I absolutely do totally want a revolution," she said. "Because I've got kids, and for my own peace of mind I need the world to change before they get out there. I totally need the world to change entirely so they can be safe and happy and never get to seventeen and look in the mirror and say, 'I'm fat and inadequate and there is no place in this world for me.'

"So that's why I have to change the world. I have six years to make it into a feminist paradise so my little girls won't get screwed up."

ELIZABETH BLACKBURN: WHY SCIENCE MUST ADAPT TO WOMEN

If Elizabeth Blackburn were male, I would never have been assigned this profile. I knew nothing about her work; I'd never even taken high school biology. I certainly didn't understand telomeres—the discovery of which would, in 2009, eventually earn her a Nobel Prize. She graciously (and patiently) explained them to me, using stuffed, chromosome-shaped pillows that were specially designed for such occasions. One of the more telling parts of this piece, which ran in November 2002, is the study in which researchers sent out fake résumés that were identical except for the gender of the job applicant. In 2017, a similar experiment was published by the San Francisco Federal Reserve Bank: forty thousand fake résumés were sent out—all identical except for the gender and the age of the candidate—to thirteen thousand online job listings. The result: "compelling evidence" that older workers, especially women, continue to experience discrimination in hiring.

Elizabeth Blackburn is talking about chromosomes, which isn't surprising: she is the biologist who in 1978 first established that telomeres, caps on the ends of chromosomes, protect critical genetic material from eroding during cell division. Seven years later, she and molecular biologist Carol Greider discovered the enzyme telomerase. Both findings offer tantalizing clues to the mysteries of aging and cancer. In as many as 90 percent of metastatic cancers, for instance, telomerase is wildly overexpressed. Blackburn's work has launched one of the hottest fields in cell biology. Her office in the Blackburn Lab at the University of California at San Francisco (UCSF) is chockablock with awards; it also sports a poster depicting dancing chromosomes tipped with merry, Day-Glo telomeres.

What has Blackburn riled up at the moment, however, has nothing to do with her research. She is focused on the Xs and Ys of chromosomes and why it is that more XX types—women—disappear from academic science. Nearly half of undergraduate science and engineering degrees are earned by women, but that number plummets to a third at the doctoral level, propped up by high numbers in fields such as psychology. Just 22 percent of doctorates in physics and 12 percent in engineering are awarded to women. At the faculty level, women's representation shrinks to 20 percent, concentrated, after controlling for age, in the lower ranks and at less prestigious institutions. In the rarefied air of the National Academy of Sciences, women's membership hovers around 7 percent. Blackburn is one of these elite survivors.

"The argument has been that the pipeline will take care

of this," Blackburn says, referring to the idea that if enough women are encouraged to enter science early, the gender gap, over time, will disappear. "But the pipeline has been good for a number of years, and it hasn't taken care of it. In biology it's especially insidious because 50 percent of grad students are female. This has been the case for quite some time. Yet when I was chair of my department, I was the only woman chair in the entire medical school. We are putting a lot of our students off continuing—both men and women, but more women. They vote with their feet."

Make no mistake, Blackburn has flourished in the culture of science. But when she entered in the 1970s, the expectation was that once the pesky problem of overt discrimination was solved, women would adapt to science. Three decades later, she believes that hypothesis was wrong. To create true equality—to ensure that the best minds continue—she feels that science will have to adapt to women.

IT IS NO SECRET WHY WOMEN SCIENTISTS FLOW OUT OF THE ACADEMIC pipeline. Numerous studies have shown that subtle, often unintentional bias combined with a tenure process that overlaps childbearing years has a corrosive effect. A study of two thousand science and engineering doctoral students sponsored by the National Science Foundation in 1996 found that men were more likely than women to report that they were taken seriously by faculty. They were also more likely to have received help designing research, writing grant proposals, coauthoring publications, and learning management skills.

According to Gerhard Sonnert, a sociologist of science at Harvard University who published a large-scale study on gender and science in 1995, women are often put off by the combative style that's rewarded in scientific research, as well as the emphasis on self-promotion. "There's an accepted language of science that has entered into the folklore and become the field," Blackburn says. "Women don't necessarily speak that exact same language, which is not to say that the language they use is not as good. It is. But all those subtle ways women present things that are different from men, even their tone of voice, play into how what they're presenting is accepted, its authority." What's more, women who do take on an aggressive style are often labeled "difficult."

Women who stick to the academic track may run into further obstacles when they go job hunting. Rhea Steinpreis, a neuroscientist at the University of Wisconsin-Milwaukee, sent more than two hundred thirty curricula vitae to randomly selected professors, asking them to evaluate the fitness of the candidate as a job applicant. The CVs were identical in every respect but one: Half were sent by "Karen Miller" and half by "Brian Miller." Fewer than half the professors would hire Karen; Brian was endorsed by two-thirds.

Sometimes women fight back: In 1999 a group of female faculty at the Massachusetts Institute of Technology presented a report to the president of the institution quantifying a culture that marginalized women. In addition to lower pay, they documented discrimination in hiring, promotions, and awards; exclusion from leadership positions; inequities in lab size; and hostility toward family responsibilities. Meanwhile, faculty ratios hadn't budged in two decades. Perhaps the saddest aspect of the report was that because female faculty members had little contact with one another, they tended to see their ill treatment as a unique, isolated event rather than the result of gender bias. When they quit, as many did, they blamed themselves for their inability to thrive.

ELIZABETH BLACKBURN IS HARD-PRESSED TO RECALL EVER BEING told that because she was female she couldn't be a scientist. Growing up in Tasmania, Australia, the second of seven children whose parents were both family physicians, she considered science a birthright. She was further insulated from stereotyping by attending an all-girls school and an all-female college.

Blackburn went on to graduate school at Cambridge and a postdoctoral fellowship at Yale, where she recalls her mentor, cell biologist Joe Gall, as particularly supportive. Looking back on her career, however, she believes she was subject to plenty of bias; like many successful women in nontraditional fields, she was just particularly adept at denying it. "I was oblivious for a long time," she recalls, "and that's the way I coped. It was very much a defense. If I had stopped and thought about it, I would've felt so vulnerable to it."

As she talks, Blackburn sits in the living room of the house she shares with her husband, John Sedat, a cell biologist and microscopy expert at UCSF who works on three-dimensional structures of chromosomes in nuclei, and their fifteen-year-old son, Ben. It's a typically chilly San Francisco summer Sunday. Wisps of fog slide by, rendering the view as undefined as the cost to a woman of blocking out an unfriendly culture. "I spent so much time exhausted and anxious," Blackburn sighs. "It was a different kind of tension than for my male colleagues. And I can't really say what that means. Was I more afraid of being wrong? I don't know."

Not until she was an assistant professor at the University of California at Berkeley and saw a talented female colleague turned down for tenure did Blackburn realize that denial might not protect her. "That was my first wake-up-and-smell-the-coffee feeling," she says. "For a long time, I was stupid enough to think it's only the science that counts. That's a great comfort because you love doing your science. But realistically I knew—I know now—that's not the whole thing."

What propelled Blackburn forward was her passion for the work. She is a driven, gifted scientist, and the exciting results of her research reinforced her commitment. If they hadn't, she wonders whether she would have persisted. Like many women, she was tempted to dribble out of the pipeline toward the end of her postdoc. "At one point I thought I was pregnant," she says. "And I thought, Oh well, I'll just have a child, and I won't have to think about this pressure. I don't know if that would've been short-term or not. I look back and think how easily one can be deflected because one is at a daunting stage such as having to go out and look for a job."

Blackburn had only one child, at thirty-eight, after her appointment to the safe haven of full professorship. When she was placed on bed rest for the last five months of the pregnancy, she offered to take the time as a sabbatical with reduced pay. Her department head, a man, informed her that she was entitled to a leave with full salary. "Here I was, all apologetic," she says. "I was *inviting* discrimination. It was pathetic. Even at the time, I realized that. But I felt like, here I am not keeping up my end of the bargain."

After Ben was born, she moved to UCSF. For years, she says, her life consisted of exactly two things: work and family, which makes her sympathetic to other parents in her lab.

"Many women wonder, 'How am I going to do this and have a family?' Because part of the culture of science is that if you're not there until late, you're not really doing it, which is the biggest pile of crap. All these hours and chatting and things like that don't make the science better."

She and Sedat were lucky and affluent enough to find a child-care provider they trusted. *Luck* is a word that Blackburn uses often. She feels lucky to have had encouraging mentors, lucky that her research vindicated her commitment, lucky to have found consistent, loving child care for Ben, lucky to have satisfying work, a happy marriage, and parenthood. Listening to her, though, one wonders: Serendipity plays a role in every life, but is it disproportionately necessary for a woman who wants to pursue academic research? "Someone once asked me how I did it as a woman," Blackburn recalls. "I said something that surprised even me at the time: 'I disguised myself as a man.' I had not really realized until that conversation that that's what I was doing. At the time, I didn't think of it as a sad thing, but it is sad."

She does not perpetuate that strategy. Her lab is half female; a bulletin board is covered with photos of pregnant grad students and postdocs. Some of her students have gone on to mentor others. And twenty years after she and Greider discovered telomerase, the research on the enzyme is largely dominated by women.

BLACKBURN PACKS ME OFF TO LUNCH ONE AFTERNOON WITH THREE OF the most promising young women scientists in her lab. Jue Lin, thirty-two, is a postdoc in molecular biology with a PhD from Cornell. Melissa Rivera, thirty, who did her undergraduate work at MIT, will soon move on to a postdoc at the University of Texas at Austin. Carol Anderson, twenty-nine, is a graduate student in molecular biology with a BS from Yale. Rivera and Anderson are single. Lin is married with two toddlers.

We stroll down the hill to a Thai place in San Francisco's Sunset District, taking a circuitous route to avoid the steepest streets. While each of these women had once assumed that she would become a principal investigator, they are no longer quite so sure. All three consider their doubts to be personal, yet they sound awfully familiar to me. "It's just, you've got to be this person that I don't want to be in order to be successful as a scientist," Rivera says. "You have to be competitive, and grab things from wherever you can get them, and be protective of what you present."

But surely they're accustomed to competition. "This is different," Lin says. "It's not just about studying and getting good grades. I've always done well at that. This is politics." In addition to, or perhaps because of, her disenchantment, the demands of work seem to conflict with family life. "When I'm in the lab, I think about what's going on in the house," she says. "At home I think, 'I could be working, I could be getting something done.'"

Rivera has put her social life on hold until she finishes her degree. At thirty, she is more interested in biology than in her biological clock, but when she projects forward, she's apprehensive. "By the time I'll be established, I'll be forty," she says. "So then I get to maybe date and get married and have children. People can do it, and they do, but meanwhile, you're working twelve hours a day. It's not human."

Anderson, the youngest, frowns. "Maybe it's not necessary to work sixteen hours a day to be successful." she says. "I wanted to be in Liz's lab, to have an example of someone who was successful but lives a balanced life." She has joined a support program for women graduate students in the sciences. Does she expect to become an advocate for change? "I would," she says, "but I'm not sure what change needs to happen. The problem isn't clearly defined."

"How do you get rid of those subtle biases?" Rivera asks of no one in particular.

"It takes effort," Anderson says. "Women mentoring other women, supporting each other—which won't happen if women don't go into academic science."

On the way back to the lab, the three enthuse about Blackburn. "Liz is really special," Rivera says. "My next principal investigator is also a woman. She's not typical either. Maybe if I see a lot of PIs like them, it will make a difference. The door is still open. Ask me again in five years. Maybe I'll see that I can do this and still be me."

BLACKBURN IS TROUBLED BY THE YOUNGER WOMEN'S PERCEPTION OF what it takes to be a successful academic. True, she says, the pressure is more intense for this generation, male or female, at all career stages. But those three could more than meet the challenge. "How many years have these women spent doing incredibly difficult, demanding work? Ten? Thirteen? They ought to get more choices and not feel intimidated after all that. If you have a passion for the work, you should be able to go for it."

Maybe they will. Recently, there have been signs of change.

A follow-up to the MIT report, issued in March, showed that while the institution still had a long way to go, it had made progress: More women had been appointed to leadership roles, salaries had increased, collegiality had improved. The university is considering innovative hiring practices and has changed the tenure process to allow time out for childbearing. Other universities have launched their own investigations. Some already offer on-site day care, part-time positions, housing, and mentoring.

For more radical thinkers like Debra Rolison, head of the Advanced Electrochemical Materials Section at the Naval Research Lab in Washington, D.C., waiting for reform isn't acceptable. She believes taxpayers shouldn't support discriminatory institutions. Title IX legislation ought to be applied to hiring practices in academic science, she says. "It's simple. We should yank all federal funds if departments are not hiring women commensurate to how they're training them. You can bet that would solve the problem quickly."

IN LATE JUNE, BLACKBURN IS IN WASHINGTON, D.C., SERVING ON the president's Bioethics Council on Stem Cell Research. Other scientists had declined to participate, believing the committee would be stacked toward conservatives. Perhaps those years of being a lone female voice make her more willing to stand up for the minority position. "This research is enormously important," she says. "There are intractable diseases out there, and we can't continue with business as usual."

When the council breaks after three days, she is cautiously optimistic. A narrow majority of the members have been swayed to her point of view: ban reproductive cloning but proceed with cloning for research under strict regulation. Will that position be reflected in the final report? "They could easily present this in a way that would hang up the research, that would effectively make it impossible to proceed," Blackburn warns. (The following month, when the report became public, it did disappoint. It advised a four-year moratorium, an option that had hardly been discussed by the group. Discouraged, Blackburn skipped the next meeting.)

For now she has brought her son, Ben, with her, and they're eager to hit the museums. I ask Ben how he copes with his mother's frequent travels. Even as the question escapes my mouth, I realize it reflects my own unconscious bias: Would I ask the son of a male biologist whether his father's travel schedule upsets him? Am I not implying that Ben *ought* to resent his mother's work?

The truth is that when Ben was younger, Blackburn's absence did make him anxious, which worried her. She cut back on trips and stayed away no more than two nights at a time. She and Sedat never traveled simultaneously. Today Ben seems enviably close to both parents and quietly proud of his mother's accomplishments. "I don't like her going away," he says thoughtfully. "But this council is a worthy cause, and it's important for her to make some good happen. I'm in agreement with her on these issues; we share the same opinion—and she didn't prime me to say that!"

It is difficult to believe there could be any barriers left for Blackburn to break through, but I can't resist asking. She has been nominated for a Nobel Prize, an honor only ten women scientists have won since it was first awarded in 1901. Will those XX chromosomes undermine telomerase's chance for glory? "If you look at the track record, it would certainly factor against it," she says, then smiles wryly. "But every now and then, you know, someone has to make a gesture to prove the track record is wrong."

MIRANDA COSGROVE: THE GOOD GIRL

Kids' media tends to market its stars' innocence as part of their appeal—Miley Cyrus, Selena Gomez, and Britney Spears all at one time wore "promise rings" indicating they would remain virgins until marriage. As they get older, to prove they're all grown up, those same stars turn their sexuality into a marketing gimmick as well—in the process teaching girls that self-objectification is a feminine, even a feminist, rite of passage. Miranda Cosgrove, star of the hugely popular Nickelodeon show iCarly, was different: she had a reputation for being diligent and sensible. I caught up with her in 2010, a few months before she turned eighteen. I wanted to find out whether she could make the transition more creatively. The piece ran in March 2011, just before she decided to enroll in the University of Southern California. Since then, she has voiced the character of Margo in the Despicable Me films and acted in two failed sitcoms. Has she achieved Miley-Selena-Britney-level status? No. But at twenty-two, she's still in school, still working, still close with her parents, and seems to be balancing fame and real life just fine.

ON VETERANS DAY AT MARY FAY PENDLETON ELEMENTARY
school on the Camp Pendleton Marine base, American
flags lined the sidewalks. Bunting festooned the windows
along with children's crayoned drawings of tanks, fighter
planes, and soldiers shooting bullets or throwing grenades.
Although the school was closed for the holiday, hundreds
of kids and parents had gathered on a playing field to break
ground for a new "teaching garden." The program was sponsored by the American Heart Association and Kelly Meyer, the
wife of the Universal Studios president, Ron Meyer. Which
explained the improbable presence of Miranda Cosgrove, the
seventeen-year-old star of the hit Nickelodeon show *iCarly*. A
photographer stopped her as she walked toward a makeshift
stage and asked her to plant a cabbage seedling, but a strand of
her long, dark hair fell across her face, ruining his shot. Cosgrove's smile never dimmed as she scooped up the plant and
tried again. This time her hair stayed put. "Perfect," said the
photographer. And it was.

If you don't recognize Cosgrove's name, you must not be
between ages two and fourteen, the parent of such a child, or,
possibly, British (nearly 8 percent of England's population
tunes into *iCarly*). You're also not of much interest to Nickelodeon, which aims for the eyeballs, as well as the prodi-
gious pocket change, of today's media-hungry tweens. *iCarly*
is the network's most popular show among that desirable
demographic—two years ago it surpassed the seemingly un-
touchable *Hannah Montana* in ratings. Cosgrove, who report-
edly earns $180,000 an episode, is the second-highest-paid
child actor on TV (bested only by Angus T. Jones, the "half"

on CBS's blighted *Two and a Half Men*). Her first album, *Sparks Fly*, was released last spring by Columbia Records and made its debut at No. 8 on the Billboard 200. She is also an official "ambassador" for Neutrogena; topped a float in the Macy's Thanksgiving Day Parade; and serenaded the president's daughters in a White House Christmas special.

That makes Cosgrove the latest in a series of "It" girls—among them Miley Cyrus, Selena Gomez, and Hilary Duff—who have emerged over the past decade: not just actresses, not just singers, these young women are industries. In addition to TV shows, they have movies, recording careers, clothing and cosmetic lines, and their images appear on everything from coloring books to nail clippers. Their popularity, in part, rises from the new perch they occupy in tween girls' hearts. Rather than wanting to be *with* their idols (as they would, say, Justin Bieber), young fans want to *be* them. That's a different relationship entirely.

Still, the secret to their juggernauts may have less to do with kids' fantasies than with the one they evoke in parents: from the smoothness of their skin to the length of their hemlines to the banality of their song lyrics and sitcom plots, these young stars embody an ideal of teenage innocence that adults are grateful to embrace. For as many seasons as the illusion can be maintained, they remain, at least on-screen, uncomplicated, untroubled good girls on the verge of, but never actually awakening to, their sexuality. There is a lot of money to be made—and a lot of parental anxiety to be tapped—by walking that line. There is also a lot of fury unleashed at those who step across it. When young stars pose seminude or get caught drinking, they threaten the notion that our own daughters' coming-of-age could be effortless. Suddenly, the "role models" who have perpetuated that myth become the vector of our fears. The betrayal feels personal and cuts deep.

Cosgrove seems to wear the pressure lightly. At Mary Fay Pendleton Elementary school, she extolled the virtues of broccoli and regular exercise, her affect appealingly, accessibly awkward—just like a real girl. Her flowered swing top (purchased, she told me, the night before to go with the garden theme), skinny jeans, and fake-distressed combat boots were fashionable yet modest; pretty but not sexy. When she leaned forward to sign a few hurried autographs, children hugged her, kissed her.

After a few more quick publicity photos, her escort suggested that Cosgrove wait for her driver inside the principal's office. "They're about to let the kids go," he explained, "and you'll be mobbed."

Cosgrove glanced hesitantly at her mother, Chris, who accompanied her to the event. "It's okay," Miranda said. "I don't mind." Chris added firmly, "She's here for the kids." Two more officials rushed over to shoo her away, and each time, Cosgrove was reassuring. Finally, the school principal called the escort's cell and said: "They're coming! Tell her to *just get in the car and go!*" So, reluctantly, she did.

As Cosgrove's Town Car pulled away, I noticed a mother hurrying forward with her two small daughters, looking expectant. "She's *leaving*?" the woman said, disgusted. "That's just terrible."

Disney has churned out more tween-girl idols, but Nickelodeon pioneered the concept back in 1991, with *Clarissa Explains It All*, starring Melissa Joan Hart. That show demonstrated that a female lead could play to both sexes. Until then, the conventional Hollywood wisdom held that girls would watch a male protagonist but that the reverse was not the case, so a show with a female star would instantly halve your market share. Additionally, *Clarissa* featured an actress who, at fourteen, was the same tender age as the part she played, intensifying fans' identification with her.

It took Disney until 2001 to broadcast its own perky-girl-centered sitcom: *Lizzie McGuire*, starring Hilary Duff, who was then thirteen. "Lizzie" books, "Lizzie" albums, a "Lizzie" movie, and a "Lizzie" clothing line soon followed. When Duff quit the brand over a contract dispute, Disney merely replicated the formula with Raven-Symoné, filming sixty-five episodes of *That's So Raven* in rapid succession, before its star could age out of her role.

Then came *Hannah Montana*, a show about a girl named Miley Stewart (played by Miley Cyrus, who also took on the role at age thirteen) with a secret: an ordinary teen by day, at night she becomes—a pop star! *Lizzie* and *Raven* were big, but nothing like this: by 2008 *Hannah* had two hundred million viewers globally, and Cyrus was on her way to becoming a billionaire. The show was an ideal fit for a generation whose increasing access to celebrities—through Web sites, Facebook, Twitter—changed the nature of their dreams: stardom was no longer confined to the distant climes of Hollywood or New York. It was available to anyone with access to a smartphone and YouTube.

iCarly, which made its debut in 2007, trades on that notion as well. In it, Cosgrove plays Carly Shay, a spunky yet relatable teenager who, when she's not attending high school, hosts a wacky yet wholesome Web show—*let's make chicken soup in a toilet!*—with her two best friends. On the program's on-line counterpart, fans can watch webisodes of those shows-within-a-show. They're also encouraged to post their own videos (a kid squirting milk out of his eyes) for the entertainment of the cast and one another, further blurring the distinction between performer and fan. Such contrived intimacy fuels brand loyalty and also the belief that *iCarly* truly is the young viewer's friend. All the more crucial, then, that the actress who plays her behave in an exemplary way. "The first time someone called me a role model," Cosgrove recalled, "I remember thinking, What does that mean? But I feel aware of it when I'm reading scripts. I want to be able to make things that the people who watch my show can see and that they would enjoy."

Cosgrove likes to say she's "doing home-school," though that is normalizing what is a very unusual situation. Child actors are required by law to spend fifteen hours a week being tutored until they complete high school or (a popular choice) test out at sixteen. Cosgrove used to do her studying in public libraries, but since the success of *iCarly*, that's become impossible. Kids recognize her, word spreads, and soon she's beset by crowds begging for autographs. "We've been told to leave about half the libraries in Los Angeles for being distracting," she said.

I joined her and her tutor, Patti Foy, one morning in a conference room on the Nickelodeon lot in Los Angeles. Cosgrove was busily composing an essay on *Macbeth*. Chris Cosgrove was there, too, getting ready to run some errands. Foy, who has been tutoring Miranda for nine years, gushed over what a model pupil her charge is: Cosgrove completed precalculus over the summer and was now taking Shakespeare, French III, economics, and government. Her progress is evaluated by a college prep "distance learning" school called Laurel Springs, from which she has always gotten straight As. While I didn't doubt her intelligence or diligence, it almost seemed too much: Could this girl be more perfect? A more glittering ideal? "There are lots of easy ways to get by," Foy added proudly. "Miranda has always chosen the hard path."

Cosgrove's acting career seems to have proceeded along an easier road, or at least a charmed one, beginning with a random Lana Turner moment at age three: an agent spied Miranda clowning around with her parents at a Los Angeles food festival and handed Chris a card. Perhaps the girl could model. Chris wasn't especially keen to put her only child in front of the camera, but after checking out the agency, her parents thought they would give it a go. "Our big plan when we decided to do this was to get money for college," she said. Within a few weeks, Cosgrove landed a commercial for the soft drink Mello Yello. More ads and a few small TV roles followed; then, at age nine, she was cast as an elementary school prig turned band manager in the movie *School of Rock*. Shortly before that film was released, she landed another role, as Megan, the diabolical younger sister on the Nickelodeon show *Drake and Josh*. The reaction of her fourth-grade classmates to that news marked the moment, Cosgrove recalled, "when I really understood I was acting. Since I did it from the time I was so little, I never thought of it as 'a job.' And I didn't realize that everybody didn't do it."

Her mother, Chris, and her father, Tom, were wary of the impact that fame could have on their daughter. They've tried, as much as they can with a superstar child, to maintain a normal life—the one they might have had if all this had not happened. They live in a middle-class suburb of Los Angeles, in the same house they have owned since Miranda was born. Tom Cosgrove still works every day at the dry-cleaning business he owns. "We don't feel like we're a part of her world," Chris explained. "Like what are we going to do later? And, you know, it's not our money. So we're doing our own thing."

For as long as they could, they also kept Miranda in public school, but by sixth grade, coordinating multiple teachers and a more complex schedule proved impossible. "It took a lot for my mom to give in," Cosgrove said. "I remember her asking: 'Are you sure you want to do this? Are you sure you want to stay in acting?'

"At first I was kind of happy to be homeschooled," she continued, "because all my friends were afraid of that first day of middle school. But actually it's harder. You're all alone." For a short time, her costars, Drake Bell and Josh Peck, shared her classroom, but they were several years older than she and quickly obtained their GEDs. "I cried when they left," Cosgrove admitted. "It's cool in a way, but I miss being in a regular school."

Child stars tend to be isolated from other kids. The perpetual scrutiny of adults—even those they love—can feel at least as intense as that of fans and the media, and it's that spotlight that seems to make Cosgrove squirm. Whenever one of her "team" praised her talent or intellect, which happened regularly, she ducked her head in the typical adolescent combination of mortification and pride. When Foy pulled out a homework essay for me to read, Cosgrove put her book over her face and moaned, "Oh, my God!"

A child performer must always be accompanied by a parent or guardian while working. A publicist shadowed Cosgrove during our interviews. Her manager is often with her, too, as is Foy. And of course, Chris (who won't appear in photos and refuses to be interviewed) is almost always near her daughter, a protective and often corrective presence. After a concert one night, she noticed that Miranda, engrossed in conversation, unintentionally ignored someone who was leaving her dressing room. It was a small thing, and completely accidental, but Chris called her on it.

"Miranda," she said sharply. "Someone said goodbye to you!"

Cosgrove stopped short and turned around. "Oh, I'm so sorry," she said earnestly. "Goodbye, it was nice to meet you."

To give Miranda a break, Chris tries to carve out time at the end of each day for her daughter to hang out with old pals from elementary school (Miranda's best friend, whom she has known since second grade, still lives next door). Yet even they are conscious of Cosgrove's image. When a young man she didn't know asked to take a picture with her during a party, her former classmates stopped him and insisted he first put down the bottle he was holding. "That could go up on the Internet," one of them cautioned. "We don't want anyone thinking Miranda is drinking a beer." She couldn't risk being perceived as doing something inappropriate—something *realistic*—like the rest of them.

With her millions of dollars, concert tours, and celebrity chums, Cosgrove would seem the enviable one, the girl with all the opportunity. Yet in some ways she is more constrained than the friends she left behind: at least they are free to explore their identities, mess up, hook up, test their limits, taste a beer. At one point, Miranda regaled me with the story of how, on one of her rare dates, she looked into the rearview mirror of the boy's car to find her mother tailing them. I glanced over at Chris, waiting for an explanation. "Well," she said slowly, "it's not the way it sounds." Then, to her daughter's amusement, she retold the story—exactly the same way, adding only, "I was going to have to pick her up at the restaurant anyway, so I figured I might as well go then and wait."

It isn't easy to watch a daughter's incipient forays into romance and sexuality. If Miranda embodies the wish that girls could engage in the former without the latter, Chris was acting out a parent's desire to ensure it. Most of us don't (and can't) chaperone our daughters at school, at concerts, at public appearances. Most of us accept, if with some ambivalence, that our daughters have to navigate the turbulence of romantic life on their own. Most of us have no choice but to let our daughters go.

NEITHER DISNEY NOR NICKELODEON WANTS ITS LUCRATIVE TEEN-age properties to become tabloid staples. When Disney retitled the last season of Cyrus's show *Hannah Montana Forever*, the studio probably wished it could be true. But little girls grow bigger every day. And often the largest threat to the tween-girl franchises are the stars themselves, whose adolescent growing pains leave them vulnerable to empire-gutting scandal. Gary Marsh, president of entertainment for Disney Channel, sounded like a fretful father when he moaned to a reporter that concern over his stars' behavior "keeps me up at night."

Yet what is a good girl to do? By sixteen, playing the

G-rated role no longer feels so sweet. After all, no one wants to be a role model to nine-year-olds forever. As a performer and a person, you have to grow up. And what is the fastest way for a young woman to shed the mantle of wholesomeness? Easy: take it off with the rest of her clothes.

A lingerie-clad Hilary Duff appeared on the cover of *Maxim* magazine. So did Melissa Joan Hart from *Clarissa*. Jamie Lynn Spears, Britney's younger sister and star of Nickelodeon's *Zoey 101*, announced at age sixteen that she was pregnant out of wedlock. As for Cyrus, she, more than anyone, was sold as the girl whom parents could trust. Much was made of her "true love waits" ring that symbolized her vow of premarital chastity. She told Oprah in 2007 that "I look way young, and that's the way that's more comfortable for me." In 2008, Barbara Walters called her "any parent's antidote to the current crop of teen train wrecks." Two months later, *Vanity Fair* published several photos of Cyrus, including one of the fifteen-year-old seemingly nude, hair and makeup mussed, a rumpled sheet clutched to her chest. Then came a pole dance at the Teen Choice Awards and a string of outré videos, including one of the underage star in a club grinding with a man who appeared to be in his mid-forties. Her former agent, Mitchell Gossett, advises his clients to "keep it clean till eighteen," but she apparently couldn't wait.

Parents who had bought Cyrus's virginal hype (and praised her to their daughters) were livid. How dare she break character that way? She was supposed to be a poster girl for purity! Yet it may be the very expectations foisted on girls like Cyrus—the fetishizing of their innocence, the dogged refusal to acknowledge their changing selves, the denial of libido that the stars themselves collude in—that prime them to push hard in the other direction. No wonder that Selena Gomez, star of Disney's popular *Wizards of Waverly Place*, recently quietly slipped off her own chastity ring—which she had called a "promise to myself, to my family, and to God"—donned a black miniskirt and stilettos, and told a fanzine, "I don't want to be stuck in a box anymore."

By last November, when eighteen-year-old Demi Lovato—star of Disney Channel's *Sonny with a Chance* and one of the girls Disney pushed forward in the wake of Cyrus's mini-scandals—landed in rehab "for emotional and physical issues," her crash seemed almost part of the script. That same month, in an AOL poll, Cyrus sank from TV's number-one role model to the bottom of the heap, below the *Dancing with the Stars* contestant and abstinence advocate Bristol Palin.

Cosgrove, by contrast, seems, at least for now, to feel less confined by her image, willing to nudge the boundaries rather than tear them down. Before a guest appearance in an episode of *The Good Wife*, in which she played a dissolute tween idol, both Patti Foy and a Nickelodeon executive vetted the script for untoward language or provocative clothing. A scene with suggestive dance moves was excised. "We want to make sure her golden-girl image is still there," Foy told me. When, in "Dancing Crazy," Cosgrove sings about "going all night" or "hot hot," she's referring solely to the dance floor. In a publicity still, her hair is blown back by invisible wind, and she's wearing a T-shirt that says I ♥ Boys. For a girl of nearly eighteen, that is indeed keeping it clean.

THE GREENROOM AT THE *JIMMY KIMMEL LIVE!* SHOW IS TRICKED OUT like the ultimate man cave. During one evening's preshow festivities, a bartender poured free drinks; a football game blared from a giant flat-screen TV. A group of guys in cowboy hats lounged on deep-cushioned couches, and some dude, maybe a friend of Kimmel's, seemed hypnotized by a game of *Pac-Man*. Cosgrove, who was there to promote her *Good Wife* appearance as well as an hour-long *iCarly* special, kept her distance from all of it. She stayed in her dressing room, chatting with her manager and publicist, as Chris and a stylist fussed around her, affixing her dress's grosgrain straps to her body with double-sided tape to avoid any possible wardrobe malfunctions. A crew member popped by with his daughter, a blond first grader with a bowl haircut. When she saw Cosgrove, she froze, shoving all the fingers of both hands into her mouth.

"Go ahead," the dad coaxed. "Say hi to Miranda."

The girl hesitated, then burst out, "I wish I was watching *iCarly!*," shoved her hands back in her mouth, and ran out of the room as if she had been set on fire.

Kimmel's first guest that evening was Kathy Griffin. She strutted onstage and, before taking her seat, bragged about the loft of her breasts (though "breasts" wasn't the word she used) and the tautness of her behind (again, different word), then twirled around, asking Kimmel over her shoulder, "Do you ever wish you tapped that?" She spent the rest of the segment riffing on the tabloid shenanigans of tween idols. She mocked Britney and Justin, then did a bit about feeling outclassed at a tony cocktail party until the hostess turned to her and asked, "Now, Kathy, what is going on with the Lohans?"

"I'm on twenty-four-hour-a-day Lohan watch," she joked. "She's got the government LoJack, and then she has the Kathy Griffin LoJack."

Watching on a monitor from her dressing room, Cosgrove laughed, but Chris was becoming visibly nervous. (Later she would tell me, "I thought maybe she'd say Miranda attacked Dakota Fanning or something.")

I turned to Cosgrove's manager, Mark Beaven, and asked how he thinks Cosgrove can age more gracefully than Griffin's foils. No matter whom I asked that question, the answer was always the same—she had to *evolve* rather than leap to adulthood, look for good material, choose her roles carefully. That is, of course, what parents of her fans hope to hear. But while the generalities were true, the specifics were always vague. One thing's for sure: no one imagines Cosgrove dancing on a pole. "Ultimately, it's really up to Miranda," Beaven said. "Miley is facing challenges because she's stepping into other parts of her career. She can do that, but her following may not respond favorably, and that's the reality."

Among the options Cosgrove discusses: walking away, at least for a while. She talked as often and enthusiastically to me about going to college in a year as she did about finding a great script or cutting a new album. During our time together, she was industriously filling out college applications, answering questions like "What is your concept of a global networked university" that would make most teenagers with a seven-figure-salary flee. But college has been the plan from the get-go, the reason she went into acting. "Yes, it could make her lose momentum," Chris said. "I understand that. But if the talent is there, it will always be there. And in a way, maybe when you come back you won't be stuck in the stigma of being the child star. So it could be an advantage."

Cosgrove's manager was politic about the possibility that she'll leave while still at her peak ("My mother was a college professor," he said), but Kimmel was not. "Why do you want to go to college?" he asked with mock-incredulity when Cosgrove came on set. She started to answer, but he cut her off. "You're already very successful and wealthy, and I see no reason to get an education." Cosgrove laughed and answered, "Well, my dad went to USC." When I pressed her on the subject later, she said: "It's weird for me. My friends are going through this thing of figuring out what they want to do with their lives. And I—at this point, I think I know what I want. But if I go to college, I can figure it out for sure." Maybe for her, it's not about finding a career path, though. Maybe college would give Cosgrove something else: four years to be a kid, or a budding adult, like any other, without everyone watching—something she's never really gotten to be.

Back on the set, the applause swelled, and the camera pulled back for a commercial. Kimmel leaned in toward Cosgrove and, almost as a throwaway, said, "I hope you don't wind up in a lot of trouble like all those other stars."

IT'S NOT QUITE THE SAME AS MATRICULATING, BUT ON A WINTER night in December, Miranda Cosgrove was attending San Jose State University. She was performing as part of a radio-sponsored holiday show called "Triple Ho." As in ho-ho-ho. Only not. The other performers on the bill—the hip-hop artists Nelly and Jay Sean, the R&B singer Taio Cruz, and the Latin crossover sensation Enrique Iglesias—skew to a decidedly older crowd. At a parking structure near the event, I overheard a conversation between two young women, students at the University of California, Berkeley, who drove down for the show. "I can't wait to see Enrique," said the first one, Anisa

Young, who wore cutoffs over tights, ballet flats, and a leather jacket. "And Nelly. Actually, everyone—except Miranda Cosgrove."

I broke in and introduced myself, asking her why Cosgrove didn't appeal. "She's too random in this lineup," Young explained. "We're looking at this cool list, and then we see her, and it's like, What's going on? She's for little kids."

And that is the bind of the tween-girl idol: If you sell your sexuality, your young fan base (and certainly their parents) will turn on you. Yet if you stay clean, you're dismissed by your peers as too bland. What's more, no one—neither young women who have gone through it nor girls who will—has patience for the mistakes and pratfalls of your transition to womanhood.

Young and her friend each made a face when I mentioned Cyrus, though they were devotees as little girls. "All that stuff she's done . . . ," Young said, trailing off. It's not the sexiness per se—they were both Katy Perry fans, and she shoots whipped cream from her breasts. It was the suddenness and the extremity of the shift. It felt disingenuous to them, overly calculated. They simply didn't buy it. Nor apparently did many others: Cyrus's last album, *Can't Be Tamed*, was, for the first time in her career, a commercial disappointment, and the domestic gross of her 2010 film, *The Last Song*, was nearly 20 percent lower than her 2009 release, *Hannah Montana: The Movie*.

When Cosgrove performed early on in the show, however, she was received warmly enough by the crowd, which seemed happy to bop along to her hit "Kissin' U." It was a likable performance, and Cosgrove seemed content with it. The following week she would go back to the studio to finish up her new single with Max Martin, the producer who, as it happens, worked with Katy Perry on several of her singles.

Perry, whom few parents would consider a role model for their girls, incited controversy last year when she appeared in a low-cut dress singing a duet with Elmo on *Sesame Street* (the segment was ultimately shelved). For the moment, anyway, Cosgrove would be welcomed in that neighborhood. By next year, who knows? Maybe she'll be in college. Maybe she'll land a slightly edgy role in an indie film, which is another of her fondest dreams. Maybe she'll be touring stadiums, or maybe her pop career will go flat. When I asked her where she'd like to be in five or ten years, she laughed and said she didn't know. And really, how can seventeen imagine twenty-five? I tried again: "Where do you think you'll be in a year?"

She paused, thoughtfully. "I really don't know," she said. "I hope at least I have my driver's license."

KATHERINE MARY FLANNIGAN: THE STORY OF MY LIFE

This essay is a meditation on the collision of dreams with reality: on growing up, on struggling with marriage, on the ways a book can shape and sustain you during hard times. If I could have, I would've added A Tree Grows in Brooklyn, *Laura Ingalls Wilder's "Little House" books and* Anne of Green Gables *to my list of formative volumes. I have read all of those to my daughter, though we have yet to tackle* Mrs. Mike. *This piece was published in December 2007, three years before Nancy Freedman died at age ninety. Her husband, Ben, followed two years later at ninety-two. I think about them often—their grit, spirit, and especially their iconoclasm. They remain among my role models; I miss them. As for Katherine Mary . . . I still love her story, regardless of its relative truth.*

HAPPENED ACROSS *Mrs. Mike* WHEN I WAS IN SIXTH GRADE; IT WAS buried under a stack of tattered comic books in my older brother's room. I'd snuck in there to snoop for contraband issues of *National Lampoon*, which my mother insisted he hide from me (already possessed of a journalist's curiosity, I took that as a challenge). But *Mrs. Mike*, with its cover illustration of a parka-clad girl on a dogsled, stopped me. The manila library pocket, its checkout card intact, was stamped SUSAN B. ANTHONY, the Minneapolis junior high my brother had attended. I didn't stop to wonder why he would have boosted a love story, first published in 1947, about a plucky sixteen-year-old girl who married a Mountie. Figuring that if he'd swiped it, it must be juicy, I hightailed it to my room, slid under the covers of my canopy bed, and dug in.

That was thirty-five years ago. *Mrs. Mike* has sat at my bedside ever since—traveling with me from Minnesota to Ohio to New York and, finally, to California. After all this time, it's held together with rubber bands and Scotch tape, the pages weathered and dog-eared. I pick it up about once a year, intending merely to leaf through, and end up as engrossed as the first time I read it; the themes of resilience, a woman's indomitable spirit, of living a life of purpose, and doing so with gusto and courage, still hook me.

A classic girl's adventure yarn, *Mrs. Mike* is the real-life tale of Katherine Mary O'Fallon, a turn-of-the-last-century Boston lass who, stricken with pleurisy (one of those literary wasting diseases about which one no longer hears), is sent to Canada to take in the bracing fresh air at her uncle's cattle ranch. She weds Mountie Mike Flannigan after seeing him a mere handful of times and joins him in the wilds of British Columbia. Yet this is no happily-ever-after trifle: every tender moment is offset by tragedy, every triumph booby-trapped with loss. Kathy announces she's pregnant, and shortly afterward a fire levels her town, destroying her home, incinerating her neighbor's son. In the absence of doctors, Mike must assist in amputating a man's leg (without anesthesia). Tension simmers among whites, "'breeds," and Indians. Mosquitoes drive men mad.

When the couple's own two children perish from diphtheria—a disease that would have been treatable had they lived closer to civilization—Kathy breaks. She leaves Mike to return to Boston. But the harsh country, as much as her husband's love, has changed her, and eventually she goes back. They adopt the children of friends (who also died in the epidemic) and begin again, knowing they may well lose this family, too. By the book's final page, Kathy is barely nineteen years old.

As a girl, I was inspired by Kathy's determination. It was the early 1970s, and the feminist movement was crashing headlong into the traditional expectations I'd been raised with. I knew I wanted something different for myself, and even if I wasn't sure what that might be, I suspected that it would involve breaking free of my family and community as Kathy had. She had defied convention and her mother, leaving behind everything she knew, perhaps forever, for a questionable future. True, she was simply following her man (the book isn't called *Ms. Kathy*, after all). But given the parameters and proprieties of the time—before meeting Mike, she'd never even worn pants—hers was a radical act. I wanted to be that fearless, that confident of my convictions, that willing to create a life on my own terms. It was Kathy I thought of at twenty-one, when my father warned me that I'd never make it as a writer. It was Kathy I thought of when I quit my day job with no money in the bank. It was Kathy I thought of when I moved to San Francisco, where I didn't know a soul.

In my late twenties, with my career blossoming, the appeal the book held for me shifted: now I was more taken with the passionate, collaborative partnership Kathy and Mike had formed. I was hoping to find my own soul mate, someone who would engage me, heart and mind. When I found that man, just to be sure, I read him *Mrs. Mike* during late, lazy nights in bed. I noticed that the story was a tad schmaltzy, its portrayal of Native people often problematic. But luckily—for him as well as me—he saw past that. He compared the book to his own all-time favorite, *Jude the Obscure*, another tale of near-inexplicable perseverance.

I'm not saying I wouldn't have married him if he didn't love my favorite book, but that certainly clinched the deal.

MRS. MIKE CAUSED A SENSATION WHEN IT WAS PUBLISHED SIXTY YEARS ago, selling more than a million copies in the first year. Since then, it's been continuously in print, though often just barely. I'd assumed its authors, husband-and-wife team Nancy and Benedict Freedman, were long dead. Even if they'd been as young as thirty in 1947 . . . well, you do the math. Still, they'd had such a profound effect on my life, I wondered what theirs had been like. So one afternoon in the fall of 2002, I did the contemporary version of sneaking into someone's bedroom: I googled them. Immediately, I found a newspaper article about how Amazon had given new life to much-loved but obscure books. *Mrs. Mike* was example A. The dozens of reader reviews—mostly from women like me who'd treasured the story in their teens—had prompted a major reissue. Interesting. But there was more: the Freedmans had been interviewed for the story. Interviewed! That meant they were alive. And not only were they alive, but in a miraculous coincidence, their home was just a short drive from mine. It felt like fate. I quickly knocked

out a fan letter explaining what their book had meant to me—
the chance to have a similar impact on even a single reader is,
as much as anything, why I became a writer—and asking if I
could meet them. Within days I received an invitation to tea.

By then, my husband and I had been married for ten
years, the last five of which had been spent—more and more
miserably—trying to have a child. We'd been through three
miscarriages, months of soulless sex, invasive tests, pills and
shots, two cycles of in vitro fertilization (IVF) using my eggs
and a third using a friend's. Nothing had worked. Along the
way, I seemed to have lost the ability to feel joy; my husband
was angry that his tenderness couldn't restore it. Now, when
I reread *Mrs. Mike* before visiting its authors, it was the trag-
edies that stood out, the cost of Kathy's willfulness. I recognized myself in the flat grief of her losses, the way pain eroded
her capacity for love. I, too, dreamed of starting over somewhere else, making different, perhaps safer, choices. Even my
usual refuge—my work—was suffering. How could I trust my
instincts as a writer, as an observer of human nature, when I'd
so screwed up my own life?

I don't know what I wanted from the Freedmans. A little
distraction, perhaps, a reminder of a better time. I was eager
to quiz them about what had happened to Kathy and Mike after
the book's final page. Had things gone well? Were they happy?
After so much sadness, had they found peace? I felt personally
invested—maybe too invested—in the answers.

NANCY FREEDMAN, THEN EIGHTY-TWO, MET ME AT HER APARTMENT
door. A tall, slender woman, she carried herself like the actress she'd trained to be. Her hair was a dramatic white, her

eyebrows dark above pale blue eyes, her features wide and vibrant. The beauty in the lines of her face was the best argument I'd seen yet against Botox. She greeted me as if we were old friends. Later I'd realize that full-throttle was the Freedmans' approach to everything—during their courtship, which took place almost entirely by mail, Benedict wrote "page 40" at the top of his first letter, as if they were already mid-conversation. "You gotta love a guy like that," Nancy would tell me. At that point they'd been married sixty-one years.

Benedict was on the couch in the living room, facing a window that overlooked a canal dotted with rowboats and waterfowl. At eighty-three, he had difficulty walking, though you'd never have known it; he made his way across the room by leaning casually on the backs of strategically placed chairs. His mind, however, was still nimble: he had just finished his day's work on a nonfiction book titled *Rescuing the Future*, which he described as a plea, for the good of humanity, to focus on looking forward rather than bickering over past wrongs.

"What appealed to us about Katherine Flannigan's story," Benedict told me right off, "was how it paralleled our own." He and Nancy had met briefly in Los Angeles in 1939. He was a junior writer on Al Jolson's radio show; she was a nineteen-year-old ingenue about to move to New York. But after a few months of hoofing around Broadway, she was diagnosed with a lethal heart infection (now treatable with antibiotics) that forced a retreat to her native Chicago, where she was confined to bed. Benedict followed her there and, though he'd seen her a mere five times, proposed marriage. Nancy burst into tears; her father, who was a doctor, explained that she probably wouldn't survive three months. Benedict didn't care. "I just didn't believe she was going to die," he said. "Also, I felt even if it's only three months, we've got three months. Better than lying in bed staring at the ceiling."

Like Mike, who fashioned a bed on a dogsled for Kathy out of boxes and fur blankets, Benedict folded back the seat of his jalopy—a convertible with a beach umbrella for a roof—to make a chaise for his bride before they headed west for their honeymoon. For years, first in Chicago and later in Los Angeles, he would carry Nancy up every flight of stairs. "She couldn't walk," he said. "On the other hand, she was always full of life."

And like Kathy, Nancy never saw another doctor. Benedict took care of her himself. Three months turned to six, turned to a year, turned to eight. Slowly, she improved. The woman who was never supposed to see 1942 now has four great-grandchildren. She credits her recovery to Benedict's love— "He hauled me back to life," she said, "he really did"—and to *Mrs. Mike*, which they wrote together from her sickbed. I could have swooned from the romance of it all.

AFTER MIKE FLANNIGAN DIED, IN HIS FORTIES, FROM A RUPTURED appendix (another preventable loss, I thought grimly), Kathy went to L.A. and tried to peddle her story to the movies. No one bit. But an agent introduced her to the Freedmans, who thought her life might be the stuff of literature (*Mrs. Mike* was eventually adapted for the screen; the film is truly ghastly). They invited her to their tiny apartment, a converted garage on what had once been the actress Mary Pickford's estate, and spent two days listening to her talk. "We were enchanted by her story," Benedict recalled. "Here was this girl, very young, incapacitated—but willing to fall in love, really fall in love,

passionately, without any care for anything else. That reinforced our own determination to live the life we wanted to live
regardless of the clouds on the horizon."

I knew the feeling. "Did any of their children survive?"

Nancy shook her head. "No. They had adopted an Indian
girl. But not the ones that are in the book. I dreamed those."

I must have looked confused. "*Mrs. Mike* is a novel," Benedict explained.

"A novel?" My stomach clenched. I felt an abrupt, almost
physical sense of displacement, the way you would if, say, you
found out at age forty-five that your mother was actually your
aunt. I'd based my life on this book. It was a core part of my
identity. As an eleven-year-old I'd accepted each word as gospel; it had never occurred to me to question that assumption.
Now I looked at my ancient library copy, which I'd brought
with me: sure enough, a red "F" was taped to the side, indicating it should be shelved in the fiction section.

"But did she really live in that town that burned down?" I
asked, my voice rising.

"Yes," said Nancy.

"No," said Benedict.

Yes? No? Which was it? I'm sure I looked as stunned as I
felt. "What's true is her spirit," Benedict added firmly. "She
was a person afraid of nothing, willing to take on anything.
And the most important scenes—for example, when she leaves
Mike and goes back to Boston—we didn't invent that. But we
also didn't check her account of things."

Part of me wanted to rush home right then and try to re-
trace the story, to follow the Flannigans' trail north. I could
google the town of Grouard. Or look up Mike's name in the
records of the Royal Canadian Mounted Police. But even as

I plotted my search, I realized its results would be irrelevant. *Mrs. Mike* might have played a lesser role in my life had I known it was, at least in part, fabrication. But Kathy—the reality, the invention, the symbol—had been there when I needed her most. And if I still needed proof that real, ordinary people could choose bold, unconventional lives, all I had to do was look at the Freedmans, whose story was as enthralling as Kathy's—maybe more so. They had lived so fully, experienced so much, crossed paths with so many great names of their day. Nancy had played Juliet in a production of Shakespeare's play staged by Fanchon and Marco, the brother-sister dance team who'd launched the careers of Cyd Charisse, Judy Garland, Doris Day, and Bing Crosby. Igor Stravinsky himself had chosen her to dance in *Petrushka*. She had studied under the director Max Reinhardt.

Meanwhile, Benedict's father, David, had created the character of Baby Snooks for Fanny Brice, written a Broadway hit, and was head writer of Eddie Cantor's radio show. When, at age thirteen, Benedict needed a date for a school dance, his father tried to fix him up with the burlesque queen Gypsy Rose Lee (who, informed of the boy's predicament, responded, "Well, for Dave's son . . ." and flipped a breast out of her bra; Benedict did not pursue the opportunity).

David died when Benedict was sixteen, leaving gambling debts that bankrupted the family. They left their tower apartment in Manhattan's swank Beresford building (the unit is now owned by tennis star John McEnroe), and Benedict, the eldest of three, dropped out of school to help support the family. He worked for an actuary by day, and wrote scripts at night and on weekends. Eventually, he snagged a job as a junior writer on the Marx Brothers' film *At the Circus* and headed off to Los Angeles. He wrote gags for Mickey Rooney, Bob Hope, and Jimmy Durante. He spent twelve years with *The Red Skelton Show*, moving with it from radio to television, and wrote episodes of *My Favorite Martian* and *The Andy Griffith Show*. He and Nancy collaborated on writing eight books. They still spend hours a day working side by side, Benedict on his humanitarian manifesto and Nancy on a novel.

"Tell her about the time you met Howard Hughes," Nancy said during that first visit, and I listened, rapt, to how the famous eccentric instructed Benedict to shower, sponge himself off with rubbing alcohol, then shower again before their meeting. It was a fine anecdote, but I was more impressed that at forty-four, with three kids and a wife to support, Benedict had walked away from his Hollywood paycheck—with Nancy's blessing—to pursue an early dream, the one he'd abandoned when his father died: studying advanced mathematics. He enrolled at UCLA, eventually earning a PhD in mathematical logic and teaching for thirty-five years at Occidental College in Los Angeles. The man had the courage to reinvent himself at midlife, to refuse to be ruled by regret. Maybe, I thought, I could do that, too.

NANCY AND BENEDICT SPENT THEIR ENTIRE *MRS. MIKE* WINDFALL on a house in the Pacific Palisades designed by the architect Richard Neutra—only to see the house severely damaged in a mud slide. A second home, in Malibu, went up in flames. At times over the years, they were penniless; once when their kids were young, Benedict had to tend bar until a writing job came through. None of it fazed them. As children of the Great

Depression, they never much trusted wealth or stability. "One of the things we learned from all of it was to celebrate bad news," Benedict said. "If a book is turned down or something goes very wrong, you go out and have a party."

"Good news, you're happy anyway," Nancy added. "But bad news, you've got to have a great dinner and kick up your heels.

"Benedict and I have had difficult periods," she continued. "And we always faced serious, scary problems. But I have a theory about courage. I don't think it's a moment of bravery when you have a rush of adrenaline. Courage is something level, a kind of force that sustains you. And that's what it takes to face difficult things, to make it through life successfully."

Maybe Nancy was right. It's easy to congratulate yourself on your wisdom, your bravery when things are going well. The challenge is to trust in yourself, your work, your marriage, your gut, when they aren't. I'd thought, as Kathy had, that seizing my destiny and finding true love would protect me from pain, bad luck, mistakes, failure. I'd clearly missed the point of the book. Those things aren't avoidable; they're actually the hallmark of a life richly lived.

One meeting with my favorite authors did not erase years of struggle. There were still plenty of nights in our California home when the atmosphere felt as chilly as the Yukon's. But over time, especially after the birth of our daughter, my husband and I found our way back to each other, just as Kathy and Mike had. Last summer, we celebrated our fifteenth anniversary, and we marked the occasion by rereading *Mrs. Mike*. This time, I felt a new appreciation for the bittersweet finale— the couple's courage to forgive and their leap of faith in reconciling. I asked my husband what he had taken away from the book. "That's easy," he said, with a half smile. "Life is hard. But love is strong."

I already have plans for my next rereading: it will be in another few years, snuggled up in bed with my daughter. Maybe *Mrs. Mike* won't be the book that changes her life. But when she hears Kathy's story, and especially how it influenced my own, I hope she'll be inspired to find the book that will.

PART 2

BODY LANGUAGE

DOES FATHER KNOW BEST?

My dad, who was a lawyer, once defended a back-alley abortionist in a criminal case. Seeing the horror of illegal abortion up close—all I know is that a coat hanger was involved—left him shaken, and adamantly pro-choice; at age ninety, his memory may fail, but he never forgets his annual contribution to Planned Parenthood. Early in my career, I wrote a number of articles on reproductive politics, mostly for Vogue. *The victories of the 1970s were already eroding; today, Roe v. Wade has been gutted, and its overturn seems imminent. I'm including this story on the attempt to block women's actions based on "father's rights," as emblematic of all my work during that earlier era. It was published in April 1989, just days before 500,000 people (myself included) convened in Washington to protest potential limits to abortion; until the Women's March of 2017, that was the largest political demonstration in our nation's history. The strategies anti-abortion activists use may have shifted over time, but most still seem ripped from the pages of Margaret Atwood's* A Handmaid's Tale. *I continue to believe what my own father taught me: that without reproductive*

*rights—the ability to choose when and whether to have
children—women have no rights at all.*

S HAWN LEWIS WAS TWENTY-FOUR YEARS OLD AND THREE MONTHS
pregnant when she was served a court restraining order
last August. She had just packed up her infant son and fled
her twenty-five-year-old husband, Carlton, a school custo-
dian in Flint, Michigan, opting for poverty and public assistance rather than continue in a relationship with a man who
had been arrested for repeatedly beating her, who regularly
harassed her, destroyed her property, and even threatened to
kill her. In dire straits, Shawn decided to have an abortion.
The injunction, issued on behalf of her husband, told her
she'd better think again: it said Carlton had the right to custody of his unborn child. Shawn Lewis was forbidden to have
an abortion.

Christine Anderson was a twenty-seven-year-old mother
of three when her court order arrived last July. It wasn't her
first surprise that summer: her fourth pregnancy, which occurred a few months after her husband Timothy's vasectomy,
had also been a shock. The Minnesota couple was paralyzed by
debt; their three-year marriage was on the rocks; and they had
agreed that another child would be a disaster. Christine decided that to continue providing for her children—as well as to
save her marriage—she had to terminate her pregnancy. Her
pro-life husband went to court to make her change her mind.

Since last March, U.S. lower courts have heard at least
twelve angry men—husbands, ex-husbands, and boyfriends—
demand that the women they've impregnated come to terms
with coming to term. The cases have generally been brought

to court under the banner of a fathers' liberation movement, the idea being that the mother isn't the only one who has an interest in the future of a fetus. "It's a balancing of rights, the father's versus the mother's," says James Bopp Jr., general counsel to the National Right to Life Committee, who has tried the majority of these cases. Bopp has also developed a "Fathers' Rights Litigation Kit" for other lawyers interested in the cause. "Roe v. Wade [the 1973 Supreme Court decision that gave women the constitutional right to choose an abortion] gives a woman the right to her own body. On the other hand, a father also has a constitutional right to the care, custody, and companionship of a child; those rights are in conflict when the mother wants to abort that child."

Men's rights groups across the country, even those that are pro-choice, support at least some aspects of the platform, but pro-choice organizations run by women are skeptical. The fathers' rights argument, they say, is a ruse. The real issue is an attempt by men to control women's bodies, and, equally dangerous, an attempt by antichoice forces to muddy the issues in the hopes of overturning the precariously perched Roe v. Wade.

So far, even when lower courts have granted men's requests, higher courts have unanimously overturned the decisions. Last fall, for the first time, Bopp took the pleas of rebuffed, estranged husbands Carlton Lewis and twenty-four-year-old Erin Conn, a toy store worker from Elkhart, Indiana, to the Supreme Court. In both instances, the court opted against hearing the cases (an earlier Supreme Court decision overturned a Missouri statute requiring written consent of a spouse for an abortion) and let the right of a woman to control her reproductive system—and her destiny—stand.

"The Constitution certainly protects Mr. Lewis's right to

be free from government intrusion in his decision to have a child," the National Abortion Rights Action League's (NARAL) lawyers wrote in a brief urging the court to turn down one of the cases. "But it is up to Mr. Lewis, not lower court judges, to find a woman who will have a child with him. No individual, male or female, has a constitutional right to have a court compel another to procreate with him or her."

And that, one assumes, is that. After all, if the highest court in the land lets a decision stand, there isn't much else a legal beagle like Bopp can do, is there? "The court simply decided not to hear the cases; they still may hear one in the future," Bopp counters. "We're still involved with two cases, both pending in the Indiana [Supreme] Court. I wouldn't be surprised if the court does decide to hear them. This issue presents legitimate, important issues that have a broad impact, since in every abortion there's either a husband or a father. The rights they have, which the lower courts have recognized, are important; and we hope the Supreme Court will eventually hear one of these cases and recognize them, too."

On the surface, the men's rights argument can't help but be compelling. Over the last twenty years, encouraged by increasingly independent women, the father's expected role has changed from that of a peripheral authority figure who brings home the bacon and promptly falls asleep under the sports section after dinner to that of a sensitive, primary caretaker who can do a dish, change a diaper, and bandage a boo-boo with equal aplomb. We take for granted that fathers can gain custody of children in divorce suits—almost unheard of in the hoary days before *Kramer vs. Kramer.* In this new, equal-opportunity atmosphere, fathers' rights groups point out, it follows that a man should have some say over the termination of a pregnancy that he helped to create.

"The fathers' rights argument is different from what the Right to Life lawyers say," says Dick Woods, executive director of the National Congress for Men and the first person to help a man obtain a court injunction against his pregnant wife. "We say that only when a father has a demonstrated interest in the unborn child, when he is ready, willing, and able to accept the emotional and financial costs of a child, does he have a valid argument going.

"In several of the cases we've seen, the pregnancies were planned over a long period of time. The couple repeatedly went to clinics to get tests; when they finally conceived, there was a real celebration. In one case, the couple took an ultrasound picture and showed it to grandparents and friends and said, 'This is our baby.' The fathers made career decisions based on planning for the child; they gave up opportunities so they could have shorter hours or better health coverage. Some had gone to gynecologic appointments. Some had made financial commitments, such as contracting to remodel a room, or buying baby furniture. All these things established commitment to children."

Women's groups, though, question whether painting the spare room is a commitment comparable to carrying through with a pregnancy. Or whether a man who would drag his wife through the legal system, in an attempt to force her against her will to endure a pregnancy and give birth to a child she doesn't want, is demonstrating the caring and compassion necessary to be a good father. In two cases in Iowa, Woods was successful in convincing women to bring their pregnancies to term, but he refuses to comment on the subsequent relationships among the members of either family.

Pro-choice advocates are quick to dismiss both Woods and Bopp. A father's rights, they say, simply do not extend to dictating compulsory pregnancy. "It's not in our tradition to compel people to undergo major medical procedures and burdens, which is what the risks and process of pregnancy are," says Sylvia Law, a New York University law school professor. "Children can't compel parents to give them a kidney or to give them blood marrow. I don't have any problem with the notion that a man can't tell a woman to bear a child."

Forcing a woman to give birth, to endure the dangers of pregnancy, pro-choice activists say, is tantamount to indentured servitude, a dystopian attempt to turn back the clock to the days before women could vote or own real property. "Fathers have the right not to engage in sexual intercourse," quips Lynn Paltrow, staff counsel for the American Civil Liberties Union (ACLU). "They do not have the right to control somebody else's body. Women are not the property of the men they happen to have slept with."

"Right to Life lawyers talk about balance," adds Marcy Wilder, staff attorney for NARAL. "But when there's a conflict, only one person can decide and it has to be the woman. Any other outcome gives the control of reproduction back to the man."

As it happens, the vast majority of the cases that Bopp and his cohorts have tried are brought by angry, estranged husbands like Carl Lewis and Erin Conn. Or Michael Reynolds, a Salt Lake City man, who had his nineteen-year-old wife served with divorce papers and a "paternity" suit on the same day. Or last summer's headline-grabbing case of wealthy Long Island orthodontist David Ostreicher, who claimed that his young wife, Toni, aborted out of malice; she was furious because he refused to rip up their prenuptial agreement. For her part, Toni insisted the abortion had been his idea, that he told her he didn't want to support a baby. Lurid installments of the Ostreichers' arguments were played out in newspapers across the country; the legal issues quickly moved from paternity to divorce.

"It's clear that these kinds of cases arise when there's already a serious conflict in the relationship," says Wilder. "The man is trying to exert control over his partner. This doesn't happen when there's a loving, caring man."

In fact, the only recent case that didn't end in divorce was that of the Andersons in Minnesota. The court injunction against Christine was lifted, and she went ahead with her abortion as planned. The Andersons split temporarily; but eventually, without changing their respective stances on abortion, they reconciled.

Both the ACLU and NARAL say there's a hidden agenda in the fathers' rights cases, especially as they're being tried by Bopp: rather than merely trying to gain custody for a hapless father, the lawyers are attempting to undermine the *Roe* v. *Wade* decision by harassing women individually. "They get a woman up on the stand and they do a brutal cross-examination," Wilder says. "They make her talk about her sex practices, her birth-control habits, all kinds of things. They hope to harass women and keep them from getting abortions on an individual basis."

Bopp, of course, takes umbrage at such a low blow. "Those people have a blind spot," he sighs. "Their conception of reality is that there is no child, therefore it's a dispute between the pregnant woman and the man. *Roe* v. *Wade* talked about the 'unborn child'; it said the unborn child didn't have a constitutional right to life, not that there was no child. The premise of our case is that there's a relationship between a father and an unborn child that's constitutionally protected."

The courts have continued to side with NARAL and the ACLU, but the victors are leery about winning a battle rather than the war. In a talk at the University of Arkansas last fall, Supreme Court Justice Harry A. Blackmun, who has always supported a woman's right to terminate a pregnancy, said that *Roe* v. *Wade* could be overturned before 1989 was out. Solicitor General Charles Fried of the Justice Department has noted that the case of *Reproductive Health Services* v. *William Webster*, currently high on the docket, may well provide the opportunity. Certainly, President Bush would applaud a reversal of the *Roe* v. *Wade* decision.

If *Roe* v. *Wade* is eliminated, the door will be open for each state to decide whether to allow, curtail, or prohibit abortions. Eleanor Smeal, the president of the Fund for the Feminist Majority, recently said that she's only confident of pro-choice legislation in five of the fifty states: Hawaii, Alaska, Vermont, Oregon, and Washington; and with states like Arizona and Missouri already preparing antiabortion laws, the future for pro-choice women looks grim. Without the constitutional guarantee of choice, the states can institute any number of restrictions: they can make abortion impossible for poor women to afford; they can demand that both parents of a minor—even a minor who has never *met* one of her parents—give written consent before an abortion can be performed; they can even enact a provision that allows a potential father, whatever his relationship to the woman in question, to force a pregnant woman to bring a fetus to term and then turn it over to him.

THIRTY-FIVE AND MORTAL: A BREAST CANCER DIARY

For weeks after my initial breast cancer diagnosis, I would jolt awake at three in the morning thinking, I might die! I would stumble out of bed to my computer, download everything that was in my head, and, only then, fall back to sleep. I had no intention of publishing the results, but after a while, largely because of my extreme youth, I believed I could tell a unique story. So I shipped off a raw, fifty-thousand-word manuscript to Adam Moss, then editor-in-chief of the New York Times Magazine *and a dear friend. "I like it," he replied. "Now cut it down to seven thousand words!" The piece ran as a cover story in June 1997. Subsequently, I would realize that much of what I wrote in it was inaccurate—especially the part about mammographic screening saving my life. That bothered me. A lot. Fifteen years later, I set the record straight in another* New York Times Magazine *cover story, "The Problem with Pink," which follows. Even so, while I repudiate science in this essay, I stand by its emotional truth. I also couldn't help but notice, in re-reading it, that I imagined (fairly accurately, I think) what contending with infertility might feel like; little did I realize that would be my next challenge.*

Dec. 19, 1996

I got my first mammogram today at a place called the Breast Health Center in San Francisco. I've never really considered whether I had healthy breasts. Healthy knees, yes. Healthy gums, maybe. But healthy breasts? I don't even do self-exams, except when I read something about cancer in the paper.

Thirty-five seems a little young to be going through this particular rite of passage, but my doctor said I should have a baseline and the health insurance pays for it, so I figured, why not? The procedure went pretty fast and it didn't hurt; it was just sort of awkward. Mostly, I hoped that an earthquake wouldn't strike while my breast was clamped in a vise.

Jan. 9, 1997

I almost skipped my second mammogram. When I got the letter saying they had to do a follow-up, I assumed they'd just botched the film. But when the technician took three rounds of pictures, I began to get nervous. I felt myself slip into shock when the radiologist showed me what they were filming: a bicycle-spoke-like pattern emanating from a central point in my left breast. No lump, just these lines in the tissue. I could barely see them. He said he is nearly 100 percent sure that it is nothing, but

I should have it biopsied, "just to be 120 percent sure."

I called my gynecologist for a list of surgeons and chose the only woman among them, Nima Grissom. She did a biopsy on a friend of mine who liked her a lot. Unnecessary biopsies. You hear about them all the time.

Jan. 14

Nima turned out to be a blond, brown-eyed gal in her mid-forties with a wry streak. She examined my breast and didn't feel a thing. Because there's no palpable lump, she has to do a surgical biopsy in the hospital. The radiologist will inject blue dye into the tissue so she can see what to cut out. I'll be home by noon. "Really, though," she said, "the chances are 98 percent that this is nothing." Steven came with me to the appointment. He's the calmer one in our marriage. When I get scared, he repeats "98 percent."

The biopsy is in two days.

Jan. 17, middle of the night

At 4:45 this afternoon I found out I have breast cancer. Breast cancer! That first moment on the phone when Nima told me, all the colors in the room seemed to go flat and I yelled to Steven to get on the extension. He stood in the dining room doorway and we stared at each other, just stared, as Nima talked.

She used comforting words. She told me it is a

slow-growing, tiny cancer—only eight millimeters.
She said lumpectomy, not mastectomy. Radiation,
not chemotherapy. She used words I'm sure I will
soon become very familiar with, words I'd rather
not know. "Well-differentiated." "Low-grade."
"Lower lymph node dissection." She told me I am a
very lucky woman, although I don't feel like I am,
and that this is what early detection is for.

"Goddamn it," I was thinking. "There is no
history of this in my family. I do aerobics three
times a week. I eat organic broccoli."

I called Mom immediately and tried to tell her,
but my hands were shaking so badly that I couldn't
keep the phone next to my ear.

I woke up an hour ago in a sweat imagining my
death and realizing I've made a terrible mistake: I
didn't have children. But I didn't even want them
until last month. Our lives had felt full enough
with work and our love for each other. I couldn't
imagine how we'd have time or energy for a child.
My thirty-fifth birthday in November and Steven's
dad's death a week later changed our minds.

Now, at best, Nima says we should wait two
years before trying to conceive, when the risk of
recurrence begins to decline. By then I'll be thirty-
seven. And it's possible we can't have children at
all. I am so sad. I want to have a baby. I want my
life with Steven. I love him so much, I can't bear
that he has to go through this, too. I want him to
be happy. I want us to be happy together. I want my
life. I don't want to do it over or do it differently,

I just want to have the next part. I will appreciate
it more. I will try to be happier. I will try to love
better, live fuller. I promise.

Jan. 18
Today was a bad day. Steven suggested we go into
San Francisco to a museum, but I couldn't focus.
Over lunch I kept tearing up, and he finally joked,
"Oh great, people will think I'm breaking up with
you." I managed a watery smile.

Seeing kids scampering around in the museum
hurt so much it made me dizzy. It's hard on Steven,
too. He said he believes I'll be okay, but when Nima
said I had to wait to have children, all the ambivalence that he'd felt on the subject evaporated. It's
like couples who discover they're infertile: you're
finally ready, and biology says no. You can't believe
it, not in this age when we control so much of our
own destinies.

But who knows what the truth is. This cancer
may have been in my body for years. For some
women in their thirties, breast cancer is more
likely to be diagnosed when they're pregnant, when
the surge in estrogen can accelerate a previously
undetected cancer. Pregnancy might've made this
cancer more aggressive, more deadly.

Later, when we got into bed, Steven began to
kiss me. I told him I was afraid he wouldn't want to
touch me anymore, that he'd see me as diseased.
He kissed me more passionately and said he would
never feel that way.

Jan. 20

I walk down the street staring at people, especially young women who look carefree, college students dressed in grubby jeans, hair just the right amount of greasy. I think, Do they know what might happen to their bodies? Would it have changed my life, changed my choices had I known?

I feel as if I'm living in this other world now, the world of illness. It has its benefits. People have to be nice to me. I have an excuse that gets me out of just about anything—sorry, can't do that, I have cancer!—and Steven is going to do my share of the housework for a few months. I can be as self-absorbed as I please. But I also feel older, more hesitant. I wonder if I would be a very good mother now; I suddenly feel so conscious of peril.

Jan. 21

Saw Nima today. She said that if this cancer hasn't spread to the lymph nodes—and that's unlikely—my chance of recurrence is only about 10 percent over ten years. But the chances that this was cancer in the first place were less than 10 percent, so I'm not so easily reassured.

I have to make a decision: I can either have a lumpectomy followed by six and a half weeks of daily radiation treatments or a mastectomy and no radiation. At first, the answer seemed obvious: Who wants to lose a breast? A lumpectomy, even in small breasts like mine, would barely leave a dent. But then I started thinking about the long-term effects of radiation on someone my age, the potential for the treatment itself to cause cancer in ten, twenty, even thirty years.

On the other hand, a mastectomy—that reconstructed breast is not much consolation. Nima described it as a squishy ball under a scar with a tattooed aureole. How could I look at that for the rest of my life? I wish there were someone to tell me what to do. When I pushed her, Nima said, "I guess I'd choose mastectomy if it were me, but I'm a surgeon."

Nima keeps repeating that I'm one of the lucky ones. Breast cancer rates began rising 1 percent a year in 1940 and accelerated in the eighties before leveling off in the early 1990s. Women under fifty now account for more than forty-five thousand cases annually, a quarter of the total. Most, like me, have no family history of breast cancer. The cruelest part is that since the disease tends to be the most virulent in its younger victims, few have prognoses as favorable as mine: cancer is the number-one cause of death among women in their forties. This is not a trend I want to be a part of.

Nima said her practice has shifted from mostly postmenopausal to mostly premenopausal women since she began in the early eighties, and only partly because young women prefer a female surgeon. "At first we thought the rise was because of exposure to DDT," she said, "but women like you are too young for that. So no one knows why: pesticides, pollution, environmental estrogen released

from plastics. Most tumors respond to estrogen,
so earlier menarche and later childbearing might
increase the risk somewhat by exposing the breasts
to more monthly hormone cycles. There's a lot of
speculation but no answers."

I asked her if there was anything I could've
done to prevent this. "Maybe it would've helped
if you'd had babies when you were eighteen," she
said, arching her eyebrows. "But that's not exactly
good public policy."

Jan. 22
I've been a busy little research bee, calling cancer hotlines, combing the hospital's public access
library, spending hours online. I seek control by
gathering information. I found pictures of reconstructed breasts on the Web: it looked as if someone had shoved one of those plastic salad bowls you
get in school cafeterias under the woman's skin
and there was a huge scar across it. Other pictures,
with the reconstructed nipple, looked better. Still,
they were pretty upsetting.

It's nearly impossible to find information
about women in their thirties; we're usually
lumped into an all-inclusive "under fifty" category. Apparently, though, I'm one of about twelve
thousand under forty who will be told she has
breast cancer this year, up from 5,120 in 1970.
Much of the jump is because there are simply a
larger number of women in their thirties than
there used to be, which means more young women

who could get cancer. Whatever the case, that's a lot of people.

No one can fully answer my questions about radiation, either. It seems to slightly increase my chances of getting cancer again someday in my other breast. Even without the radiation, because I was diagnosed so young the chances of that are now 25 percent: one of the biggest risk factors for getting breast cancer is having already had it once. Grim.

Staring at these numbers makes nothing clear. They exhaust me.

Jan. 23

Everyone has a friend about my age for me to call "who had this and is now fine." Most of them scare the bejesus out of me. One has already got cancer again in her other breast and had a double mastectomy. Another now has ovarian cancer. The youngest ones are in the worst situations, and no one is thinking about having children. Either they had them already, or they're single, or they've had chemotherapy, which puts you into menopause, sometimes permanently. At least, if everything goes as expected, I won't have to make that decision: my tumor is two millimeters shy of the size where chemo is an issue.

One woman, a friend of a friend named Candace, was a true gem. She found out she had cancer at forty-seven and had to have a mastectomy. "They took me in kicking and screaming," she said. Candace said her reconstructed breast looks fine in clothes, even in a bathing suit. She doesn't have a nipple yet. "You get used to it," she said. "You miss sensation. You miss the feeling of cloth against your skin. I wouldn't say that it isn't horrible, but it's not the worst thing. It's not like it's your face."

Her neighbor, also a breast cancer survivor, had a lumpectomy and radiation. "In a way, I suppose I'm jealous," Candace said. "Psychologically, she could move on much more easily than I can." That got to me. Which choice will make it easier for me to continue with my life? There's a risk with radiation, but it's one I think I'll take. I'm going to have the lumpectomy, although I'm nervous about it. I almost asked Candace if I could come over and see her breast, but I figured if she didn't offer, it would be rude.

I remember a picture I saw somewhere of a woman who'd had a mastectomy and then had a beautiful vine tattooed along the scar. I never understood those body-piercing, tattooing kids before, but maybe it's about trying to turn something you feel is mutilated and ugly into something you can love again.

Tomorrow I'm going to New York. I am going to spend a few days reporting for a book I'm writing on life choices among women from their twenties through their mid-forties—can you believe it?—and trying to live my own previous life as much as possible. Then Steven will come join me for a final weekend before the surgery.

Jan. 24

I am the person whose life is officially not worth saving. According to today's paper, a panel convened by the National Institutes of Health has declined to recommend mammograms for women in their forties because they don't save enough lives. I know I wouldn't have bothered with a mammogram if I'd read this. If I hadn't had that test, if I had waited until I found a lump myself, my prognosis would have been far worse. I certainly would have needed chemotherapy. I might have even found the cancer while pregnant, when treatment is much more difficult. Either way, death would have been a greater possibility.

I am sitting in the airport waiting for my flight to New York. It was impossibly hard to leave Steven. I cried when he dropped me off. I feel superstitious about him, that if I'm with him nothing bad can happen.

Another article in the paper alarmed me even more than the one about the mammography panel. I didn't even clip it, it made me so queasy. It talked about a gene called BRCA1, which, when it is mutant, is linked to breast and ovarian cancers. Apparently it has a higher mutation rate among Ashkenazi Jews—and I am one—especially if there was already reproductive cancer in the family. My aunt died of ovarian cancer, and although my doctors have said that is not especially significant, it haunts me.

I have already had one ovary and part of the

second removed because of cysts that Nima assured me, have nothing to do with the cancer. Still, I want my ovary gone. I want to have children. I want to have children right now and then get that sucker cut out.

I feel so defective, so unable to trust my body. It is like losing faith in a God whose power you were sure of, even if you had the teensiest doubts.

Last night I lay awake and wondered about what defines us as female. If it is, indeed, biology, then what am I becoming? I have only 80 percent of a single ovary and may, in a few years, decide to remove that. I will only have part of my breasts and may, some day, lose those. Will I be less female? Will I be less of a woman?

Jan. 31

I couldn't stand it anymore yesterday and I pulled the tape off the incision from the biopsy. It's longer than I thought—about an inch and a half—and prominent on the top of my breast. It's true, if this hadn't turned up anything, I would've been really ticked about the big scar. On the other hand, I wouldn't have cancer.

Over lunch today, an old friend asked me in all seriousness whether I thought I had a "cancer personality." What would that be? Someone who holds anger in, she said. She's been on antidepressants for over a year, and I have the cancer personality?

Maybe deep down the reason it bothers me so much when people say I should change my diet or get rid of stress is that I am afraid I really did do something wrong, that this could be a punishment for . . . what? Being on the Pill? Waiting to have children? Independence?

It doesn't help that there is a distinct undercurrent of accusation in many of the books supposedly promoting "healing." I can't believe what I've found skimming bestsellers in the health sections of bookstores. Bernie Siegel writes, "There are no incurable diseases, only incurable people." Louise Hay claims that cancer returns when a person doesn't make the necessary "mental changes" to cure it. Those are tidy ideas, placing the onus of the illness on the ill and letting the healthy off the hook.

Still, I doubt I gave myself cancer because I'm reluctant to tell one of my best friends she's an idiot.

Feb. 1
The pressure to have a positive attitude is intense. Steven came to town on Thursday. We went to the Guggenheim and I stood in front of a Picasso, a study of a woman's head in grays, blacks, and whites. Her face is broken up and put together in a way that is beautiful but frightening and awful. I thought, That is exactly how I feel.

Steven says I should allow myself to be depressed. But I feel that there are those who expect me to be upbeat, and I expect it of myself. And then, even though I know it's ridiculous, I fear that if I give in to my sorrow—over being ill, over possibly not having a child, over the loss of my youth and descent into a feeling of fragility that ought to be reserved for the very old—that I will cause my cancer to spread.

I am glad Steven is here, but it has brought me back to the disease. For most of the week I was able to ignore it, to throw myself into work. But Steven's presence forces me to confront my life. I ask him how he can love me if, because of me, we can't have children, if our lives cannot be as we wanted them to be. He holds me and says that what we have is enough. I know he is not a person who says what he doesn't mean, but I wonder if somewhere, deep in his soul, he feels I've failed him. I have failed him. I have failed us.

Sex feels out of the question. I cannot feel pleasure. I want more than ever to express how deeply I feel for Steven, how married I feel to him, but I can't: my body betrays me again by refusing to respond. I am sure this is a normal reaction. That doesn't help one bit. I want to go home.

Feb. 5

Surgery tomorrow. Nima called to see how I was doing. Mom and Dad just got in from Minneapolis, and they seem more nervous than I am. We were all supposed to go out for a "last supper," but Steven's office has been robbed and he has to wait for the police. Tensions are running high: Mom is continually on the verge of tears and Dad has barely said a word. We eat our roast chicken in a state of forced cheerfulness.

Feb. 6

Sitting in the hospital room before the lumpectomy. An elderly man on the other side of the curtain is listening to Rush Limbaugh on the radio. Really loudly. Steven goes to ask him politely to turn the thing down. I know this is a mistake, sending my big, brawny Asian husband to reason with a Dittohead. The guy yells, "Well, it's too damned bad because I'm not turning it down." We retaliate by turning on the TV, cranking up Barney until both programs become a blur of background noise. This ought to scare the cancer away.

In the operating room, Nima and I briefly discussed the mammography panel again. She rolled her eyes. "I see too many young women in here," she said. "A lot of my patients are younger than I am. It's overwhelming."

This is one of those areas, Nima said, where people of goodwill disagree. "Maybe it doesn't find every tumor and maybe there are more biopsies," she said, "but to me, finding early breast cancer is more important than that. Tumors found early do better. Look at you. If you had waited six months, things would've been different. If you'd waited until you'd found a lump, we wouldn't be looking at the same prognosis."

I had left Mom crying in the waiting room, and she cried again when I was wheeled out, smiling. I know this is hard on her. Steven said that as soon as the door to surgery swung shut she fell apart. "It should be me going in there," she said.

I was discharged within an hour. I'm not in a lot of pain: the spot under my arm where she removed some lymph nodes to biopsy hurts more than the lumpectomy. I can take the dressing off in two days. I wonder what my breast looks like under all this gauze. How bad is it? I'm anxious about getting The Call about the lymph nodes. I know the news should be good, but there is that small chance the cancer has spread there. I thought the news on my original biopsy would be good, too.

Feb. 7

The nodes are negative!

I am so relieved, even though it was the expected result. I didn't realize how tense I've been these last few weeks. Like a bad episode of *thirtysomething*. (Oh, God, am I Nancy? I would hate being Nancy!)

Nima called while Mom and I were out on a walk, something I shouldn't have done, and that—along with making dozens of phone calls to my brothers, Steven's sisters, his mom, and all my friends to tell them about the nodes, as well as checking in on my parents every two minutes all day and not napping—caused me to pass out over our celebratory dinner. The books all said to get back to normal routines as soon as possible after surgery—I guess they didn't mean twelve hours later.

I made an appointment with an acupuncturist. Acupuncture and Chinese medicine are supposed to ease the fatigue that can go along with radiation and, over the long term, help prevent recurrence. I start next week.

Feb. 9

I removed the big white bandages on my chest and armpit today. I was apprehensive, but I stared into the mirror as they came off. Steven came in and stood behind me. I considered asking him to leave, feeling I needed to face my new body alone, but it turned out to be difficult to remove the adhesive from my skin.

There was my breast in the mirror. It has a large, raw wound covered by surgical tape and the surrounding area is blue, the color of veins show-ing through pale skin. But it appears to be the same size and shape as before. Steven leaned over and gently kissed the scar, a sweet welcome home. It is all I want.

Feb. 10

I read an interesting tidbit in *Dr. Susan Love's Breast Book*: women who participated in sports in high school and college have lower rates of breast cancer than other women. Physical activity reduces their estrogen levels. So as a public health policy,

to lower breast cancer rates she suggests pouring
money into girls' athletics.

Feb. 13

Last night Steven and I went to see Mare Win-
ningham's band, tried to have a normal evening
out. But we ended up coming home early and
having a meltdown. I suppose it had to happen.
Steven has been distracted, and I fretted that he
no longer found me attractive, that he was going
to dump me for a younger, healthier, more fertile
woman who wasn't obsessed with cancer. I asked
what was wrong and he said he was just feeling sad. I asked why and he said he felt that bad
things just kept on happening. Now, he has a right
to feel that way: his father and one of his best
friends died last year. His work has been difficult
lately, his office was robbed, and his wife has cancer. But I read this as further confirmation of my
fears and flipped. Somehow, things just escalated
from there.

    In the best of times, I hate it when we fight.
But last night I panicked, because I tend to feel our
fights in my chest. I thought: Oh God, what if this
is bringing the cancer back? What if fighting with
Steven is why I got sick in the first place?

    Maybe I will look into cancer support groups.

Feb. 14

This morning I got up and took some vitamin C
and E, selenium, my various potions from the acu-

puncturist, and now I'm drinking green tea at my computer. With these amulets I ward off evil. They are the modern-day versions of saying *kinehora* and spitting three times.

I am seeing the acupuncturist once a week. He shoots six small, fine needles through a tube into my ankles and calves and three more as a bonus into my left arm to ease the pain in my tendon from typing all day. He also gave me supplements to boost my immune system.

Does it all help? I don't know. I feel rested when I leave his office, and my typing arm feels great. I believe and I don't believe, but I do it.

I have several friends who have said that they, too, feel they inhabit a parallel universe of the ill. One has Crohn's disease, another is depressive, a third is having fertility problems. The issues are surprisingly similar. We develop weird obsessions and counter them with talismans: mantras from 12-step programs, or advice dispensed from shrinks, or controlled diets. Our bodies feel like petulant, spoiled children who must be spoken to carefully to avoid a tantrum.

Meanwhile, I've become obsessed with what I eat. Food that isn't good for me doesn't seem like food. Yesterday I baked some organic sweet potatoes and ate them like apples for snacks. On the other hand, I have managed to force down a couple of the chocolates Dad sent me for Valentine's Day.

Feb. 15

Steven and I continue to be testy with one another. I want him to be overjoyed—delirious—that
the nodes are clear, but he's just not. He says that
he assumed all along I was going to be fine, given
what Nima said. He says if he'd let himself think
about anything worse, he would've become so
depressed that he couldn't function, he couldn't
take care of me.

    I want him to react right along with me, but
the truth is, I only want him to do it on my terms.
As shameful as it is to say, I hate it when Steven's
depressed: it scares me. I look to him to be emotionally what he is physically—rock solid. When
he says he's upset that we can't start trying to have
a child this spring, I want to shove the sentiment
down his throat. I don't like his having feelings
that hurt me.

    Meanwhile, he's angry that I'm acting as if
this is just about me. "If something happens to
you, Peg, it happens to both of us," he said. "If you
can't have a child, we both can't have a child. If you
die"—he began to cry—"if you die, my life ends, too.
You have to think about us together, not just you."

Feb. 18

My oncologist, Ari Baron, looks like a teenager.
But once I got over my shock (and determined
his competence), we got along famously. In his
opinion, there's no reason to wait two years to get
pregnant with my good prognosis—I should just

go ahead whenever I feel healthy again after the radiation. It turns out the research on pregnancy after breast cancer is outrageously meager: since the 1930s there have been data on fewer than six hundred patients. The first large-scale study on the subject is going to be started this summer. But Ari says there's no danger to the fetus once the radiation is over, and based on what's known, pregnancy doesn't appear to affect my survival. In other words, if I'm not going to die anyway, it shouldn't kill me. He thinks it doesn't make sense to wait when you balance my chance of recurrence against my age and the psychological value of moving on with my life. "You don't want to feel like you're sick," he said. "That's what cancer is about: realizing how fragile life is, but because you're aware of that, enjoying life, seizing it with both hands. And that includes, for you, having a baby.

"So go, be fruitful and multiply."

March 5
Tonight was my first radiation session. I went into a room hung with a biohazard warning that says CAUTION: HIGH RADIATION ZONE, lay on my back under a machine that looks like a small spaceship, removed the left side of my hospital gown, raised my arm over my head, and held a handle while the technician manipulated me into place. I know I'm supposed to pretend it's normal to lie with my breast exposed in front of a bunch of fully clothed strangers while they draw on me with a Sharpie,

but, hey, call me uptight, I found it a little distressing. Then they left the room—they don't want to get nuked—and watched me on a TV monitor.

The treatment itself is short and painless. Radiation isn't like chemotherapy. The main side effects are fatigue and skin irritation. I won't lose my hair. Steven came with me for my inaugural dose and stood against the wall while they prepped me. I couldn't see him, because I'm not supposed to move, but I could feel that he was upset. When the technician came back into the room for a second to adjust something, he ran in after her. "Forgot to kiss you," he mumbled.

I stared at the ceiling. They have removed some of the panels and installed a triptych photograph of a park in springtime with a lake, groves of tulips, and budding trees. I willed myself into the picture as hard as I could and felt my body trembling. I really don't want this poison shot into me. The machine whirred for maybe thirty seconds. When it stopped, they moved it to another spot. A minute of whirring and it was over. Only thirty-two more treatments to go.

March 6

I found a support group for women under forty with breast cancer. Tonight was my first meeting. There were eleven of us and a social worker. The women were in all stages of treatment. I sat between Jeanne, whose silver-streaked blond hair is just growing back from chemotherapy, and

Natalie, who, since her diagnosis, has become an activist.

Some of the women wore scarves around bald heads, making them look Hasidic. Some had mastectomies, and I found myself sneaking peeks at their chests to see if I could tell. (I couldn't.) Most had small children, but a few, like me, were thinking about the safety of pregnancy. When I told my story, I felt a wave of relief. Everyone in the room had been through what I've been through—at least—and understood.

Only one person, Sue-Jane, a Chinese American woman with a very good prognosis, was younger than I. "When I go in for radiation, everyone in the waiting room is dying of curiosity," she told me. "They look down when I tell them. They say, 'You have breast cancer and you're thirty?'" She shrugged. "I say, 'It happens.'"

The main topic of discussion was whether to close the group to new members. There are sixteen women registered in all. That's just too many—there was a lot of warmth in the room but not much focus. The trouble is, there are new women calling to inquire about the group virtually every week, and where would they go? None of us would want to be locked out, least of all me, the newest member.

Afterward, I called a friend in New York, who asked me if it was scary being around women whose prognoses were worse than mine. "I just don't think of you as having the same thing they have," she said.

March 31

The American Cancer Society has announced
that it's recommending annual mammograms
for women in their forties. The National Cancer
Institute is expected to do the same later this week.
Everyone is calling to tell me, as if it is a personal
victory. And I suppose it is, although I'm suspicious
that endorsing mammograms has become the
cause du jour in Congress. It's an easy way to look
righteous to female voters without having to do
anything, like finance research on a more precise
detection system, more effective treatment, or the
connection between pesticides and cancer. I really
was one of the lucky ones: only about half the cancers among the women in my support group were
visible on mammograms.

I am tired of information. An epidemiologist
from the American Cancer Society sent me statistics on how much more likely women whose cancers are diagnosed in their thirties are to get other
cancers—breast, ovarian, lung, leukemia—than
older women. Someone else sent me a new Sloan-
Kettering report that says all the studies on the
safety of pregnancy after breast cancer are flawed.
I'm beginning to know too much.

April 3

There were only a few people at the support group
tonight. Someone had her daughter's soccer practice; someone else didn't feel well, and everyone
else—maybe the weather was just too good. There

are nights when life is more important than cancer. But the smaller group was, in fact, better. There was less eyeing the clock to make sure everyone got a chance to talk.

One of the women, Sue, had lumpectomies in both breasts a little over a year ago, when she was thirty-eight. Last week she felt pea-size lumps underneath the scars and she's afraid that it's back. "Maybe it's nothing," she said, smiling nervously. "But it's opened the door again." Opened the door just days after she and her boyfriend had decided to try to have a baby. Both Susan's mother and grandmother died of breast cancer. I asked if she worried about passing it along to a daughter.

"I do," she said. "But is that a reason not to have children? I'm not sorry my mother was alive. I'm not sorry I'm alive.

"It's good to be able to come here and talk. My friends want to tell me I'll be fine. They don't get it. I don't want to die, but I have to consider it. It's possible. That's what feels so unfair dealing with this at our age. I said to my friend, 'I need to know if I have a child that you'll take care of it if I go.' She said, 'That goes without saying.' But it doesn't for me. I want to live. I'm planning my future. But it does not go without saying."

Natalie, who had a mastectomy at thirty-six, is struggling, too. She has one child and would like to have more, but has decided that the risk to her health is too great. Last week a pregnant friend tried to convince her to change her mind. "She kept saying, 'Everything's a risk,'" Natalie said. "'You could get hit by a bus tomorrow.'"

We groaned. "I hate when people say that," I said.

"Yeah," Natalie agreed. "You could get hit by a bus, but they're all up on the curb and I'm already standing in the road.

"I'm not saying it's not a tragedy to get cancer at sixty," she continued, "but this is different. I don't think about it in terms of me. I think in terms of my son, the markers of his life: if I can get him through high school, into a good college. I don't want to die when he's five. To me, sixty sounds pretty good."

I felt sadder and sadder. When Jeanne said her pet dog, who was ten years old and blind, had wandered out of her yard and been hit by a car, I burst into tears.

"People are always asking me how I am in that significant way," she said. "You know, 'How *are* you?' When I say I'm feeling terrible because my dog died, they roll their eyes and say, 'Is that all?' But you know, it's a loss. I had that dog before I had my kids."

April 15

Steven and I finally had that normal night out I'd hoped for two months ago. We went back to the same club where I'd been so miserable before, this time to hear an old friend, George Kahumoku Jr., play Hawaiian slack-key guitar. Last time we saw him was on Big Island, a few days before we were married.

Steven put his arm around me. "We've had a good five years since then," he said as I leaned against his shoulder. I can't say I didn't think about cancer during George's set—it's still in my mind every second—but for the first time since January, it faded into the background.

April 16

How do you tell a child that you have cancer? Most of the women in my support group are mothers of young children; usually they found their tumors shortly after giving birth. Jeanne's was diagnosed when her son was ten months old and her daughter was five. "I ended up saying, 'Mommy's sick under her arm,'" she said, "'and she takes very special medicine.' My daughter thinks it's all better now. I don't know what I'll tell her if there's a recurrence."

Natalie lends out a picture book, *Sammy's Mommy Has Cancer*. She says her son wants to be a doctor and a builder when he grows up. "He has this elaborate plan to build special beds in the hospital so that mommies with one breast can hold their babies close without having to pick them up," she told me. "Why does a four-year-old have to deal with this?"

Susan talks not from the perspective of a mother but from that of a daughter. "My mom didn't want us to grow up worrying about cancer," she said. "She taught us how to handle the fear. I

feel I can pass that on. And I have the same hope
she did: that either my kids won't get this or there
will be better screening and treatment by the time
they get to the age when it might happen."

May 21

I went out hiking and came back covered with
poison oak. I couldn't be happier: it's such a normal
affliction. I'm working my way back down the crisis
ladder—first cancer, then poison oak, maybe next
I'll get a really bad hangnail.

Someone in my support group said she's
been "visiting her terror" a lot lately, as if it were
a geographical place. A month after completing
radiation, I find myself visiting my terror, too, at
unexpected moments: during a busy workday, for
instance, or over dinner with friends. My stomach
suddenly clenches and I think, I'm a thirty-five-
year-old who just had cancer. It seems simultaneously unreal and the most real thing there is.

Keeping up with the news on breast cancer is
tough; things change so quickly. Last week, a study
found that the BRCA1 mutant gene, the one that
makes breast and possibly ovarian cancer nearly
inevitable, is neither as common nor as definitive
as was thought. I was so relieved. When I think of
the frequent-flier miles I racked up visiting my
terror—and its twin city, confusion—over that one!
Then, yesterday, it turned out the women who do
have to worry about it are those with both early-
onset breast cancer and ovarian cancer in their

families. I was right back on that plane. But that's part of this difficult journey, from screening to treatment and beyond: making life-and-death decisions based on information that is ever-shifting and contradictory. Then not looking back.

Slowly, though, this disease is becoming a part of my life, rather than its center. I don't believe that I will die of breast cancer, at least not anytime soon. I don't know whether we'll have a child, although I hope we do. I don't know anything for sure anymore, and I guess I'm learning to live with that. It's as if I fell off a cliff on January 17. Maybe I still haven't landed.

THE PROBLEM WITH PINK

Readers seemed surprised that I was willing to retract something I'd written fifteen years earlier, but as someone whose life may depend on the future of breast cancer research, it was important to me to get it right. I was so frustrated by pink ribbon groups that continued to funnel millions of dollars into promoting the idea that annual screening should begin at age forty while ignoring the mounting evidence that it did not actually extend the lives of those with cancer. What's more, universal screening was causing significant harm to healthy women. A cover story in the New York Times Magazine, I knew, would have an impact on this debate like nothing else and had the potential to shift the national conversation. That was both a daunting responsibility and an exciting prospect. Still, although I considered writing the story for years, I never seemed to get around to it. I didn't relish the idea of returning to Cancerland, not even as a reporter. Then, my own disease returned, and, as it did with the first diagnosis, my material chose me. I reported and wrote this piece in the months following my mastectomy; it ran in April 2013.

USED TO BELIEVE THAT A MAMMOGRAM SAVED MY LIFE. I EVEN wrote that in the pages of this magazine. It was 1996, and I had just turned thirty-five when my doctor sent me for an initial screening—a relatively common practice at the time—that would serve as a baseline when I began annual mammograms at forty. I had no family history of breast cancer, no particular risk factors for the disease.

So when the radiologist found an odd, bicycle-spoke-like pattern on the film—not even a lump—and sent me for a biopsy, I wasn't worried. After all, who got breast cancer at thirty-five?

It turns out, I did. Recalling the fear, confusion, anger, and grief of that time is still painful. My only solace was that the system worked precisely as it should: the mammogram caught my tumor early, and I was treated with a lumpectomy and six weeks of radiation; I was going to survive.

By coincidence, just a week after my diagnosis, a panel convened by the National Institutes of Health made headlines when it declined to recommend universal screening for women in their forties; evidence simply didn't show it significantly decreased breast-cancer deaths in that age group. What's more, because of their denser breast tissue, younger women were subject to disproportionate false positives—leading to unnecessary biopsies and worry—as well as false negatives, in which cancer was missed entirely.

Those conclusions hit me like a sucker punch. "I am the person whose life is officially not worth saving," I wrote angrily. When the American Cancer Society as well as the newer Susan G. Komen foundation rejected the panel's findings, saying mammography was still the best tool to decrease breast-cancer mortality, friends across the country called to congratulate me as if I'd scored a personal victory. I considered myself a loud-and-proud example of the benefits of early detection.

Sixteen years later, my thinking has changed. As study after study revealed the limits of screening—and the dangers of overtreatment—a thought niggled at my consciousness. How much had my mammogram really mattered? Would the outcome have been the same had I bumped into the cancer on my own years later? It's hard to argue with a good result. After all, I am alive and grateful to be here. But I've watched friends whose breast cancers were detected "early" die anyway. I've sweated out what blessedly turned out to be false alarms with many others.

Recently, a survey of three decades of screening published in November in *The New England Journal of Medicine* found that mammography's impact is decidedly mixed: it does reduce, by a small percentage, the number of women who are told they have late-stage cancer, but it is far more likely to result in overdiagnosis and unnecessary treatment, including surgery, weeks of radiation, and potentially toxic drugs. And yet, mammography remains an unquestioned pillar of the pink-ribbon awareness movement. Just about everywhere I go—the supermarket, the dry cleaner, the gym, the gas pump, the movie theater, the airport, the florist, the bank, the mall—I see posters proclaiming that "early detection is the best protection" and "mammograms save lives." But how many lives, exactly, are being "saved," under what circumstances, and at what cost? Raising the public profile of breast cancer, a disease once spoken of only in whispers, was at one time critically important, as was emphasizing the benefits of screening. But there are unintended consequences to ever-greater "awareness"—and they, too, affect women's health.

Breast cancer in your breast doesn't kill you; the disease becomes deadly when it metastasizes, spreading to other organs or the bones. Early detection is based on the theory, dating back to the late nineteenth century, that the disease progresses consistently, beginning with a single rogue cell, growing sequentially, and at some invariable point making a lethal leap. Curing it, then, was assumed to be a matter of finding and cutting out a tumor before that metastasis happens.

The thing is, there was no evidence that the size of a tumor necessarily predicted whether it had spread. According to Robert Aronowitz, a professor of history and sociology of science at the University of Pennsylvania and the author of *Unnatural History: Breast Cancer and American Society*, physicians endorsed the idea anyway, partly out of wishful thinking, desperate to "do something" to stop a scourge against which they felt helpless. So in 1913, a group of them banded together, forming an organization (which eventually became the American Cancer Society) and alerting women, in a precursor of today's mammography campaigns, that surviving cancer was within their power. By the late 1930s, they had mobilized a successful "Women's Field Army" of more than one hundred thousand volunteers, dressed in khaki, who went door-to-door raising money for "the cause" and educating neighbors to seek immediate medical attention for "suspicious symptoms," like lumps or irregular bleeding.

The campaign worked—sort of. More people did subsequently go to their doctors. More cancers were detected, more operations were performed, and more patients survived their initial treatments. But the rates of women dying of breast cancer hardly budged. All those increased diagnoses were not translating into "saved lives." That should have been a sign that some aspect of the early-detection theory was amiss. Instead, surgeons believed they just needed to find the disease even sooner.

Mammography promised to do just that. The first trials, begun in 1963, found that screening healthy women along with giving them clinical exams reduced breast-cancer death rates by about 25 percent. Although the decrease was almost entirely among women in their fifties, it seemed only logical that eventually, screening younger (that is, finding cancer earlier) would yield even more impressive results. Cancer might even be cured.

That hopeful scenario could be realized, though, only if women underwent annual mammography, and by the early 1980s, it is estimated that fewer than 20 percent of those eligible did. Nancy Brinker founded the Komen foundation in 1982 to boost those numbers, convinced that early detection and awareness of breast cancer could have saved her sister, Susan, who died of the disease at thirty-six. Three years later, National Breast Cancer Awareness Month was born. The khaki-clad "soldiers" of the 1930s were soon displaced by millions of pink-garbed racers "for the cure" as well as legions of pink consumer products: pink buckets of chicken, pink yogurt lids, pink vacuum cleaners, pink dog leashes. Yet the message was essentially the same: breast cancer was a fearsome fate, but the good news was that through vigilance and early detection, surviving was within women's control.

By the turn of the new century, the pink ribbon was inescapable, and about 70 percent of women over forty were undergoing screening. The annual mammogram had become a near-sacred rite, so precious that in 2009, when another federally financed independent task force reiterated that for most women, screening should be started at age fifty and conducted every two years, the reaction was not relief but fury. After years of bombardment by early-detection campaigns (consider: "If you haven't had a mammogram, you need more than your breasts examined"), women, surveys showed, seemed to think screening didn't just find breast cancer but actually prevented it.

At the time, the debate in Congress over health care reform was at its peak. Rather than engaging in discussion about how to maximize the benefits of screening while minimizing its harms, Republicans seized on the panel's recommendations as an attempt at health care rationing. The Obama administration was accused of indifference to the lives of America's mothers, daughters, sisters, and wives. Secretary Kathleen Sebelius of the Department of Health and Human Services immediately backpedaled, issuing a statement that the administration's policies on screening "remain unchanged."

EVEN AS AMERICAN WOMEN EMBRACED MAMMOGRAPHY, RESEARCHers' understanding of breast cancer—including the role of early detection—was shifting. The disease, it has become clear, does not always behave in a uniform way. It's not even one disease. There are at least four genetically distinct breast cancers. They may have different causes and definitely respond differently to treatment. Two related subtypes, luminal A and luminal B, involve tumors that feed on estrogen; they may respond to a five-year course of pills like tamoxifen or aromatase inhibitors, which block cells' access to that hormone or reduce its levels. A third type of cancer, HER2-positive, produces too much of a protein called human epidermal growth factor receptor 2; it may be treatable with a targeted immunotherapy called Herceptin. The final type, basal-like cancer (often called "triple negative" because its growth is not fueled by the most common biomarkers for breast cancer—estrogen, progesterone, and HER2), is the most aggressive, accounting for up to 20 percent of breast cancers. More prevalent among young and African American women, it is genetically closer to ovarian cancer. Within those classifications, there are, doubtless, further distinctions, subtypes that may someday yield a wider variety of drugs that can isolate specific tumor characteristics, allowing for more effective treatment. But that is still years away.

Those early mammography trials were conducted before variations in cancer were recognized—before Herceptin, before hormonal therapy, even before the widespread use of chemotherapy. Improved treatment has offset some of the advantage of screening, though how much remains contentious. There has been about a 25 percent drop in breast-cancer death rates since 1990, and some researchers argue that treatment—not mammograms—may be chiefly responsible for that decline. They point to a study of three pairs of European countries with similar health care services and levels of risk: in each pair, mammograms were introduced in one country ten to fifteen years earlier than in the other. Yet the mortality data are virtually identical. Mammography didn't seem to affect outcomes. In the United States, some researchers credit screening with a death-rate reduction of 15 percent—which holds steady even when screening is reduced to every other year. H. Gilbert Welch, a professor of medicine at the Dartmouth Institute for Health Policy and Clinical Practice and coauthor of last November's *New England Journal of Medicine* study of screening-induced overtreatment, estimates that only 3 to 13 percent of women whose cancer was detected by mammograms actually benefited from the test.

If Welch is right, the test helps between four thousand and eighteen thousand women annually. Not an insignificant number, particularly if one of them is you, yet perhaps less than expected given the one hundred thirty-eight thousand whose cancer has been diagnosed each year through screening. Why didn't early detection work for more of them? Mammograms, it turns out, are not so great at detecting the most lethal forms of disease—like triple negative—at a treatable phase. Aggressive tumors progress too quickly, often cropping up between mammograms. Even catching them "early," while they are still small, can be too late: they have already metastasized. That may explain why there has been no decrease in the incidence of metastatic cancer since the introduction of screening.

At the other end of the spectrum, mammography readily finds tumors that could be equally treatable if found later by a woman or her doctor; it also finds those that are so slow-moving they might never metastasize. As improbable as it sounds, studies have suggested that about a quarter of screening-detected cancers might have gone away on their own. For an individual woman in her fifties, then, annual mammograms may catch breast cancer, but they reduce the risk of dying of the disease over the next ten years by only 0.07 percentage points—from 0.53 percent to 0.46 percent. Reductions for women in their forties are even smaller, from 0.35 percent to 0.3 percent.

If screening's benefits have been overstated, its potential harms are little discussed. According to a survey of randomized clinical trials involving six hundred thousand women around the world, for every two thousand women screened annually over ten years, one life is prolonged but ten healthy women are given diagnoses of breast cancer and unnecessarily treated, often with therapies that themselves have life-threatening side effects. (Tamoxifen, for instance, carries small risks of stroke, blood clots, and uterine cancer; radiation and chemotherapy weaken the heart; surgery, of course, has its hazards.)

Many of those women are told they have something called ductal carcinoma in situ (DCIS), or "Stage Zero" cancer, in which abnormal cells are found in the lining of the milk-producing ducts. Before universal screening, DCIS was rare. Now DCIS and the less common lobular carcinoma in situ account for about a quarter of new breast-cancer cases—some sixty thousand a year. In situ cancers are more prevalent among women in their forties. By 2020, according to the National Institutes of Health's estimate, more than one million American women will be living with a DCIS diagnosis.

DCIS survivors are celebrated at pink-ribbon events as triumphs of early detection: theirs was an easily treatable disease with a nearly 100 percent ten-year survival rate. The hitch is, in most cases (estimates vary widely between 50 and 80 percent) DCIS will stay right where it is—"in situ" means "in place." Unless it develops into invasive cancer, DCIS lacks the capacity to spread beyond the breast, so it will not become lethal. Autopsies have shown that as many as 14 percent of women who died of something other than breast cancer un-knowingly had DCIS.

There is as yet no sure way to tell which DCIS will turn into invasive cancer, so every instance is treated as if it is po-tentially life-threatening. That needs to change, according to Laura Esserman, director of the Carol Franc Buck Breast Care Center at the University of California, San Francisco. Esser-man is campaigning to rename DCIS by removing its big "C" in an attempt to put it in perspective and tamp down women's fear. "DCIS is not cancer," she explained. "It's a risk factor. For many DCIS lesions, there is only a 5 percent chance of inva-sive cancer developing over ten years. That's like the average risk of a sixty-two-year-old. We don't do heart surgery when someone comes in with high cholesterol. What are we doing to these people?" In Britain, where women are screened ev-ery three years beginning at fifty, the government recently decided to revise its brochure on mammography to include a more thorough discussion of overdiagnosis, something it previously dispatched with in one sentence. That may or may not change anyone's mind about screening, but at least there is a fuller explanation of the trade-offs.

In this country, the huge jump in DCIS diagnoses poten-tially transforms some fifty thousand healthy people a year into "cancer survivors" and contributes to the larger sense that breast cancer is "everywhere," happening to "everyone." That, in turn, stokes women's anxiety about their personal vulnerability, increasing demand for screening—which, in-evitably, results in even more diagnoses of DCIS. Meanwhile, DCIS patients themselves are subject to the pain, mutilation, side effects, and psychological trauma of anyone with cancer and may never think of themselves as fully healthy again.

Yet who among them would dare do things differently? Which of them would have skipped that fateful mammogram? As Robert Aronowitz, the medical historian, told me: "When you've oversold both the fear of cancer and the effectiveness of our prevention and treatment, even people harmed by the system will uphold it, saying, 'It's the only ritual we have, the only thing we can do to prevent ourselves from getting cancer.'"

What if I had skipped my first mammogram and found my tumor a few years later in the shower? It's possible that by then I would have needed chemotherapy, an experience I'm profoundly thankful to have missed. Would waiting have affected my survival? Probably not, but I'll never know for sure; no woman truly can. Either way, the odds were in my favor: my good fortune was not just that my cancer was caught early but also that it appeared to have been treatable.

Note that word "appeared": one of breast cancer's nastier traits is that even the lowest-grade caught-it-early variety can recur years—decades—after treatment. And mine did.

LAST SUMMER, NINE MONTHS AFTER MY MOST RECENT MAMMO-gram, while I was getting ready for bed and chatting with my husband, my fingers grazed something small and firm beneath the scar on my left breast. Just like that, I passed again through the invisible membrane that separates the healthy from the ill.

This latest tumor was as tiny and as pokey as before, unlikely to have spread. Obviously, though, it had to go. Since a lumpectomy requires radiation, and you can't irradiate the same body part twice, my only option this round was a mastectomy. I was also prescribed tamoxifen to cut my risk of metastatic disease from 20 percent to 12. Again, that means I should survive, but there are no guarantees; I won't know for sure whether I am cured until I die of something else— hopefully many decades from now, in my sleep, holding my husband's hand, after a nice dinner with the grandchildren.

My first instinct this round was to have my other breast removed as well—I never wanted to go through this again. My oncologist argued against it. The tamoxifen would lower my risk of future disease to that of an average woman, he said. Would an average woman cut off her breasts? I could have preventive surgery if I wanted to, he added, but it would be a psychological decision, not a medical one.

I weighed the options as my hospital date approached. Average risk, after all, is not zero. Could I live with that? Part of me still wanted to extinguish all threat. I have a nine-year-old daughter; I would do anything—I need to do everything—to keep from dying. Yet, if death was the issue, the greatest danger wasn't my other breast. It is that despite treatment and a good prognosis, the cancer I've already had has metastasized. A preventive mastectomy wouldn't change that; nor would it entirely eliminate the possibility of a new disease, because there's always some tissue left behind.

What did doing "everything" mean, anyway? There are days when I skip sunscreen. I don't exercise as much as I should. I haven't given up aged Gouda despite my latest cholesterol count; I don't get enough calcium. And, oh, yeah, my house is six blocks from a fault line. Is living with a certain amount of breast-cancer risk really so different? I decided to take my doctor's advice, to do only what had to be done.

I assumed my dilemma was unusual, specific to the anxiety of having been too often on the wrong side of statistics. But it turned out that thousands of women now consider double mastectomies after low-grade cancer diagnoses. According to Todd Tuttle, chief of the division of surgical oncology at the University of Minnesota and lead author of a study on prophylactic mastectomy published in *The Journal of Clinical Oncology*, there was a 188 percent jump between 1998 and 2005 among women given new diagnoses of DCIS in one breast—a risk factor for cancer—who opted to have both breasts removed just in case. Among women with early-stage invasive disease (like mine), the rates rose about 150 percent. Most of those women did not have a genetic predisposition to cancer. Tuttle speculated they were basing their decisions not on medical advice but on an exaggerated sense of their risk of getting a new cancer in the other breast. Women, according to another study, believed that risk to be more than 30 percent over ten years when it was actually closer to 5 percent.

It wasn't so long ago that women fought to keep their breasts after a cancer diagnosis, lobbying surgeons to forgo radical mastectomies for equally effective lumpectomies with radiation. Why had that flipped? I pondered the question as I browsed through the "Stories of Hope" on the American Cancer Society's Web site. I came across an appealing woman in a pink T-shirt, smiling as she held out a white-frosted cupcake topped by a pink candle. In a first-person narrative, she said that she began screening in her mid-thirties because she had fibrocystic breast disease. At forty-one, she was given a diagnosis of DCIS, which was treated with lumpectomy and radiation. "I felt lucky to have caught it early," she said, though she added that she was emotionally devastated by the experience. She continued screenings and went on to have multiple operations to remove benign cysts. By the time she learned she had breast cancer again, she was looking at a fifth operation on her breasts. So she opted to have both of them removed, a decision she said she believed to be both logical and proactive.

I found myself thinking of an alternative way to describe what happened.

Fibrocystic breast disease does not predict cancer, though distinguishing between benign and malignant tumors can be difficult, increasing the potential for unnecessary biopsies. Starting screening in her thirties exposed this woman to years of excess medical radiation—one of the few known causes of breast cancer. Her DCIS, a condition detected almost exclusively through mammography, quite likely never would become life-threatening, yet it transformed her into a cancer survivor, subjecting her to surgery and weeks of even more radiation. By the time of her second diagnosis, she was so distraught that she amputated both of her breasts to restore a sense of control.

Should this woman be hailed as a survivor or held up as a cautionary tale? Was she empowered by awareness or victimized by it? The fear of cancer is legitimate: how we manage that fear, I realized—our responses to it, our emotions around it—can be manipulated, packaged, marketed, and sold, sometimes by the very forces that claim to support us. That can color everything from our perceptions of screening to our understanding of personal risk to our choices in treatment. "You could attribute the rise in mastectomies to a better understanding of genetics or better reconstruction techniques," Tuttle said, "but those are available in Europe, and you don't see that mastectomy craze there. There is so much 'awareness' about breast cancer in the U.S. I've called it breast-cancer

overawareness. It's everywhere. There are pink garbage trucks.
Women are petrified."

"NEARLY FORTY THOUSAND WOMEN AND FOUR HUNDRED MEN DIE EV-
ery year of breast cancer," Lynn Erdman, vice president of
community health at Komen, told me. "Until that number dis-
sipates, we don't think there's enough pink."

I was sitting in a conference room at the headquarters of
Susan G. Komen, near the Galleria mall in Dallas. Komen is not
the country's largest cancer charity—that would be the American Cancer Society. It is, however, the largest breast-cancer
organization. And although Komen's image was tarnished last
year by its attempt to defund a Planned Parenthood screening program, its name remains virtually synonymous with
breast-cancer advocacy. With its dozens of races "for the cure"
and some two hundred corporate partnerships, it may be the
most successful charity ever at branding a disease; its relentless marketing has made the pink ribbon one of the most recognized logos of our time. The ribbon has come to symbolize
both fear of the disease and the hope it can be defeated. It's a
badge of courage for the afflicted, an expression of solidar-
ity by the concerned. It promises continual progress toward
a cure through donations, races, volunteerism. It indicates
community. And it offers corporations a seemingly fail-safe
way to signal goodwill toward women, even if, in a practice
critics call "pinkwashing," the products they produce are
linked to the disease or other threats to public health. Having football teams don rose-colored cleats, for instance, can
counteract bad press over how the NFL handles accusations
against players of rape or domestic violence. Chevron's dona-

tions to California Komen affiliates may help deflect what Cal OSHA called its "willful violations" of safety that led to a huge refinery fire last year in a Bay Area neighborhood.

More than anything else, though, the ribbon reminds women that every single one of us is vulnerable to breast cancer, and our best protection is annual screening. Despite the fact that Komen trademarked the phrase "for the cure," only 16 percent of the $472 million raised in 2011, the most recent year for which financial reports are available, went toward research. At $75 million, that's enough to give credence to the claim that Komen has been involved in every major breast-cancer breakthrough for the past twenty-nine years. Still, the sum is dwarfed by the $231 million the foundation spent on education and screening.

Though Komen now acknowledges the debate over screening on its Web site, the foundation has been repeatedly accused of overstating mammography's benefits while dismissing its risks. Steve Woloshin, a colleague of Welch's at Dartmouth and coauthor of the "Not So Stories" column in *The British Medical Journal*, points to a recent Komen print ad that reads: "The five-year survival rate for breast cancer when caught early is 98 percent. When it's not? It decreases to 23 percent." Woloshin called that willfully deceptive. The numbers are accurate, but five-year survival rates are a misleading measure of success, skewed by screening itself. Mammography finds many cancers that never need treating and that are, by definition, survivable. Meanwhile, some women with lethal disease may seem to live longer because their cancer was found earlier, but in truth, it's only their awareness of themselves as ill that has been extended. "Imagine a group of a hundred women who received diagnoses of breast cancer because they felt a breast lump at age sixty-seven, all of whom die at age seventy," Woloshin said. "Five-year survival for this group is 0 percent. Now imagine the same women were screened, given their diagnosis three years earlier, at age sixty-four, but treatment doesn't work and they still die at age seventy. Five-year survival is now 100 percent, even though no one lived a second longer."

When I asked Chandini Portteus, vice president of research, evaluation, and scientific programs at Komen, in January why the foundation continued to use that statistic, she didn't so much explain as sidestep. "I don't think Komen meant to mislead," she said. "We know that mammography certainly isn't perfect. We also know that it's what we have and that it's important in diagnosing breast cancer." (The statistic was subsequently removed from its Web site.)

In *Pink Ribbon Blues*, Gayle Sulik, a sociologist and founder of the Breast Cancer Consortium, credits Komen (as well as the American Cancer Society and National Breast Cancer Awareness Month) with raising the profile of the disease, encouraging women to speak about their experience and transforming "victims" into "survivors." Komen, she said, has also distributed more than $1 billion to research and support programs. At the same time, the function of pink-ribbon culture—and Komen in particular—has become less about eradication of breast cancer than self-perpetuation: maintaining the visibility of the disease and keeping the funds rolling in. "You have to look at the agenda for each program involved," Sulik said. "If the goal is eradication of breast cancer, how close are we to that? Not very close at all. If the agenda is awareness, what is it making us aware of? That breast cancer exists? That it's important? 'Awareness' has become narrowed until it just means 'visibility.' And that's where the movement has failed. That's where it's lost its momentum to move further."

Before the pink ribbon, awareness as an end in itself was not the default goal for health-related causes. Now you'd be hard-pressed to find a major illness without a logo, a wearable ornament, and a roster of consumer-product tie-ins. Heart disease has its red dress, testicular cancer its yellow bracelet. During "Movember"—a portmanteau of "mustache" and "November"—men are urged to grow their facial hair to "spark conversation and raise awareness" of prostate cancer (another illness for which early detection has led to large-scale overtreatment) and testicular cancer. "These campaigns all have a similar superficiality in terms of the response they require from the public," said Samantha King, associate professor of kinesiology and health at Queen's University in Ontario and author of *Pink Ribbons, Inc.* "They're divorced from any critique of health care policy or the politics of funding biomedical research. They reinforce a single-issue competitive model of fund-raising. And they whitewash illness: we're made 'aware' of a disease yet totally removed from the challenging and often devastating realities of its sufferers."

I recalled the dozens of news releases I received during last October's National Breast Cancer Awareness Month, an occasion I observed in bed while recovering from my mastectomy. There was the one from Komen urging me to make a "curemitment" to ending breast cancer by sharing a "message about early detection or breast self-awareness that resonates with you"; the one about the town painting itself pink for "awareness"; the one from a Web site called Pornhub that would donate a penny to a breast-cancer charity for every thirty views of its "big-" or "small-breast" videos.

Then there are the groups going after the new hot "awareness" demographic: young women. "Barbells for Boobies" was sponsoring weight-lifting fund-raisers to pay for mammograms for women under forty. Keep A Breast (known for its sassy "I ♥ Boobies" bracelets) urges girls to perform monthly self-exams as soon as they begin menstruating. Though comparatively small, these charities raise millions of dollars a year—Keep A Breast alone raised $3.6 million in 2011. Such campaigns are often inspired by the same heartfelt impulse that motivated Nancy Brinker to start Komen: the belief that early detection could have saved a loved one, the desire to make meaning of a tragedy.

Yet there's no reason for anyone—let alone young girls—to perform monthly self-exams. Many breast-cancer organizations stopped pushing it more than a decade ago, when a twelve-year randomized study involving more than two hundred sixty-six thousand Chinese women, published in *The Journal of the National Cancer Institute*, found no difference in the number of cancers discovered, the stage of disease, or mortality rates between women who were given intensive instruction in monthly self-exams and women who were not, though the former group was subject to more biopsies. The upside was that women were pretty good at finding their own cancers either way.

Beyond misinformation and squandered millions, I wondered about the wisdom of educating girls to be aware of their breasts as precancerous organs. If decades of pink-ribboned early-detection campaigns have distorted the fears of middle-aged women, exaggerated their sense of personal risk, encouraged extreme responses to even low-level diagnoses, all without significantly changing outcomes, what will it mean to direct that message to a school-age crowd?

Young women do get breast cancer—I was one of them. Even so, breast cancer among the young, especially the very young, is rare. The median age of diagnosis in this country is sixty-one. The median age of death is sixty-eight. The chances of a twenty-year-old woman getting breast cancer in the next ten years is about 0.06 percent, roughly the same as for a man in his seventies. And no one is telling him to "check your boobies."

"It's tricky," said Susan Love, a breast surgeon and president of the Dr. Susan Love Research Foundation. "Some young women get breast cancer, and you don't want them to ignore it, but educating kids earlier—that bothers me. Here you are, especially in high school or junior high, just getting to know your body. To do this search-and-destroy mission where your job is to find cancer that's lurking even though the chance is minuscule to none. . . . It doesn't serve anyone. And I don't think it empowers girls. It scares them."

Rather than offering blanket assurances that "mammograms save lives," advocacy groups might try a more realistic campaign tagline. The researcher H. Gilbert Welch has suggested, "Mammography has both benefits and harms—that's why it's a personal decision." That was also the message of the 2009 task force, which was derailed by politics: scientific evidence indicates that getting mammograms every other year if you are between the ages of fifty and seventy-four makes sense; if you fall outside that age group and still want to be screened, you should be fully informed of the downsides.

WOMEN ARE NOW WELL AWARE OF BREAST CANCER. SO WHAT'S NEXT? Eradicating the disease (or at least substantially reducing its incidence and devastation) may be less a matter of raising more money than allocating it more wisely. When I asked scientists and advocates how at least some of that awareness money could be spent differently, their answers were broad and varied. Many brought up the meager funding for work on prevention. In February, for instance, a Congressional panel made up of advocates, scientists, and government officials called for increasing the share of resources spent studying environmental links to breast cancer. They defined the term liberally to include behaviors like alcohol consumption, exposure to chemicals and radiation, and socioeconomic disparities.

Other researchers are excited about the prospect of fighting or preventing cancer by changing the "microenvironment" of the breast—the tissue surrounding a tumor that can stimulate or halt its growth. Susan Love likened it to the way living in a good or bad neighborhood might sway a potentially delinquent child. "It may well be," she told me, "that by altering the 'neighborhood,' whether it's the immune system or the local tissue, we can control or kill the cancer cells." Taking hormone-replacement therapy during menopause, which was found to contribute to escalating rates of breast cancer, may have been the biological equivalent of letting meth dealers colonize a street corner. On the other hand, a vaccine, the current focus of some scientists and advocates, would be like putting more cops on the beat.

Nearly everyone agrees there is significant work to be done at both ends of the diagnostic spectrum: distinguishing which DCIS lesions will progress to an invasive disease as well as figuring out the mechanisms of metastasis. According to a *Fortune* magazine analysis, only an estimated 0.5 percent of all National Cancer Institute grants since 1972 focus on metastasis; out of more than $2.2 billion raised over the last six years, Komen has dedicated $79 million to such research—a lot of money, to be sure, but a mere 3.6 percent of its total budget during that period.

"A lot of people are under the notion that metastatic work is a waste of time," said Danny Welch, chairman of the department of cancer biology at the University of Kansas Cancer Center, "because all we have to do is prevent cancer in the first place. The problem is, we still don't even know what causes cancer. I'd prefer to prevent it completely, too, but to put it crassly, that's throwing a bunch of people under the bus right now."

One hundred and eight American women die of breast cancer each day. Some can live for a decade or more with metastatic disease, but the median life span is twenty-six months. One afternoon I talked to Ann Silberman, author of the blog *Breast Cancer? But Doctor . . . I Hate Pink*. Silberman started writing it in 2009, at age fifty-one, after finding a lump in her breast that turned out to be cancer—a Stage 2 tumor, which she was told gave her a survival rate of 70 percent. At the time she was a secretary at a school in Sacramento, happily married and the mother of two boys, ages twelve and twenty-two. Over the next two years, she had surgery, did six rounds of chemo, took a trio of drugs including Herceptin, and, finally, thought she was done.

Four months later, a backache and bloated belly sent her to the doctor; the cancer had spread to her liver. Why didn't the treatment work? No one knows. "At this point, you know that you're going to die, and you know it's going to be in the next five years," she told me. Her goal is to see her youngest son graduate from high school next June.

It isn't easy to face someone with metastatic disease, especially if you've had cancer yourself. Silberman's trajectory is my worst fear; the night after we spoke, I was haunted by dreams of cancer's return. Perhaps for that reason, metastatic patients are notably absent from pink-ribbon campaigns, rarely on the speaker's podium at fund-raisers or races. Last October, for the first time, Komen featured a woman with a Stage 4 disease in its awareness-month ads, but the wording carefully emphasized the positive: "Although, today, she has tumors in her bones, her liver and her lungs, Bridget still has hope." (Bridget died earlier this month.)

"All that awareness terminology isn't about us," Silberman said. "It's about surviving, and we're not going to survive. We're going to get sick. We're going to lose parts of our livers. We're going to be on oxygen. We're going to die. It's not pretty, and it's not hopeful. People want to believe in 'the cure,' and they want to believe that cure is early detection. But you know what? It's just not true."

Scientific progress is erratic, unpredictable. "We are all foundering around in the dark," said Peter B. Bach, director of the Center for Health Policy and Outcomes at Memorial Sloan Kettering Cancer Center. "The one thing I can tell you is some of that foundering has borne fruit." There are the few therapies, he said—like tamoxifen and Herceptin—that target specific tumor characteristics, and newer tests that estimate the chance of recurrence in estrogen-positive cancers, allowing lower-risk women to skip chemotherapy. "That's not curing cancer," Bach said, "but it's progress. And yes, it's slow."

The idea that there could be one solution to breast cancer—screening, early detection, some universal cure—is certainly appealing. All of us—those who fear the disease, those who live with it, our friends and families, the corporations who swathe themselves in pink—wish it were true. Wearing a bracelet, sporting a ribbon, running a race, or buying a pink blender expresses our hopes, and that feels good, even virtuous. But making a difference is more complicated than that.

It has been four decades since the former first lady Betty Ford went public with her breast-cancer diagnosis, shattering the stigma of the disease. It has been three decades since the founding of Komen. Two decades since the introduction of the pink ribbon. Yet all that well-meaning awareness has ultimately made women less conscious of the facts: obscuring the limits of screening, conflating risk with disease, compromising our decisions about health care, celebrating "cancer survivors" who may have never required treatment. And ultimately, it has come at the expense of those whose lives are most at risk.

MOURNING MY MISCARRIAGE

I was initially hesitant to publish this story. Miscarriage was not something people talked about, let alone wrote about. More than that, I was afraid that readers would judge me, blame me for waiting too long to try to conceive. Journalists (especially women, especially post-internet) get used to taking a certain amount of flack for our work. But my emotional resources were depleted by cancer and pregnancy loss; I was too raw to cope with haters. So I waited a year. And I thought about it. Finally, I asked Ilena Silverman, my editor at the New York Times Magazine *whether she knew someone I could talk to at a smaller publication where she had previously worked. "Maybe if fewer people saw it . . . ," I said. "If you're not ready to have the largest audience you can get," she replied, "then you're not ready to publish it." I trusted her. And she was right. The piece ran in April 2002, and remains, for me, one of the most meaningful I've written.*

HEARD THE BELLS BEFORE I SAW THEM, FOLLOWING THE SOUND across the courtyard of Zozo-ji, a Buddhist temple in Tokyo. There they were, lining a shady path: dozens of small statues of infants, each wearing a red crocheted cap and a red cloth bib, each with a bright-colored pinwheel spinning merrily in the breeze. Some had stone vases beside them filled with flowers or smoking sticks of incense. A few were surrounded by juice boxes or sweets. A cap had slipped off one tiny head. Before replacing it, I stroked the bald stone skull, which felt surprisingly like a newborn's.

The statues were offerings to Jizo, a bodhisattva, or enlightened being, who (among other tasks) watches over miscarried and aborted fetuses. With their hands clasped in prayer, their closed eyes and serene faces, they are both child and monk, both human and deity. I had seen Jizo shrines many times before. They're all over Japan, festive and not a little creepy. But this was different. I hadn't come as a tourist. I was here as a supplicant, my purse filled with toys, ready to make an offering on behalf of my own lost dream.

I was in Tokyo for three months reporting on Japan's rapidly declining birthrate. I hadn't expected to be pregnant, though I had long hoped to be (and appreciated the coincidence, not to mention the humiliation, of succumbing to morning sickness midway through an interview on the new childlessness). I called my husband, Steven, across the Pacific, eager to share the news. We agreed that I would stay and find an English-speaking doctor. After all, we reasoned, Japanese women have babies, too. He would come in about a month to visit as planned. I imagined a sweet reunion.

Steven's response, however, was more guarded. I'd already had one miscarriage, more than a year earlier, and he was leery of giving way to excitement before that first, tentative trimester had passed. I knew he was right, but couldn't share that cautiousness—nor, I suppose, did I really try. I found myself engaged in a running conversation with the growing embryo, narrating the details of daily life in Tokyo, telling it stories of our home back in California. The connection I felt was unanticipated, electric: as if a frail, silvery thread ran between us. That link was the first thing I checked for when I woke up, the last thing I focused on when drifting to sleep.

Then, in my eighth week, walking to the subway, I felt it snap. Just like that. It's over, I thought. Is that possible? Could I have truly known? Of course there are concrete indicators that things have gone amiss—nausea abates, breast pain dwindles—but those had not yet occurred. It could have been my imagination, a momentary blip that in a viable pregnancy would have been forgotten. Or maybe the bond itself was a product of wishful thinking. I can't say.

Either way, I could never conjure the connection again. I tried not to think about it. I tried to convince myself that I was being superstitious and absurd. But I was not surprised at my next prenatal exam when the doctor looked at the wavy lines of the ultrasound and intoned, "Egg sac is empty." I just slipped further into the numbness of medical emergency. Steven caught a plane to Tokyo, and we faced the D&C procedure together, grimly, with little incident. A week later, I decided to stay and finish my work. Steven flew home. And it was over.

Or at least it was supposed to be. There's little acknowledgment in Western culture of miscarriage, no ritual to cleanse the grief. My own religion, Judaism, despite its meticulous attention to the details of daily life, has traditionally been silent on pregnancy loss—on most matters of pregnancy and childbirth, in fact. (At the urging of female rabbis, the Conservative movement in which I grew up has, for the first time, included prayers to mark miscarriage and some abortions in its most recent rabbis' manual.) Christianity, too, has largely overlooked miscarriage.

Without form, there is no content. So even in this era of compulsive confession, women don't speak publicly of their loss. It is only if your pregnancy is among the unlucky ones that fail that you begin to hear the stories, spoken in confidence, almost whispered. Your aunt. Your grandmother. Your friends. Your colleagues. Women you have known for years—sometimes your whole life—who have had this happen, sometimes over and over and over again. They tell only if you become one of them.

Women today may feel the disappointment of early miscarriage especially acutely. In my mother's generation, for instance, a woman waited until she had skipped two periods before visiting the doctor to see if she was pregnant. If she didn't make it that long, she was simply "late." It was less tempting, then, to inflate early suspicions into full-blown fantasies—women often didn't even tell their husbands until the proverbial rabbit died.

Now, according to Linda Layne, an anthropologist who is the author of the forthcoming book *Motherhood Lost*, new technologies and better medical care encourage us to confer "social personhood" on to the fetus with greater intensity, and at an ever-earlier stage. Prenatal care—including watching every milligram of caffeine, every glass of wine, every morsel of food, as well as choking down that daily horse pill of a prenatal vitamin—begins before we have even conceived. Meanwhile, drugstore kits can detect a rise in key hormones three days prior to a missed period, increasing our knowledge but also the possibility of dashed hopes. Web sites ply the newly pregnant with due-date calculators, "expecting clubs," and photographs of "your baby's" development. Ultrasounds reveal a nearly imperceptible heartbeat at six weeks of gestation. Women confide in family and friends and begin to sort through names. In an era of vastly reduced infant mortality, they assume all will go well. When it doesn't, Layne says, "the very people participating with us in the construction of this new social person—your mother-in-law or your friend or whoever was saying, 'Everything you do is important to the health of the baby, and every cup of coffee matters'—they suddenly revoke that personhood. It's like nothing ever happened."

There are so many reasons that discussion of miscarriage is squelched. Americans don't like unhappy endings. We recoil from death. Some women also may be reacting against a newly punitive atmosphere toward older mothers. Miscarriage rates increase with maternal age, and those of us who have pushed our attempts at childbearing to the furthest frontiers of time worry that we'll be blamed for our losses, that we'll be harshly judged for "waiting too long." Sometimes we feel that judgment toward ourselves.

But for me, there is another uncomfortable truth: my own pro-abortion-rights politics defy me. Social personhood may be distinct from biological and legal personhood, yet the zing of connection between me and my embryo felt startlingly real, and at direct odds with everything I believe about when life begins. Nor have those beliefs—a complicated calculus of science, politics, and ethics—changed. I tell myself that this wasn't a person. It wasn't a child. At the same time, I can't deny that it was something. How can I mourn what I don't believe existed? The debate over abortion has become so polarized that exploring such contradictions feels too risky. In the political discussion, there has been no vocabulary of nuance.

For days after the miscarriage, I walked around in a gray haze, not knowing what to do with my sadness. I did my work, I went out with friends, but my movements felt mechanical, my voice muffled. Then I remembered Jizo. I phoned the mother of a Japanese friend to ask where I might make an offering. "I can't tell you," she responded. "You'll have to find the temple that is your *en*—your destiny."

Eventually, a Japanese American friend back home told me that Zozo-ji, a fourteenth-century temple where the Tokugawa clan once worshiped, was a common spot to make offerings to Jizo. As it happened, the temple was a few blocks from Tokyo Tower, just a short walk from where I was living. On my way, I stopped at a toy store to buy an offering. What do you get for a child who will never be? I considered a plush Hello Kitty ball, then a rattle shaped like a tambourine, then a squeaky rubber Anpanman—a popular superhero whose head is made of a sweet azuki bean-filled pastry. This was no time to skimp, I decided, and scooped up all three.

"Present-o?" the sales clerk asked, reaching for some wrapping paper. I hesitated. Was it a gift? Not exactly.

"Is it for you?" she asked. I didn't know what to say.

"It's okay," I finally said. "I'll just take them like that."

There are few street names in Tokyo, which makes navigating a continual challenge, so I kept my eye on Tokyo Tower, a red and white copy of the Eiffel Tower, as I triangulated the winding side streets. The neighborhood was unusually quiet, full of low-slung old-fashioned buildings. I caught glimpses of dark interiors: an elderly woman selling bamboo shoots, something that looked like a homemade still, a motorbike parked inside a murky restaurant.

Finally, I came across a temple gate and, assuming I'd arrived, stepped into a courtyard. Down a garden path I could see a contemporary marble statue holding a baby in one arm, a staff in the other. Two naked infants, their tushes lovingly carved, clutched the robes at its feet, glancing over their shoulders. At the base of the statue, someone had left a Kewpie doll.

"Is this Zozo-ji?" I asked an old woman who was sweeping up leaves. My Japanese is good enough to ask a question but not to understand the response. She motioned for me to wait, then fetched a monk, gray-haired in black robes. I was in the wrong place, he explained politely in reasonably good English, then offered directions. For a moment I thought, Why not just do it here? But I had my mind set on Zozo-ji. As I left, I felt the tug of missed opportunity.

I HAD NEVER PREVIOUSLY CONSIDERED THAT THERE IS NO WORD IN English for a miscarried or aborted fetus. In Japanese it is *mizuko*, which is typically translated as "water child." Historically, Japanese Buddhists believed that existence flowed into a being slowly, like liquid. Children solidified only gradually over time and weren't considered to be fully in our world until they reached the age of seven. Similarly, leaving this world—returning to primordial waters—was seen as a process that began at sixty with the celebration of a symbolic second birth. According to Paula K. R. Arai, author of *Women Living Zen* and one of several authorities I later turned to for help in understanding the ritual, the *mizuko* lies somewhere along the continuum, in that liminal space between life and death but belonging to neither. True to the Buddhist belief in reincarnation, it was expected (and still is today) that Jizo would eventually help the *mizuko* find another pathway into being. "You're trying to send the *mizuko* off, wishing it well in the life that it will have to come," Arai says. "Because there's always a sense that it will live at another time."

Jizo rituals were originally developed and practiced by women. According to William R. LaFleur, author of *Liquid Life: Abortion and Buddhism in Japan*, there is evidence of centuries-old roadside shrines marking miscarriages, abortions, stillbirths, and the deaths of young children (particularly by infanticide, which was once widespread in Japan). But it wasn't until the late 1970s, when abortion rates peaked, that *mizuko kuyo*, the ritual of apology and remembrance, with its rows of Jizo statues, became commonplace. Abortion was legalized in Japan after World War II; it is viewed, in that country, as a regrettable necessity. Rates remain high—perhaps twice as high as the officially reported figure of 22 per 1,000 women, which is the same as the rate in the United States. The greater incidence of abortion is partly a result of the fact that access to the Pill was restricted until 1999 because of fears about its safety and its impact on the environment, concerns that it would encourage promiscuity and disease, and, not incidentally, because of pressure from doctors for whom abortion is lucrative.

Even so, the procedure itself has been neither particularly controversial nor politicized. There is no real equivalent in Japan to our "pro-life" movement. The Japanese tend to accept both the existence of abortion and the idea that the *mizuko* is a form of life. I wondered how they could reconcile what seem to me such mutually exclusive viewpoints. But maybe that's the wrong question: maybe I should wonder why we can't.

LaFleur estimates that about half of Japanese women perform *mizuko kuyo* after aborting. They may participate in a formal service, with a priest officiating, or make an informal offering. A woman may light a candle and say a prayer at a local temple. She may leave a handwritten message of apology on a wooden tablet. She may make an offering of food, drink, flowers, incense, or toys. The ritual may be a onetime act or it may be repeated monthly or annually. She may purchase her own Jizo statue (costing an average of about $500) or toss a few hundred yen into a coin box at a roadside shrine. Sometimes couples perform *mizuko kuyo* together. If they already have children, LaFleur says, they may bring them along to honor what is considered, in some sense, a departed sibling: the occasion becomes as much a reunion as a time to grieve. *Mizuko kuyo* contains elements that would both satisfy and disturb Westerners on either side of the abortion debate: there is public recognition and spiritual acknowledgment that a potential life has been lost, remorse is expressed, yet there is no shame over having performed the act.

THERE WAS NO MISTAKING ZOZO-JI. IT WAS A HUGE COMPLEX OF EPIC buildings with a football-field-size courtyard. I walked among the rows of *mizuko* Jizos searching for a spot to place my toys. Some of the babies' caps, which women crochet by hand, had rotted with age to just a few discolored strands. It was dank and gloomy under the trees. A black cat eyed me from a ledge. It seemed a bad omen.

I wouldn't find out until months later, when I returned

to America, that there is another, darker side to *mizuko kuyo*. Over the past few decades, temples dedicated solely to the ritual have sprung up all over Japan, luring disciples by stressing the malevolent potential of the fetus: whether miscarried or aborted, it could become angry over being sent back. If not properly placated, it could seek revenge. In the mid-eighties, when *mizuko kuyo* was at its peak, some entrepreneurial temples placed ominous advertisements in magazines: Are your existing children doing poorly in school? Are you falling ill more easily than before? Has your family suffered a financial setback? That's because you've neglected your *mizuko*.

Given the price tag on a Jizo statue, preying on women's fears is big business. At the Purple Cloud Temple, for instance, Japan's most famous modern *mizuko kuyo* site, thousands of Jizos dot the hillside. Such extortion was troubling. Could something so coercive still offer consolation? "One way of looking at this is that all these women are duped or manipulated into doing this," Elizabeth G. Harrison, a professor at the University of Arizona who studies *mizuko kuyo*, would tell me. "But what is that saying about women in Japan? So you have to look at the other side: there are women who get something out of this." Perhaps like the practice itself, in which conflicting realities exist without contradiction, both readings are true.

Standing amid the scores of Jizos at Zozo-ji that afternoon, I considered: maybe I had found that little temple earlier for a reason. In retrospect, the garden had been cozy, the monk had been kind. There were no rows of statues, no decomposing bonnets. It promised hope as well as comfort. I wanted to return but suddenly feared that the temple had been some kind of chimera, a Brigadoon that had already receded into the mists. More practically, I wasn't sure, without street names, how to find my way back.

Somehow I did, through a vague hunch and a good deal of blundering. The monk was dusting off a late-model Mercedes with two ostrich feather dusters. So much for the mendicant's life, I thought. For certain Buddhists, cleaning is enlightenment. Paula Arai writes that polishing a wooden temple floor is like polishing the heart. I wondered if spiffing up a Mercedes counted.

He saw me and smiled. "Did you find it?"

"Yes," I said, "but I liked it here better. Is it okay if I stay awhile?"

"Do as you wish," he said. And I thought, I'm trying.

As it turned out, the statue at the temple was not Jizo; it was Kannon, goddess of compassion, to whom *mizuko kuyo* offerings are also sometimes made. Her androgynous face was tranquil but not warm. The expressions of the chubby stone babies at her feet were difficult to read. Had I surprised them? Distracted them? Was their backward glance a reminder that even as they played happily with the mother goddess, they would never forget the women whose bodies had been their hosts? Were they sad? Or was I projecting my own sorrow, now a gnawing presence in my stomach, onto them? I focused on the reassuring image of the Kewpie doll that had been placed there, the happy and dimpled Western baby. It seemed less ambivalent.

As I arranged my offering at Kannon's feet, a distant bell tinkled, similar to the sound of the pinwheels. I looked up, startled. It stopped a second later and didn't start again. I am a cynic by nature with a journalist's skeptical heart. But increasingly, I was in the mood to believe.

My toys looked right surrounding Kewpie, the whole place a little cheerier. I liked them there. I liked the delicate lavender bushes surrounding me in the garden, the wild irises with their ruffled edges, the azaleas, the fleabane, and camellias. They were the same plants as in my garden back home. Crows cawed—the constant soundtrack of Tokyo—and traffic passed in a steady hum. Still, for that city it was a meditative spot. I relaxed, at last. Maybe my *en* was finally back on track.

Twilight was falling, and the garden turned cold, but I wasn't yet ready to go. I prayed for a moment for things that are too tender to tell. Then I clapped my hands three times as I'd seen done at other shrines and backed away, gazing once more at the impassive marble face. Was there compassion there?

The temple grounds were empty. The monk in his Mercedes, the lady sweeping leaves were both gone. I rummaged in my purse for an envelope and 5,000 yen—about $40. "To the monk I met at five p.m. from the foreign woman looking for Zozo-ji," I wrote. "Could you please chant a lotus sutra for me and my miscarried fetus? Thank you."

I slipped it under the door. I don't know whether it was appropriate or whether he even did it. But there were so many things I couldn't know. Maybe learning to live with the question marks—recognizing that "closure" does not always occur—is all I really needed to do. I hadn't expected, coming from a world that fights to see life's beginnings in black and white, to be so comforted by a shade of gray. Yet the notion of the water child made sense to me. What I'd experienced had not been a full life, nor was it a full death, but it was a real loss. Maybe my *mizuko* will come back to me more fully another time, or maybe it will find someone else. Surprisingly, even that thought was a solace.

I wasn't exactly at peace as I left the temple—grief is not so simply dispensed with—but I felt a little easier. I had done something to commemorate this event; I'd said goodbye. I'm grateful to have had that opportunity. As I was walking home, the sky deepened from peach to salmon to lavender, and motorists switched on their headlights. The bittersweet smell of fish grilled with soy sauce permeated the air. I breathed it in deeply and felt a little lighter. I decided to try a new route through the unnamed backstreets, not sure of the direction, but trusting that eventually I would find a way home.

BABY LUST

As my husband and I descended into the quagmire of infertility treatment, I became increasingly skeptical of the specialists—both conventional and alternative— who claimed they could help us. This piece, which ran in April 2007, reflects my evolving thinking on the ethics, politics, and social meaning of reproductive technology.

HERE IS A SMATTERING OF THINGS I DID DURING THE SIX-YEAR quest to conceive my daughter: interrupt lovemaking to squirt raw egg whites into myself with a turkey baster (it's reputed to abet the feminine fluid that speeds sperm to egg); substitute two teaspoons of Robitussin for my morning coffee (its main ingredient thins and loosens mucous in the lungs, and although there is no actual proof, it's thought to work similar juju farther south); down ovulation-stimulating pills that triggered fits of rage; inject myself with the urine of postmenopausal Italian nuns (the original source of some fertility drugs, though it's hard to imagine how the goods are gathered); chug unidentifiable herbal potions that tasted like garden mulch; squander what would have been the college fund on long-shot in-vitro-fertilization treatments; imperil my marriage.

Here is what I did not do: stock up on Häagen-Dazs. That, apparently, was my mistake. According to data gleaned from the Nurses' Health Study at the Harvard School of Public Health, and published earlier this year in the journal *Human Reproduction*, women who consume ice cream at least twice a week have a 38 percent lower risk of ovulation-related infertility than those who indulge a mere once a week. What's more, the piously health-conscious—women who eat two or more servings of low-fat dairy products, particularly yogurt, a week—are twice as likely to have trouble becoming pregnant as those who eat less than one serving of the skinny stuff.

Health advice is notoriously fickle, but never are we more willing to follow it, no matter how scant or contradictory the evidence (consider the saturated fat lurking in whole-milk dairy), than when that second pink line refuses to appear. In *The Empty Cradle*, a history of infertility, Margaret Marsh, a dean at Rutgers University, and Wanda Ronner, a physician, reported that eighteenth-century women paid fortunes to lie on the vibrating electrical "celestial bed" that was said to have cured the duchess of Devonshire of her sterility. They soaked in ice water and guzzled patent medicines of "ether, electricity, air or magnetism." A century later, they douched with silver nitrate and flocked to a physician who claimed success through "transplanting" a pea-size segment of a healthy woman's ovary into infertile women's bodies. If that didn't work, there was always the other miracle cure of the day: cervical amputation.

John Rock, a Boston physician who in 1944 became the first scientist to successfully fertilize human eggs outside the body, often observed that infertile women make better research subjects than those trying to prevent pregnancy because they are so desperate. It is impossible to overestimate the frantic despair that comes with multiple miscarriages or endless months of dashed hopes. We women will even pay for the privilege of being guinea pigs—or injecting ourselves with them: another fertility drug I was prescribed was derived from the pulverized, genetically engineered ovaries of Chinese hamsters.

Men, it is worth noting, will not. "Male factor" accounts for up to 40 percent of infertility cases ("female factor" is implicated in about another 40 percent, and the rest is unexplained or a combination), though—perhaps because infertility is often confused with impotence—that fact is less often discussed. In the 1950s, according to Marsh and Ronner, women claimed that they'd rather go childless than request that their husbands get their sperm checked. Forty years later, in a survey of couples using sperm donors, one infertile husband told researchers that he didn't believe the problem was his. Even today some doctors will mix in the sperm of an infertile husband with that of a donor to perpetuate the possibility, however unlikely, that the resulting offspring is genetically the husband's.

Men's drive to procreate is certainly as strong as women's—for both sexes, it is, on a biological level, the primary purpose of our existence—but whether because of denial or something else, they tend, as the sociologist Arthur Greil has written, to experience infertility as "disappointing but not devastating." Women find it "intolerable, identity threatening."

That wound to the psyche may cut even deeper today than in generations past, at least the recent past. Women in the post-Pill, newly libbed 1960s and '70s proclaimed "childless-ness by choice" to be the ultimate emancipation, a defiant, even sexy stance. Several decades later, although living "child free" is surely an option, motherhood has been emphatically re-embraced, rebranded not only as an essential feminine right but also as a feminist one—to be claimed whether you are single or married, gay or straight, twenty-five or fifty-nine. Having children when we want them has become a symbol of our autonomy, more central to our concept of self than ever.

And if our bodies say no? That's when the infertility in-dustry steps in. For the lucky few for whom technology works (a mere one-third in the case of IVF), it is a blessing. For the rest of us, its existence has created a new drive, as profound as either the biological or psychological: call it the techno-medical imperative, the need to exhaust every "option," to do "whatever you can" to have a baby—regardless of the cost to self, marriage, or pocketbook—or feel that you have not done enough. It is now possible to remain hostage to perpetual hope for years, unable to explore alternatives, to make peace, to move on. After all, what if the next cycle is the one? How will you know unless you try? And if you don't, will you be left always wondering what might have been? The uncertainty is agonizing.

I sometimes wonder whether, if I lived in a culture that fetishized motherhood less—one that didn't expect celeb-rity moms to coo that motherhood is the "best thing I've ever done," that didn't use babies to sell everything from toilet paper to automobiles—I would have felt as compelled to go to such extremes to attain it (which I eventually did, no thanks to the fertility docs). It's impossible to say, though Marsh and Ronner found that even in the 1960s and '70s, involuntarily childless women submitted to operations, high doses of infertility drugs, and risky experiments with IVF in order to conceive. Apparently even then there was a world of difference between declaring you might not want a baby and being told you couldn't have one.

So maybe it's inevitable that a woman struggling to conceive will live her life in fourteen-day bursts. She will plot her charts and time intercourse with the precision of a five-star general. She will insist on the missionary position and stand on her head postcoitally. She will shoot herself up with whatever the next crazy concoction may be. And she will hope for the best. But now, at least, she can do all that while eating a hot fudge sundae.

BREAST FRIENDS

Women with breast cancer are expected to join support groups, told that doing so will actually improve their odds of survival. Personally, I'm not much of a joiner but I didn't want to die because of that. So I decided to go to one meeting. Then I went to another. And another. I doubt that has extended my life, but it certainly touched my heart. And Natalie, who hosted most of our meetings, remains one of my dearest friends. This story, published in October 2003, is about our group's final reunion, though Natalie and I have talked of having another one some day. It's also my response to the magical thinking one hears so often in discussions of cancer: that idea (so disrespectful to those who have died) that you can survive it through positive attitude or sheer force of will.

N O ONE LOOKED TOO SICK. THAT WAS MY FIRST THOUGHT. TRUE, about half the women in the room were bald and frail from chemotherapy, but in some cases the effect was surprisingly fetching, a fashionable first cousin to heroin chic. This was my first foray into the Breast Cancer Support Group for Women Under Forty. I'd come because as a thirty-five-year-old cancer patient, I felt like a freak: getting cancer was like being forcibly repatriated to a country in which nothing I previously cared about, nothing beyond illness and its treatment, mattered. More important, I'd heard vaguely that group support could increase the chance of survival—something about learning to express emotions. Joining up was one of the things the take-charge patient did, along with finding a reputable acupuncturist, enrolling in yoga, and buying organic carrot juice (which I despised but now drank daily). It didn't occur to me not to do it.

That first night, I told my story and listened while everyone else told hers. The intimacy, a kind of foxhole sisterhood, was electric, although many of us had little beyond our illness in common. Two were devout Christians who believed in the healing power of prayer. Several others, including me, were skeptical Jews. One was a corporate lawyer. One was in the Navy Reserve. A few were stay-at-home moms. Three of us were childless. Two were single. We were, however, with one exception, white, and all of us were college educated, a reflection both of who is most likely to get breast cancer and who's most comfortable seeking group support. [This is actually only partly accurate: historically African American women have been less likely to contract the disease than white women, but when they did were younger and had far higher mortality rates. However, the incidence among both black and Asian American women has steadily risen since 2012, while those among white and Latino women have remained stable.] We were also all still relatively close to our initial diagnoses, and, to a woman, our cases seemed hopeful.

Over the following weeks, we traded notes on the most responsive oncologists and the best times to schedule radiation to avoid long waits. We talked about the strain cancer put on our marriages, our sex lives. And we talked about the possibility of living lives that might be shorter than we'd imagined. One night Sue, who had the most empathic smile I've ever seen, told us her surgeon thought her cancer had come back. Her mother and grandmother had died of the disease, and although it turned out to be a false alarm, she was still shaky. "It's good to be able to come here and talk," she said. "My friends want to tell me I'll be fine. They don't get it. I don't want to die, but I have to consider the possibility."

Another time, I mentioned that I'd never seen a reconstructed breast. So many women pulled up their tops, it looked like cancer day at Mardi Gras. Someone flung her prosthesis across the room. Natalie even let me touch her saline implant, the only time I've felt up an adult woman.

That was six years ago, and my group has been together in some form ever since. Yet, as the years have gone on I've often wondered about the supposed benefits of group support. How exactly does it make you live longer? Are support groups like medicine, with a precise amount one should take? And as the courses of our diseases diverged—as the health crisis receded for some and deepened for others—I've wondered what "support" over the long haul really means, whom it ought to come from, and at what point this form of "treatment" ought to end.

FOR A WHILE, THE SUPPORT GROUP WAS THE ONLY PLACE WHERE I didn't feel like I had a big red "C" stamped on my head. Even now, when I tell new acquaintances that I had the disease, they look stricken, as if I might wither on the spot, then ask,

"Did you have a family history?" I suppose it's a natural question, though fewer than a third of breast cancers are hereditary (and, for the record, only two in my group appear to be among them), but it's also a way for people, under the guise of caring, to reassure themselves that they won't get it. I'm slim, eat right, and exercise, so no comfort there. I hadn't yet had children when I was diagnosed, but that wasn't so unusual for a thirty-five-year-old. The truly bold (or paranoid) will ask about my mental health: Had I been depressed before my diagnosis?

The fact that I answer such questions politely is probably the best indication that I do have a few teeny, tiny issues with expressing anger. Although I've chosen a profession that strives to uncover some notion of truth, in my personal life I strenuously avoid confrontation. And yes, I have secretly worried that my emotional dishonesty fueled my tumor—that group therapy geared toward unearthing buried emotions could apparently extend my life only amplified those fears. Wouldn't that imply the disease was my fault?

"That's a concern," admitted David Spiegel, a psychiatry professor at Stanford. "It's the bane of my existence that my name is one consonant away from Bernie Siegel's, who says you 'needed' your cancer and all that crap." Spiegel—with the "p"—was the lead investigator on a landmark 1989 study which found that women with metastatic breast cancer (cancer that has spread to the organs or bones) who attended a weekly "supportive-expressive therapy" group lived an average of eighteen months longer than those in a control group. The study garnered massive media attention and almost single-handedly launched the support group movement that is now ubiquitous for those suffering a whole range of maladies. I didn't know it at the time, but it was Spiegel's work—or more accurately, the mythology that has grown out of it—that inspired me to seek out support.

The catch is, the findings don't actually apply to women like me, whose cancer was early-stage and confined to the breast. What's more, depending on whom you ask, Spiegel's results haven't been replicated even for metastatic patients. He points to four subsequent studies that had similar outcomes, though they didn't look specifically at breast cancer. Four that did showed no impact on survival, including the largest and most recent breast cancer study, designed in consultation with Spiegel, and published in 2001 in *The New England Journal of Medicine*. Which isn't to say that the groups conferred no benefits. Participants reported less pain than others, and those who were anxious or dejected felt better—itself a worthy outcome. (Among those who weren't distressed, the groups didn't help at all.)

According to study author Pamela Goodwin, those conclusions allow women to opt out of groups without feeling guilty. "That was the worst fallout of the attention paid to Spiegel's original results," she said. "There was someone in our study who, when she saw me just before she died, apologized, saying she must not have done the support group properly."

But the idea that emotions are not linked to survival could be a hard sell. The flip side of believing that anger, depression, or other "bad" feelings caused your cancer or contributed to it is believing you have the power to cure it. People want to believe that. In a 2001 Canadian study of two hundred ovarian cancer survivors, almost two-thirds believed that stress had caused the disease. More than 80 percent attributed their survival to a positive attitude, and nearly as many to prayer.

A related study of four hundred women who had breast cancer produced similar results—fewer than 5 percent chalked up their survival to the medicine often used to prevent recurrences, tamoxifen.

"The mind-body connection has been oversold and overbought by a culture that wants to believe that if you will something, it will be true," said Jimmie Holland, chair of the department of psychiatry and behavioral sciences at the Memorial Sloan Kettering Cancer Center in New York. "But it's one of those things: If you believe in it, no evidence will change that, and if you don't, you'll always be a skeptic."

Meanwhile, Spiegel, whose own long-term study on therapy groups is still in the works, isn't willing to concede the survival question just yet. He speculates that the "dose" of Goodwin's groups was off—they should have lasted longer. Or perhaps his original outcome was an artifact of another era. A lot has changed since Betty Rollin's 1976 groundbreaking book, *First, You Cry*, when cancer was the Voldemort of diseases, its name never spoken out loud. Now you can't buy a container of yogurt without being reminded of it. "It's harder to be as isolated now than it was in the seventies," Spiegel said. "There's more social support in general. Chemotherapy and hormonal therapies are better, too; people live longer. You can't improve survival twice."

Spiegel's original groups were therapist-led, met weekly, and accepted new members only when someone died or moved away. They were somewhat structured, focusing on seven tasks that ranged from improving communication styles to learning self-hypnosis to help manage pain. My initial group was also facilitated by a therapist, but had no set agenda. New members joined regularly, and when they did, we'd have to backtrack, repeating the diagnosis stories from which we desperately wanted distance.

I also noticed that after a couple of months, I began leaving meetings feeling anxious. "Are you sure you want to keep doing this?" my husband asked one night. "You're more depressed when you get home than before you leave." He was right. I'd had my surgery, finished my radiation. Although I'd always be vulnerable to getting cancer again, I wanted as much as possible to emigrate back to the land of the healthy. I attended the group sporadically for a while longer, mostly because I genuinely liked the women in it, but eventually, without saying goodbye, I drifted away.

A YEAR LATER, NATALIE CALLED. SHE WAS ORGANIZING A POTLUCK reunion at her house. Would I like to come? I don't remember much about that night, but by its conclusion, almost unintentionally, we re-formed. Without a leader, we weren't precisely a therapy group anymore, nor were we quite friends—I haven't been to most of my fellow members' homes, couldn't tell you all of their last names. But our intimacy remained intense.

Yet oddly, as we grew closer, we also grew more careful with each other. Although we talked about cancer in a general way—decoding the latest research, debating genetic testing or the value of tamoxifen—we stopped asking direct personal questions. Two out of ten of us had recurrences to the breast, but I didn't really know what that meant. Sharon had bone metastasis, but I was unsure about her status. Maybe I no longer felt I had the right to inquire, or perhaps I didn't want to know. Yet, I didn't consider abandoning the group any more than I would have expected others to leave if I'd been the one to relapse. It felt wrong, especially once Robin was dying.

Robin's cancer had spread to her lungs and was growing rapidly. Her ex-husband, meanwhile, had died of a heart attack, leaving her as the sole parent of two young boys. She talked frequently about to whom, among her siblings, she might entrust the children. She talked about her treatment and the toll it was taking on her. But the subject of her imminent death came up only once, at a surprise forty-first birthday party we threw for her, which we suspected would be her last. She blew out the candles on her cake and announced that her wish was to have sex one last time. "I'm thinking of taking out a personals ad," she joked. "It would say, 'Single White Female Looking for Good Time. No Long-term Commitment Required.'" We all laughed—Robin was a big presence, fiercely funny and resistant to pity—but then she grew serious. "I have to be able to talk about dying. When I try to talk to my friends, they tell me, 'Oh Robin, if anyone can beat this, you can.' It's not a matter of beating it anymore." We all fell quiet, but then Meredith's new baby cried, and Robin went to soothe him. The moment passed, the conversation changed, and we never found our way back. Later I realized how Robin's comments echoed Sue's several years before. In those days, we could listen to one another talk about death without flinching. We were, after all, in it together. But now, even in this group, Robin was on her own.

Robin died on September 9, 2001. Her funeral was two days later. All morning I watched the Twin Towers collapsing on TV. Then I drove along the empty freeway, the jetless sky above me, to the service. About half of our group attended. Along with hundreds of those who'd loved and respected her, we listened to the James Taylor songs she'd chosen, heard the eulogies of old friends and family, and cried. We promised to get together soon. But here's the thing: we didn't. We stopped meeting entirely. In the weeks and months that followed, as no one, including me, called the group together, I began to think it was for the best. I'd joined during a crisis. I'd stayed, in part, to see someone else through hers. And now? How much did I want cancer to define me? What, exactly, was my commitment to my fellow survivors? What did I want theirs to be to me?

A year later I still felt unsettled. I mentioned my quandary to David Spiegel. "I think that's where a good leader would come in," he said. "There's a point where people who've had primary cancer don't want to identify themselves as a cancer patient. But if I were running your group, I'd say, 'That may be true, but grieve the loss of Robin first. Then if you decide it's time to stop, fine.'" I realized he was right. I couldn't leave it like this. In the end, I was the one who gathered us together, with this article as my pretext.

As always, seeing these women filled my heart with gratitude. Esther's hair, which had fallen out during a new round of treatment, was now long and lush. Sue had just given birth to a second daughter; four months pregnant myself with my first, I was eager to talk to her about pregnancy after cancer. Sharon, who was in remission, passed around pictures from her daughter's bat mitzvah. There was sad news, too: one member, who had moved out of the area, had discovered her cancer had returned and was now metastatic. She'd been clean for seven years.

As we caught up, I asked why we hadn't met since Robin's death. "It's true," Natalie said, "we didn't naturally draw back together. If I'd said, 'Okay, we're all coming back to my house—'"

"And why didn't I do it?" Sharon cut in. "I think I just withdrew."

I'm no therapist, but that night, as a reporter, I felt a little like I had in the group's early days, when we were strangers and the rules of polite friendship didn't apply. Why did we now avoid difficult topics? I pressed. "I didn't even tell the group about my metastasis for a long time," Sharon admitted, "because . . ." She paused, searching for words. What did it mean that she couldn't tell her cancer support group that she had cancer? "It felt like a betrayal," she finally said. "Here you were all moving on. I felt . . . different."

"For me," added Laurie, whose cancer returned in her chest wall two years after her initial diagnosis, "I didn't want to talk about it much. Maybe it was a form of denial."

At that moment, Natalie's kitchen phone rang. Usually her canary mimicked the sound, but this time it was silent. "Hey, what happened to the bird?" someone asked.

Natalie rolled her eyes. "It died of a brain tumor." We laughed so hard her husband shut the door to block out the noise. We all found out new things about one another that night, particularly about Sharon. I hadn't known that she had stopped working when the metastasis was discovered or that her disability payments had been in jeopardy. I didn't know that she was dogged by fatigue, or how she felt about the chance that the cancer would kill her. "I do think of myself as somebody who has metastatic breast cancer," she said. "I appreciate that I'm in this great period of being able to be blissfully ignorant of it. But I know what a remission is. It delights me to go for days without thinking about cancer. But it also makes me feel secure to know that when I do dip into it, it doesn't totally throw me."

I asked Sharon how she thought the group could improve. Her answer was immediate: "If we went back to meeting more often," she said. I felt a stab of apprehension. Earlier that evening, I'd confessed that I'd felt relieved to give up the group after Robin died, ready, possibly, to let go, or just attend the occasional reunion. Yet tonight, I'd also realized that this group held a part of me that no one else could reach. I honestly wasn't sure where to go from here. So I said what was true, but not the whole truth. "Seeing everyone again makes me so happy."

Laurie nodded. "It's like a miracle," she said, and I saw tears spring to Natalie's eyes.

"You know," Esther added, "we've seen each other reach milestones that at one time we thought we might never see."

"And we've always had fun," Natalie said.

We were quiet. "I say, we all pitch in and buy Natalie a new bird," I said, and the mood broke. A good therapist might not have let me get away with ending on a joke, but as in life, a good therapist is not always around. It's just us, muddling through.

PUT TO THE TEST

I wasn't tested for the gene mutations indicating a predisposition to breast cancer until a decade after my diagnosis. I didn't want to know the results unless I was sure of what I'd do with the information. Then I had a daughter and I thought: it's time. This piece was published in October 2007. In the future, more of us will be able to find out whether we have an inherited tendency toward specific, sometimes life-threatening conditions. Already, companies such as 23 and Me can predict your chances of contracting Parkinson's disease or Alzheimer's for a couple hundred bucks and a vial of spit. Yet, more knowledge may not always be better. Incidentally, I did eventually have an oophorectomy, which was a huge relief, but I waited until after menopause, when attendant risks of cardiovascular disease, dementia, and Parkinson's disease (among others) dropped.

THE THING I REMEMBER MOST ABOUT BEING TOLD I HAD BREAST cancer was how the colors in my home office—where I'd been tidying up for the day, preparing to go to a movie with my husband—went flat. Isn't that odd?, I thought, looking down at my newly alien torso. My red shirt has turned gray. My red shirt has turned gray, and I might die.

That spectrum shift was the first sign that I'd passed through an invisible membrane into the parallel universe of the ill. I turned to my husband, Steven, who was standing in the doorway, listening in disbelief on the extension as the surgeon told us that I was a lucky woman, that the cancer was low-grade and slow growing, eminently treatable with a lumpectomy and six weeks of radiation. We stared at each other for a beat, as close and as distant as we had ever been. He reached his hand out, as if to keep me with him. "But I eat organic broccoli!" I wailed, and then began to cry.

That was January 1997, only six weeks past my thirty-fifth birthday. The odds of being diagnosed at that age were one in 233. A fluke. "Do you have a family history?" an acquaintance asked when I told her the news. I suppose it was a natural question, although fewer than a quarter of breast cancers are familial. "No, I don't," I said, perhaps a little too harshly. "No one in my family has had breast cancer. I'm just like you."

As far as I knew, that was true.

A week later, I read an article in the paper about a blood test that could detect inherited mutations in the BRCA genes, BRCA1 and BRCA2. In most women the BRCA genes suppress tumor growth. In some families, however, the gene contains a flaw, passed along by either the mother or the father, that makes it do the opposite, predisposing its carriers to breast and ovarian cancers. About one in eight hundred people in the general public carry the BRCA1 mutation, but among Ashkenazi Jews—those whose ancestors emigrated from middle or Eastern Europe—the rate of mutations in either gene is closer to one in forty. I'm an Ashkenazi Jew. My aunt had died of ovarian cancer at fifty-four. At the time, we thought that was a fluke, too. Yet even as the thought This could be me entered my head, I rejected the idea. No one else in my extended family had been sick. Besides, I already knew my lifetime breast cancer risk: it was 100 percent.

There is a little bit of Vegas in predictive genetic testing, a roll of the statistical dice. Even if you found, let's say, that you had an 80 percent risk for some disease, who's to say you wouldn't be in the other 20 percent? What if the known risk-reducing treatments come with risks of their own, the way tamoxifen, the widely used breast cancer drug, raises the risk of uterine cancer? Increasingly, all of us will be running the numbers and weighing the trade-offs on one scary condition or another—we all have skeletons lurking in our skeletons. In its zeal to find them, science has outpaced the medical, psychological, and ethical implications of its discoveries.

Cardiovascular disease. Diabetes. There will be gene tests for all of them and more, and each will bring with it the same questions: Who should be tested? What is the benefit of knowing you're at risk, especially if, as with the degenerative and ultimately fatal Huntington's disease, there is no cure available? What responsibility does a person who tests have to family members, including those who might not want to know the status? Should genetic testing be a factor in choosing whom you marry? Would some couples want to abort if their fetuses were found to have a tendency toward cancer? Mutations are not a guarantee of cancer, remember, and cancer is by no means a death sentence. Maybe there are some things we can't, or shouldn't, control.

The BRCA tests were among the first gene tests to hit the marketplace, and since they involve half the population and are harbingers of so much to come, they're important and bear watching. That doesn't make them any easier to deal with. "There are people who come in for their first genetic counseling session, then we never see them again," said Richard King, director of the division of genetics and molecular medicine program at the University of Minnesota, in Minneapolis. "The risks are scary to face. But I've also seen the benefits of testing, even with Huntington's disease. Families can get things organized and understand things better, be more prepared.

"Would I be tested in that position?" He paused. "I don't know. I can't give a direct answer without thinking about it. Just like everyone else."

My mother mentioned something in passing: my great-aunt Golde had died of a "stomach ailment."

"You mean she had ovarian cancer?" I asked.

She hesitated. "It's possible," she said. "Though who knows? Back then, it could've been appendicitis."

Oh, she continued, and Great-Aunt Jane? On Grandpa's side? She had breast cancer in her seventies. And Anice, my first cousin once removed? The one who'd lived on a ranch in Montana? Breast cancer killed her in her early forties. Then there was Great-Aunt Minnie; she died of breast cancer, too. "But she was phobic," my mom assured me, as if mental illness explained the physical one. Minnie wore only white and lived in an all-white house in Los Angeles with all-white furniture, including her grand piano. When she got sick, she refused to go to a hospital for treatment—she was afraid there'd be germs there. It seemed to me that Minnie had a lot more to worry about than breast cancer.

I, on the other hand, was getting progressively more nervous—maybe cancer really did lurk in my family's gene pool. I still hoped to have children; what might I be passing on to them? A year after finishing my breast cancer treatment, I finally mentioned it to my GP. "Everyone has some family history of cancer," he said, shrugging. But he suggested I make an appointment with a genetic counselor, saying, "I think it will ease your mind."

I EYED THE OTHER PATIENTS AT THE COMPREHENSIVE CANCER CEN-ter at the University of California, San Francisco (UCSF). Were they getting treatment, or were they also waiting for someone to read their genetic tea leaves? An elderly couple shuffled in with his-and-hers walkers, the legs of which had been made scuff-proof by attaching Day-Glo tennis balls. In another context I might have pitied them their frailty, but now I found myself envious. At least they'd made it this far.

My counselor was a young, sweet-faced woman named Lisa, who would assess my risk of a mutation from what was already known; then the decision of whether to get tested would be mine. She took my family history, tapping her pencil on her desk a few times before explaining that a Jewish family with just one case of early-onset breast cancer, combined with one case of ovarian cancer at any age, was statistically likely to have a mutation. Then she pulled out a pie chart. "See this section?" she asked, pointing to a large white slice. "This is sporadic breast cancer. It's random. It represents about 70 percent of all breast cancers. These women have no previous family history of disease."

I nodded. That, I had assumed, was me. "Now see this section?" she continued, pointing to a smaller, striped area. "These are people with familial cancer, but without any known cancer-gene involvement; they may have other behavioral or inherited factors at work, such as body size or a naturally higher level of estrogen. This represents about 20 percent of cases."

I nodded again. "Now this section," she said, pointing to a thin, black sliver of the pie. "This is where I think you fall. These are people with a genetic mutation. My suspicion would be that you have a BRCA1 mutation. It carries a 60 to 85 percent lifetime risk of breast cancer and a 20 to 50 percent risk of ovarian cancer." She went on to say that if I did have children, there was a 50 percent chance that I would pass the mutation on. She continued, but my mind had already floated away. It was so tacky to make that pie segment black, I was thinking, so insensitive. Couldn't they make it green? Or polka-dotted? Less of a grim reaper?

I focused my anger on the chart; I couldn't absorb what the counselor was saying. Not yet. If she was guessing right, that meant I could get cancer again and again? And the next time, it could be in my ovaries? If I had children and they got sick, it would be my fault. Should I not have them? What if my mother hadn't had me?

If I did have the mutation, I heard Lisa say, the most effective risk-reducing options for carriers were a double mastectomy and an oophorectomy, removal of one or both ovaries. That is: amputation of healthy body parts. Once again, I gazed down at my body, which suddenly seemed like an assassin, a stranger. I'm a journalist, someone who believes in the power of knowledge. But for the first time in my life, I was weary of information. I wanted to go back to the land of the well; I wanted my visa to this other, desolate country permanently revoked.

A LONG TIME LATER, I WOULD FIND A KIND OF TERRIBLE BEAUTY, a poetry in the BRCA mutations. They are ancient flaws, which some say date back to about 75 CE, around the time when the Romans sacked Jerusalem and forced the Jews into an exile that would last nearly two thousand years. There are now as many as eleven million Ashkenazim scattered throughout the world, but, since we've had a tendency to intermarry, we mostly descend from the same few thousand forebears. As devastating as the thought of having a mutation was, it was still a tangible connection to my deepest past, to a web of ancestors stretching across millennia. One of my grandparents had carried that legacy, deadly yet sacred in its history. So had his or her grandparents. And their grandparents. And theirs. The schism in our DNA had flowed through each of them into my own mother's blood and finally into mine. Somehow, knowing they were all in me—with me—through this made me feel stronger.

I also read about a study of people with perfect pitch. That trait, too, may be partially genetic and, as it happens, may be disproportionately found in Ashkenazi Jews. My brother has it, as does his son. I do not. Great, I thought. They got the perfect pitch gene, while it looks like I got the cancer gene—and I might add, the *zaftig* upper arms.

Why is there no exact feminine equivalent of the word "emasculated"? That's how I felt about the idea of prophylactically removing both of my breasts. Maybe they aren't the only source of my femininity, my sexuality, but I'm rather attached to them (as they are to me). We have a lot of history together, me and the girls: standing up to those junior high boys who called me a pirate's dream (because of my "buried treasure"); chanting the legendary bust-increasing mantra from *Are You There God? It's Me, Margaret.* (It didn't work.) Giving pleasure. Getting pleasure.

I had chosen lumpectomy in part because I felt it would leave me less scarred, psychologically as well as physically, by my illness. Some women feel the opposite—a mastectomy, even when clinically unnecessary, is a reassertion of control over their bodies, their destinies—but I needed to be able to look into the mirror each day and see, more or less, what I always had. I was willing to wager that the kind of breast cancer I had was the kind my body would always make: slow growing and treatable. I had no idea whether that was actually true.

Ovarian cancer was a different story—it's hard to detect, and nearly 65 percent of sufferers die within five years of diagnosis. I'd seen my aunt's abdomen swell to the size of a basketball and watched the mischief and vitality drain from her lovely face. "Numbers aren't the only way women make these decisions," said Beth Crawford, manager of UCSF's cancer risk program. "If you've experienced loss, you may make a different choice than someone with little history of cancer in her family. I've met women who don't have retirement accounts, they're so convinced that they'll die young. For them, knowing they can reduce risk with a mastectomy or oophorectomy comes as a relief."

ABOUT A THIRD OF THE WOMEN WHO TEST POSITIVE IN CRAWFORD'S program have risk-reducing double mastectomies, and two-thirds undergo a risk-reducing oophorectomy. Seventeen percent of the latter group have turned out to have early stage, highly treatable cancers, tumors that without the surgery, would probably not have been caught until they were lethal. That was a pretty powerful argument. On the other hand, I wasn't eager to experience the jarring discomforts or health risks of early, surgical menopause. "Risk tolerance is different for everyone," Crawford said. "Some women can just monitor themselves closely and sit comfortably with that; others can't. Everyone has to come to the decision that best allows them to go forward."

And what would that decision be for me? I stood at the craps table, feeling truly crappy, wondering what testing would mean to my mind, my body, my heart. I kept shaking those dice for the next six years. Then, at age forty-one, I gave birth to my daughter, and it became clear: I wanted to be here for her first day of kindergarten, to dance at her wedding, and to meet my grandchildren. I needed to be tested. Either way, I'd keep my breasts, but if it came out positive for the mutation, I wanted my ovaries gone. Now. And so one day, in between the breast-feeding and diaper changing, I drove to the hospital, had my blood drawn, and let those dice roll. The strangest thing was, I wasn't even sure which result I was rooting for.

It came out negative.

"We were as surprised as you are," Crawford told me. "We calculated that you had a 90 percent chance of being positive.

"We call this an uninformed rather than a true negative," she added, explaining that if you thought of the BRCA gene as a document, the current test functioned as a spell and grammar check: it could find missing, extra, or transposed letters and words. But if a whole sequence or chapter was gone, the test wouldn't know anything was missing and would come out clean. So I might still have a mutation, they just couldn't yet find it. I'd expected a yes or a no—or, more precisely, I'd expected a yes. But a maybe? No one told me that was a possibility. "Do I still have the oophorectomy?" I asked.

"Well, we can't really make any recommendations beyond regular surveillance, because you don't have a known mutation. Maybe in another year or so we'll have something new to offer you." She smiled sympathetically. "I'm afraid this is a bit like peeling an onion."

I WALKED OUT OF THE HOSPITAL INTO THE NORTHERN CALIFORNIA fog more lost and frightened than when I'd gone in. Perhaps my body really was a time bomb. Or maybe my cancer and my aunt's were totally unrelated. A fluke, after all. I'd finally gambled on the test, and what did I learn? Bupkes. Part of me wished I had tested positive. At least then I'd know how to protect myself. Instead, I was left with the unknown—like everyone else.

The truth is, it's not possible to ward off all evil, all disease, all ill luck. Maybe, someday, there will be much better detection, better treatment of breast and ovarian cancers, more understanding of the causes, even cures. I'll be pushing for all of that, for myself and for my daughter, regardless of our risks. Meanwhile, simple as it sounds, I'm left with one last, best choice: living my life as it comes, every day . . . just as I always have.

WHAT MAKES A WOMAN A WOMAN?

When I wrote this piece, in September 2009, the notion that sex was a continuum rather than a binary was, to many liberals as well as conservatives, largely incomprehensible. This was before Laverne Cox graced the cover of Time, *before Caitlyn Jenner transitioned, before the hit series* Transparent. *What and who decides a person's sex or gender is now at the front lines of the culture wars, with battles raging—as they did historically for people of color, cis women, and gays and lesbians—over the use of public restrooms and the right to serve in the military. If I were to write this piece today, then, less than a decade after it was published, I would approach it quite differently, a shift for which I'm grateful. Caster Semenya, meanwhile, continues to make headlines: In 2017, the International Association of Athletics Federations announced that it will go to court to reinstate a regulation, suspended two years earlier, that sets limits on the natural testosterone levels allowed in female competitors. If the organization prevails, Semenya and athletes like her would either have to withdraw from their sport or undergo hormone replacement therapy. Who's right? What's fair? I don't know, but I'll be watching to see how the complications of sex, gender, biology, and ethics play out on this high-stakes public stage.*

THERE IS A PAINTING BY RICHARD PRINCE HANGING IN THE Walker Art Center in Minneapolis, a purple canvas bisected by one line of chartreuse type that reads: "I met my first girl, her name was Sally. Was that a girl, was that a girl. That's what people kept asking." That refrain echoed in my head as I pored over the photos of eighteen-year-old Caster Semenya, the South African track star whose biological sex was called into question last month after she annihilated her competition and won the 800-meter race at the World Championships in significantly less time than her own previous finishes.

Was that a girl, was that a girl. That's what people kept asking. Semenya's saga was made for the news media. A girl who may not be a girl! That chest! Those arms! That face! She was the perfect vehicle for nearly any agenda: Was this another incidence of people calling into question black female athletes' femininity (the Williams sisters, the basketball legend Sheryl Swoopes)? Was it sexist to assume that women were incapable of huge leaps in athletic performance? Should all female athletes be gender-verified, as they were in Olympic competition until 1999? (The practice was dropped because no competitive edge was proved for the few women with rare disorders of sex development—it served only to humiliate them.) Should the entire practice of sex-segregating sports be abandoned?

Was that a girl, was that a girl. That's what people kept asking.

I had my own reasons to be fascinated by Semenya's story: I related to it. Not directly—I mean, no one has ever called my biological sex into question. No one, that is, except for me. After my breast-cancer diagnosis at age thirty-five, I was told I almost certainly had a genetic mutation that predisposed me to reproductive cancers. The way I could best reduce my risk would be to surgically remove both of my breasts and my ovaries. In other words, to amputate healthy body parts. But not just any parts: the ones associated in the most primal way with reproduction, sexuality, with my sense of myself as female. Even without that additional blow, breast cancer can feel like an assault on your femininity. Reconstructing the psyche becomes as much a part of going through treatment as reconstructing the body.

In the weeks that followed my diagnosis, during that heightened, crystalline time of fear and anxiety, I was not, I admit, at my most rational. So I began to fret: Without breasts or hormone-producing ovaries, what was it that made me female? Who got to decide? How much did it matter?

When I was in college, in the early 1980s, the gospel was that the whole enchilada of gender was a social construct: differences between boys and girls were imposed by culture, rather than programmed by chromosomes and chemicals, and it was time to divest ourselves of them. That turned out to be less true than feminists of the era might have wished: physiology, not just sisterhood, is powerful. While femininity may be relative—slipping and sliding depending on the age in which you live, your stage of life, what you're wearing (quick: do tailored clothes underscore or undercut it?), even the height of the person standing next to you—biology, at least to some degree, is destiny, though it should make no never mind to women's rights or progress.

Even as I went on as a journalist to explore ideas about

gender, I took the fact of my own for granted: as for most people—men and women alike—it was so clear to me as to be invisible. I was unnerved, then, to discover not only that it could be so easily threatened, but also how intense that threat felt. That, too, gave me pause: Why should being biologically male or female still be so critical to our self-definition? Is it nature—an evolutionary imperative to signal with whom we can reproduce? Is it nurture? Either way, and regardless of our changing roles and opportunities, it is profound.

Was that a girl, was that a girl. That's what people kept asking.

And yet, identity is not simply the sum of our parts. That's what makes Semenya—whose first name is usually conferred on a boy but happens to be Greek for "beaver"—so intriguing. Science may or may not be able to establish some medical truth about her, something that will be relevant on the playing field. But I doubt that will change who she considers herself to be. According to Sheri Berenbaum, a professor of psychology and pediatrics at Penn State who studies children with disorders of sex development, even people with ambiguous biology tend to identify as male or female, though what motivates that decision remains unclear. "People's hormones matter," she said, "but something about their rearing matters, too. What about it, though, no one really knows."

THERE IS SOMETHING MYSTERIOUS AT WORK, THEN, THAT MAKES US who we are, something internally driven. Maybe it's about our innate need to categorize the world around us. Maybe it arises from—or gives rise to—languages that don't allow for neutrality. My guess, however, is that it's deeper than that, something that transcends objectivity, defies explanation. That's what I

WHAT MAKES A WOMAN A WOMAN?

concluded about myself, anyway. Although I have, so far, opted to hang on to my body parts (and still wonder, occasionally, if I would feel differently were, say, a kidney or an arm at issue), I know that my gender could never really be changed by any surgeon's scalpel. Why not? Perhaps because of the chemistry set I was born with, one that Semenya may or may not share. Perhaps merely because . . . I say so. And maybe that will have to be enough.

CALL OF THE WILD

An editor from MORE *emailed me one day asking for ideas for a new travel section the magazine was launching. The only criteria were that the trip had to be adventurous (no lolling on the beach) and outside the United States. I submitted a long list of ideas, most of which were in warm weather climes (maybe a little lolling on the beach would be okay . . .). On a whim, I also threw in, "dogsledding in the Arctic Circle." I don't know why. But I knew, as I hit the send button, that was where I'd end up—it was obviously the most interesting story. The article was published in September 2013; the trip is still among the most memorable of my life.*

Nico Hobi, a sharp-eyed, deeply dimpled thirty-four-year-old Swiss man, peered at me. "Will you take an ice bath?" he asked expectantly. I'd just traveled for two days from California to Finland's slice of the Arctic Circle, lugging my suitcase the last quarter mile through snowdrifts and subzero temperatures. This was to be my last night in civilization—a cozy inn—before a five-day dogsledding expedition through Pallas-Ylläs National Park. After that I'd be sharing a one-room cabin, lacking heat and running water, with seven strangers, including Nico and his perpetually amused wife, Michaela. The weather report predicted record cold. An ice bath—whatever that was—was the last thing on my to-do list. "After the sauna," Nico persisted in clipped, Swiss-German-accented English, "will you take a bath in a hole in the ice in the lake?"

Michaela laughed. "He's joking," she said. Nico only nodded. "I will dig a hole, and you will see," he said. "You will take an ice bath." This was not the first time—and would not be the last—that I wondered what I was doing here.

Six months earlier, I had weathered a different sort of extreme: lying in an intensive care unit recovering from a mastectomy after a return of breast cancer. I had first been diagnosed and treated at age thirty-five; by fifty, recurrence free, I figured I had it beat. Then one evening my fingers grazed a small, hard knot under my lumpectomy scar. My passport to the land of the healthy was revoked. In most cases, you can't have radiation to the same body part twice, so though my tumor was low-grade and small and I would almost surely survive it, the whole breast had to go. My doc sculpted a new one out of my abdominal fat, essentially giving me a tummy tuck in the process (now aren't you jealous?). The downside was a grueling double surgery—eight hours under the knife—followed by a long, slow recovery. A month after leaving the hospital, I couldn't stand up straight. Two months after, a walk around the block left me gasping for breath. The idea of dog-sledding in the Arctic Circle seemed preposterous; it was also, on my darkest days—when my energy ran low and my terror ran high—a hope I could cling to.

MARKKU AND MARI RAUHALA, THE OWNERS OF PALLAS HUSKY, gathered our group after breakfast: there were Nico and Michaela; a pair of twenty-seven-year-old German PhD candidates in physics (whose habit of explaining the mechanics of virtually everything earned them the nickname "the Einstein brothers"); a photographer in his late thirties based in Los Angeles; and an Australian architect in his fifties. There was also Margarete, another German, who was seventy. At least, I thought selfishly, I won't be the weakest on the trip. In my woolen long underwear, fleece pants and hoodie, down jacket, two pairs of socks, gloves, scarf, neoprene balaclava, and goggles, I looked like the love child of a ninja warrior and the Pillsbury Doughboy. Yet I could already feel the cold seeping in. At the Rauhalas' farm, we added bib overalls, anoraks, fur-lined caps with earflaps, clunky polar boots, and leather driving mittens that looked like oven mitts. When I stepped outside again, the day felt almost balmy. I recalled my childhood in Minnesota, with a climate not unlike Finland's—one, incidentally, I'd eagerly left behind—when my mom bundled me in so many layers that I was red-faced and sweating by the time I left the house. Dressed like that, I could play in the snow for hours. And I did, making forts, snowmen, stockpiles of snowballs, and fields of angels.

Markku showed us our sleds, simple birch contraptions with boatlike prows and runners about two-thirds the width of my boots. There were two foot-operated brakes: a metal bar with claws that dug into the snow, stopping the dogs immediately, and a flat pan we could step on to slow them down. We'd each have our own team of five. Everything else, Markku said, we could pick up as we went along. "Um . . . how do we steer?" someone asked. Finnish is an uninflected language that makes anything Finns say in English sound vaguely ironic. So it was unclear to me whether Markku intended to be quite so deadpan when he answered, "You don't."

I'd expected sled dogs to have a touch of the wolf in them, but my lead pooch, Bambi, looked at me with the melting brown eyes of her namesake and immediately tried to crawl into my lap. Her daughter, Ninni (named after a character in a Finnish children's book), was equally sweet. All the dogs were, instantly forgiving me for jamming their harnesses on upside down or mercilessly torquing their paws as I tried to hook them to the sled. The howling of some forty dogs eager to run spiraled from din to pandemonium. They didn't even sound like dogs: they screamed like monkeys, yowled like cats, shrieked like parrots. Their energy built like fizz in a fast-shaken can of soda. I began to worry about what would happen when it was released.

At last I stood on my runners, one foot planted on the main brake. Markku took off first, followed by Margarete and one of the Einstein brothers. I was next. Mari, standing a short distance from me, called out one last piece of advice in that laconic Finnish intonation: "Hold on with both hands!"

For years I had thought of myself as a Weeble, one of those roly-poly children's toys that "wobble but they don't fall down." I had, after all, survived breast cancer in my thirties, an age when it tends to be especially deadly; after three miscarriages and six years of infertility, I got pregnant in my forties with my daughter. There were other crises, too, of the heart and the head as well as the body—how could there not be after five decades of living?—but they didn't define me. I'd always popped up fine. Yet lately, incrementally, I had begun to feel defective, emotionally diminished rather than strengthened by trauma, in danger of becoming the sum of my pain. Had that happened after this latest bout of cancer or before? I couldn't say. But I felt cleaved, a word that also means its opposite: cleaved to this body, whether I liked it or not, and from it by its many betrayals. I wanted to bounce back, but this time I just couldn't.

My dogs lunged forward. The sled tipped left, listed right; I felt myself start to tumble. Then I stomped on the pan brake with one foot, and magically the team slowed. My whole body thrummed, but I stayed on the sled. The barking had stopped the second the dogs took off. Now it was quiet, the only sounds their rhythmic panting, the creak of the wooden sled, the scrape and skitter of the pan brake along the powder. I relaxed my death grip on the handlebar and looked around: at spruce trees whose needles were individually etched in crystals of ice, at birches laden so heavily with snow that they'd bent into arches over the trail. I'd heard that Eskimos have fifty words for snow and that Finns have nearly as many. I understood why. We sledded through crystallized snow and powder snow, compacted layers, and snow as granular as salt.

I zoomed over moguls, catching air and momentarily taking flight. In truth, we averaged about seven miles an hour and covered up to nineteen miles a day, but when you're balanced on two thin wooden planks, trust me, that is blazing. One of my dogs, Harald, lifted his leg to pee whenever I rode the brake or neglected to help on hills by pushing with one foot. Maybe it was my imagination, but his gesture felt personal.

Too soon we pulled into our camp for the week: a cabin on a snow-covered lake with an outhouse, a wood-burning sauna, and a *kota*—a traditional hexagonal cottage with a conical roof and a central fire pit—in which we'd eat our meals. Although we'd been out in the cold for hours, pausing only for a lunch of sausages roasted over an open fire, we now tended to the dogs' comfort before our own. I stroked shoulders and cradled paws, cuddled Bambi, gave Ninni a belly rub. I chained each one to a little straw-filled house where they built their nightly nest. Mari, meanwhile, pulled around a sled weighed down with kibble and a barrel of broth studded with animal fat and parts I preferred not to contemplate.

Nico spied a volunteer staffer heading toward the sauna with an ice pick. There was a hole in the ice of a stream there, just wide enough for the bucket. The staffer cut it open twice a day to haul water for washing dishes and sluicing ourselves in the sauna (the nearest we'd get to bathing). Nico offered to take over, plotting to enlarge the hole so he could fit through it. The ice was nearly two feet thick. Michaela laughed at him. The rest of us did, too. Even Nico laughed. But he kept chipping away. "Now we have soup," Mari said when the dogs were settled, as if this were normal, as if the whole world took a soup break at around five o'clock. Maybe they should: it turns out there is nothing so comforting or convivial. On successive days we warmed to steamy bowls of cream of mushroom, potato-leek, tomato, vegetable, and ginger-carrot accompanied by tea, bread, white Finnish cheese, and a little cake.

We laughed and shared stories of the trail, holding our hands and stocking feet out to the fire. When Mari said it was sauna time, I hesitated. Finnish women used to give birth in saunas. There is an entire wing devoted to saunas in the country's Parliament House. And an estimated two million private homes in a country of about five million people have them. There is even a sauna about four thousand six hundred feet below sea level, in a Finnish metal mine. Taking a sauna was virtually obligatory for a visitor, but this would be the first time since my surgery that I'd disrobe in front of anyone but my husband and my daughter.

Dressed, I looked fine—better than fine: my new breast passed for natural, and my stomach was flatter than it had been since puberty. I may have felt lousy about myself, but I looked great. Beneath my clothes, however, a jagged purple scar slashed from hip to hip. My reconstructed belly button was ringed by scars, and another scar cupped the underside of my breast. They were the price of staying alive, and I was grateful for them, but I didn't want to discuss them. Not even with other women. Still, I couldn't skip such an integral part of the experience. Besides, I was *freezing*. On our way to the sauna building, I told Michaela and Margarete as briefly and casually as I could, precluding any pity. They were sympathetic, but that wasn't the point: I was here to transcend the identity of illness, not confess it.

Here is what you are supposed to do in a Finnish sauna: sit on a wooden bench until the sweat cascades off you, until you are flushed and slimy and so hot that you can't bear it any longer. So hot that you will do this mad thing: you will run outside, stark naked, and fling yourself into the snow. It is not something I imagined I would ever do—*could* ever do—yet with the others urging me on, I dashed outside, screaming, and flung myself face-first into a snowdrift. It was cold. *Burning* cold. And the snow was the texture of sandpaper. I stood up, turning toward the sauna, but Margarete stopped me. "Now on the back!" she said. So I threw myself backward, tush first. Then, laughing and still whooping, living nowhere but in that moment, I returned to the heat.

That night I dreamed my dogs were pulling my sled without harnesses—no ropes, no clips. We simply floated together, a unit, through the snowy nights and days. There was no cold. There was no heat. There was just being.

By morning the cup of water I'd left on the windowsill for toothbrushing had frozen solid. So had my toothpaste. So had my contact lenses. My camera would also freeze, as would the ink in my pens. I shimmied into an extra layer of long underwear inside my sleeping bag, then climbed out to check the thermometer; it was nine degrees in the cabin and twenty-seven below outside. And although I had been trying to drink as little as possible, I had to pee. I steeled myself for the task by piling on pants, a jacket, a hat, mittens, socks, and boots. The outhouse was a short jaunt down a snowy path: a deceptively quaint, snow-covered log structure with diamond cutouts in the door and back wall for ventilation. A Styrofoam seat covered a wooden hole—it wasn't cold to the touch, exactly, but neither was it warm, and an Arctic breeze whooshed up from below. On my way back to the cabin, I passed Margarete, who waved cheerfully. She was wearing an undershirt and leggings—no jacket, nothing on her head or hands. I glanced down: her feet were bare, in flip-flops.

That second day, my sled shot out from under me; I hung suspended in midair, flailing like a cartoon character, then was dumped headfirst into the snow. The dogs kept going, until Markku grabbed them. Everyone waited while, in the musher's equivalent of the walk of shame, I struggled through the snow to fetch them back. I'd go down three times before realizing that mushing was in the legs: the trick was to go with the motion, not fight it—to dance with your dogs. We burst onto a snow-covered lake, a glittering expanse under a crystalline sky. It was spectacular, that emptiness, a vista of frozen potential. I took a deep breath. Northern Finland has some of the cleanest air in Europe; every inhale felt like a sip of spring-water, delicious and pure. I'd assumed that we'd sled the same terrain every day and that while lovely, it would get a little dull. Now we circled upward to the top of a fell—a small Finnish mountain—stopping at the edge of the tree line. Moisture in the air had condensed on the branches in layers, forming wild, Seussian phantasms: a child fishing, a queen in a white fur cape, flying dragons, sentinels. I would say it felt like another planet, but it didn't, not at all. It felt, at last, as if we were in the Arctic.

My nostalgia for Rudolph aside, I'd been excited about trying reindeer meat, common in the Finnish diet, but it proved less succulent than I'd imagined. It's a little chewy, like a lesser cut of beef, but Mari cooked it into a tasty stew. For dessert there were sour lingonberries she had picked and frozen over the summer, topped with yogurt and caramel sauce. Afterward, we duly donned our Arctic gear and trudged into the moonless night, walking single file along the trail (to avoid sinking into the snow) until we reached the lake. A faint green stripe fanned across the horizon, then changed direction and shot straight up. The northern lights. The Einstein brothers began to natter on about the science—something about collisions of gaseous particles—but I turned away. I preferred the Finnish explanation: the lights are sparks swept from the snow by the tail of a magical fox as it runs across the fells. I gazed up at the firmament, at stars brighter than any I might ever see again. There were Orion, the Big and Little Dippers. There were the Pleiades and Cassiopeia. There was the bright North Star, glittering like an icy gem, leading lost travelers home.

We mushed uphill all the next morning. On the steepest slopes I jogged behind my sled, pushing until the crest, then hopping back on before the dogs could pull off without me. I sweated through my many layers, that fresh Finnish air now searing my lungs. The arm on my mastectomy side ached from the dogs' yanking. Harald lifted his leg. A lot. I can't do this, I thought. It was too soon. I was too weak. I would have to quit. I focused on Margarete, straight and sinewy, two teams ahead of me. Hanging on to the pretense of youth mattered to her not at all. Her hair was white, clipped short for ease, not style; her face was lined; her teeth were yellowed. Yet she was tougher than the rest of us: the first one up every morning, the last one inside at night. Her beauty ran deep, a product of spirit, not cosmetics. And if she could do this, dang it, I could, too.

NICO'S ICE BATH WAS READY ON OUR LAST AFTERNOON AT CAMP. Michaela snapped pictures as he streaked to the hole. Somehow he persuaded the other men, one by one, to follow his lead. They returned to the cabin pink and swaggering, urging us ladies to give it a try. "*Anyone* can roll in snow," Nico announced. "*This* is special." It was twenty-two degrees below zero outside, but I am a sucker for a dare. So I sat in the sauna until I thought my eyeballs would blister. Then, before rationality could set in, I sprinted, naked and steaming, to the hole's icy ledge, slipping and sliding my way in. The water was surprisingly gentle on the skin, less scratchy than snow. I dunked to my armpits, grinning crazily, desperate to get out, loving that I was in. Back in the sauna, I felt as shining and phosphorescent as the aurora itself. For months my body's limits had defined me, but not anymore. It wasn't that I felt invulnerable—those days are gone. But I was resilient. And in the end, isn't that better?

PART 3

NOT YOUR MAMA'S MOTHERHOOD

THE PERFECT MOTHER TRAP

During the "Mommy Wars" of the early 2000s, women who stayed home with children were pitted in the media against mothers who worked for pay and neither side emerged a winner. Womens' insecurites were ripe for exploitation: after all, in what I would come to call a "half-changed world," others' choices can feel like a rebuke. We may be headed for another round of conflict: according to a survey that has monitored attitudes of high school seniors over the past forty years, the percentage of both sexes who believe that the best family arrangement is one with a male breadwinner and a female homemaker has risen steadily since the mid-1990s, growing fastest among boys. And while young women's confidence that employed women are as good mothers as those who stay home has gradually risen, young men's has dropped to the point where those aged 18 to 25 have become more traditional on the subject than their elders.

I was not yet a mother myself when I wrote this piece, which ran in July 2000, nor was I sure I ever wanted to become one. It was adapted from Flux, *my second book, which I began, in part, as an attempt to make that deci-*

sion, sort through my own ambivalence and fears about motherhood.

On a lush summer day in suburban New Jersey, Carrie Pollack,* thirty-eight, strides through a shopping mall toward the red-hot center of what she calls the parallel universe of stay-at-home moms. She pulls up short in front of a playground designed to look like a lily pond: dozens of children leap in gleeful chaos, plunging from plastic toadstools, squirming through hollow logs, and rolling around the bluemat "water," while the adults supervise from carpeted steps. "Well, ladies and jelly beans," Carrie says, beaming at four-year-old Julia and eighteen-month-old Sam, "what do you think?"

Carrie is just shy of five feet tall, dressed in blue jeans, a T-shirt, and sandals. Her dark hair is pulled back into a ponytail; her large brown eyes, under straight-cut bangs, are slightly asymmetrical, giving her a friendly, quizzical look. It's easy to see why, back when she was a district attorney prosecuting child abuse cases—before Julia and Sam were born— she could win the trust of even her most traumatized clients.

She takes a seat as the children skitter stockingfooted into the fray. Around us, the stairs are filled with women. It may be 1997 in the real world, but here in the parallel universe, it looks more like the 1950s. There is a smattering of grandmothers and nannies, but mostly these are full-time moms. I see exactly two fathers during our visit here, and only one is without his wife. As that man walks by, Sam stops what he's doing and stares, eyes wide, until the man is out of sight. Sam always stares at men, Carrie explains: "He's not used to seeing fathers during the day."

OVER THE LAST FOUR YEARS, I HAVE INTERVIEWED MORE THAN TWO hundred women for my book *Flux: Women on Sex, Work, Love, Kids and Life in a Half-Changed World*. The women I talked to were married and single, with and without children, working and staying home. Most, but not all, were college graduates; all were currently in the broad swath considered middle-class, although many were raised in blue-collar homes or in poverty. They ranged in age from their mid-twenties to their mid-forties, which meant that by the time they became adults, sexual norms, marital patterns, relationships with family, and women's career expectations—the warp and woof of what it means to be an American female—had undergone a radical transformation.

I was interested in how, as teenagers, they had imagined their lives would unfold; how their aspirations had changed over time; what they expected from marriage and mother-hood; what they'd learned about managing conflicting de-mands and choices. Ultimately, I hoped these conversations would yield a deeper understanding of the forces that shape our lives—as well as help break down some of the barriers that keep women from talking to one another.

By their mid-thirties, many of the mothers I spoke with, including Carrie Pollack, seemed surprised by where they had ended up, describing a kind of whiplash turnaround from their younger, single selves. Back then, they'd imagined that they would divide housework and child care equally with their future husbands. Somehow, though, that's not what happened. Whether or not they worked outside the home, the vast majority of women had made concessions to parenthood in a way that men, for the most part, still do not. That's why words like "balance," "trade-off," and "work-family conflict" have become as feminine as pink tulle.

Women complained to me that their husbands didn't pull their domestic weight, but time after time, I heard them let men off the hook. A thirty-eight-year-old technical writer I interviewed in San Francisco was typical: "You know," she mused after running down a litany of frustrations, "my husband is really involved compared with his own father."

I pushed, pointing out that this sets the bar too low. Shouldn't we be comparing men's involvement with that of their wives instead? "Well," said another mom, "you can't really expect that." I tried putting it another way: "It seems to me that women, whatever their arrangements, feel like lesser mothers than those of the previous generation. Meanwhile, men, even with minimal participation at home, feel like better fathers."

"You're right," the first woman acknowledged, "because most of the men we know are better fathers. But I don't know any woman who doesn't struggle."

Carrie Pollack was a little different, and that's what had drawn me to her. More than almost anyone I met, she and her husband, Brian,* thirty-six, were in a position to make good on the promise of equal parenting. He was one of the rare men in America to take a six-month unpaid paternity leave when his daughter was born. Meanwhile, Carrie loved her job prosecuting child molesters and had felt strongly about her economic independence. She even earned more than her husband did. Even so, here she was, sitting by the plastic lily pond while her husband, a mid-level lawyer in the federal government, was off at work. What, I wondered, had led someone who valued equality so fiercely to make such a traditional choice?

The answers, I discovered, revealed a great deal, not just about Carrie and Brian but about modern women's and men's deepest expectations about parenthood and the real range of choices we allow ourselves to consider. They also say something about what needs to change psychologically as much as culturally for men to do more in the home and for women to let them.

A FEW HOURS AFTER WE RETURN HOME FROM THE MALL, BRIAN Pollack comes through the door and yells a greeting. He's a bearish man, with an unruly mop of red hair and a warm, patient expression. He sweeps his daughter off her feet for a hug, and she dissolves in giggles. "It has surprised me that our love has grown," Carrie confides. "I never thought that I could love him more than the day we married. But I'm just crazy about him. And I think part of that is the joy of seeing him with our kids."

The Pollacks have strong views about child-rearing, and they've made significant personal sacrifices to accommodate them. Brian's government job is both less interesting and lower-paying than one in the private sector or academia, but the hours are regular, and twice a month he works a four-day week. With just one income, they take no out-of-town vacations, forgo nights out as a couple, and have passed on the kinds of luxury items most Americans take for granted, such as a CD player and a VCR. Brian's parents chip in by helping with the mortgage on their modest home, and Carrie's mom

provides child care when they need it. They are both adamantly against day care. Carrie says that because of the nature
of her work, she is fearful of abuse, and both she and Brian
mentioned observing what they called "benign neglect" by
nannies and day-care workers. "The bottom line," says Brian,
"was that one of us was going to stay home."

Which one of them that would be, however, was an open
question. Brian would have seemed the more likely candidate for full-time parenthood. Carrie liked her job far more
than he did and was more dedicated to it. Here is how Brian
describes his job with a government agency: "It's pretty easy. I
can goof off for days at a time."

When Julia was born, they figured they'd each take a leave,
then work out the next step from there. Carrie would go first,
taking the four-and-a-half paid months that her job allowed,
then Brian would put in for the six months' unpaid parental
leave his office provided. He was the first man to avail himself
of the policy. "I got mostly stroked," Brian tells me after dinner. "Other guys said, 'That's really cool.'"

"'Really cool,'" I counter, "but none of them did it themselves?"

"Yeah," he says. "And there was some 'No way I would have
done it.'"

Brian says he was fully prepared to make fatherhood his
vocation, yet even before he left work, subtle cues from friends
and family let him know he was expected to return to his job.
Carrie's girlfriends told her how lucky she was that Brian was
"trying to understand your experience." Brian's parents proclaimed the leave "wonderful for the baby," as long as it didn't
hurt his long-term earning potential. All around, Brian was

hailed as "a progressive and New Age-y dad"—provided he went back to work when it was over.

Women may have been integrated into the male enclave of the workforce, but men have neither entered nor been accepted into the parallel universe of mothers. Brian enjoyed the attention of being the token dad at Gymboree, but it's hard to imagine most men feeling as comfortable. Some of the women I met confessed that they think of full-time fathers as "losers." Few young, single women imagined marrying a man who would want to be a stay-at-home dad. "I don't need to be the test case for that," one told me. "I mean, *Mr. Mom* was a great movie, but the reality seems more unsavory."

Meanwhile, the men who were trying to do their part complained that day-care providers and teachers always instructed them to tell their wives when a child needed Popsicle sticks for a project or a packed lunch for a field trip. The assumption persists, as sociologist Pepper Schwartz has pointed out, that a child's primary parent is her mother and the father is a temporary substitute.

Looking back on it, Brian believes he could have withstood such social pressures if he had enjoyed his early caretaking time with Julia. But when he discusses those six months, a tone of defeat creeps into his voice. "Staying home with her was really tedious," he says. "I was surprised by the constantness of it, the lack of breaks that we so much take for granted in life. By mid-afternoon, my entire mental focus would be on how long it would be until Carrie returned."

I ask Brian if there was anything he loved about staying home with Julia. He grins. "Oh, absolutely," he says. "Little things, like when she'd fall asleep with her tiny arms around my neck. And also there was the sort of general psychic feeling of being a father. The feeling of parental love was absolutely tangible. On the other hand, it was tinged with a lot of guilt at not being a better one. Not spending more time, not having more energy."

What struck me, listening to Brian, was that the experience he described mirrored that of so many new mothers. Studies have shown that professional women in their thirties are particularly likely to feel isolated after a child is born. Not only do they feel numbed by the monotony, they worry that their feelings make them bad parents. But women have two things Brian didn't: a support network—other mothers and family members to help them cope with the boredom—and a social expectation that they would simply endure it. After all, there is no shame in a father admitting that he finds infants exasperating and retreating to the workplace. But when a mother does the same, her devotion is called into question—by others and by herself.

As it turned out, that is what happened to Carrie. At first, she reveled in being the working parent. "It was great," she told me. "I took care of Julia in the mornings, then I disappeared to work. Then I came home and took care of her some more. And I knew that during the day she was with Brian. But on the other hand, I started to feel like I was missing it, like he was home and I was missing all of this stuff."

As Brian's paternity leave wore on, Carrie and Brian each began to articulate reasons why she would be the better full-time parent: Brian watched C-Span all day, and Carrie didn't want Julia exposed to that much TV. Carrie was "more disciplined, more able to get the job done through the tedium." Carrie was ambivalent, but less ambivalent about leaving work.

"Carrie missed Julia," Brian says. "Either she missed her genuinely emotionally or felt that she should be here for her." He shrugs. "It probably was a combination. I think the truth is, Carrie didn't want to be seen as 'that kind of mom'—the mom who was working and not staying home with her kids." Bad Mother: the phrase affects women like kryptonite, and it's one of the most effective checks against those who want fuller lives or more help on the domestic front. The Bad Mother— "that kind of mother"—is thought to risk damaging her children through her independent needs and outside interests. It's why so many working mothers protest that they "have" to work, while no father feels compelled to make such a justification. The Bad Mother is the evil twin of the Perfect Mother, who lives solely for her children, whose needs are completely in sync with theirs. In her book *When Mothers Work*, journalist Joan Peters found that working mothers in particular respond to the threat of being tagged a bad mother by unconsciously clinging to control. Micromanaging their children's lives— retaining a sense of authority over packing lunches, choosing clothes, and coordinating their kids' schedules—makes them feel that they are good mothers, even as the responsibility for "doing it all" overwhelms them.

"I'm scared my husband wouldn't do things right," admits a thirty-six-year-old insurance executive in Minneapolis. "Like, one day he dropped our oldest daughter off at a Brownie event where I thought lunch would be provided. It wasn't. Luckily, the troop leader worked something out for her, but I cried that night. I kept thinking, What a failure I am as a mother to not even think of what my daughter is going to eat for lunch." She looks at me to make sure I understood what she is saying. "I didn't think, He's a bad father," she emphasizes.

"I didn't blame him. I feel like if my house is messy or my kids don't have clean clothes, people are going to judge *me*."

The stay-at-home mom is just as vulnerable as the working mom to Perfect Mother pressure. In addition to basic nurturing, Peters points out, she's now expected to be a creative playmate, a developmental psychologist, and an educational expert, not to mention a ready volunteer. Carrie strives to imbue every activity that her kids engage in with a "purpose" and talks wistfully about her lost connections with old friends. "It's not about who you want to be friends with," she says about spending an afternoon with a mom she clearly didn't connect with. "It's based on who the kids are friends with, what's good for them." Although she spends a lot of time with her children, Carrie feels guilty because she sometimes drifts off when Julia chatters at her or feels exhausted by Sam's perpetual motion. Other women told me they felt they'd "failed as mothers" when they couldn't breast-feed. ("I tried for six-and-a-half weeks. I really bonded with that pump," one joked.) The impossible standards they set for themselves, shared by so many women, reminded me of teenage girls who, no matter what their weight, see themselves as fat. I don't know whether there's a Perfect Mother equivalent to an eating disorder, but I wondered: How good does a mother have to be before she feels good enough?

I ask Carrie—since she's given up her job, her financial independence, and time with friends for her children's well-being—if there is anything that would make her feel she's gone too far, that she has become too subsumed in her role as a mother. "If I suddenly felt totally satisfied with motherhood alone," she says slowly, "that would be a warning sign. There's got to be ambivalence. Because I can't imagine ever being totally satisfied with this role."

THAT EVENING, WHEN I LEFT TO TRAVEL ON TO PHILADELPHIA, I FELT disturbed. In many ways, I admired Carrie. Like other mothers I met, she raised important questions about our culture's definition of success, about the lure of materialism, and about the value of home and regeneration in our overly busy lives. But instead of being part of a larger discussion involving both men and women, these questions had fallen into the cracks of women's choices and were getting lost in the defensiveness and anger of the Mommy Wars.

The next morning I interviewed a group of female medical students from a variety of racial and economic backgrounds. As it happened, these young women had just attended a forum of women physicians discussing how they'd met the challenge of mixing work and family. "How many men came to the session?" I asked, remembering Carrie and the other mothers I'd met. They looked blank. "Did they have their own panel in which male doctors advised them on how to be good fathers and good physicians," I continued, "or don't they expect to have to be both?"

Their male classmates, they informed me dryly, would never show up for such an event. Maybe they're right. But it sounded to me like a younger version of "Well, you can't expect that." Suddenly I felt I could see these young women's futures as clearly as any psychic.

The truth is, women will grapple with these contradictions and compromises until work-family balance transcends the ghetto of women's issues. No matter what we do, our "choices" will remain both real and illusory until we reach the point where men feel obliged to struggle as deeply as we do with the trade-offs at work and the rewards of home. That requires not just economic and cultural change, but changes in our own psyches: we need to have greater expectations of men and more realistic ones of ourselves. It requires loosening our grip as micromanagers of our children's lives, even a little bit, and most of all, letting go of the Perfect Mother.

That, perhaps, is something on which both women who work and those who stay home can agree.

Names in this story have been changed.

YOUR GAMETE, MYSELF

Reproductive technology shattered conventional definitions of "parent," and the legal system still struggles to catch up. Do children have a right to know that they were conceived through third-party reproduction? Should they have the right to meet their genetic or biological parents? What claims might donors or gestational surrogates have on such children? What rights do social/legal parents have to privacy? Whose story is this to tell? The issues in this piece, published in July 2007, were personal to me, as someone who went through multiple rounds of infertility treatment—including a donor egg cycle—before conceiving spontaneously. Since this piece was published, the use of third party reproduction has continued to rise: in 2014, the most recent year for which data is available, there were 20,481 donor egg cycles and between 30,000 and 60,000 children conceived via artificial insemination. Meanwhile, the number of cycles employing gestational surrogates more than quadrupled between 1999 and 2013 (as the first edition of this book went to press, Kim Kardashian and Kanye West announced they had hired a surrogate to carry their third child). The ethical questions, however, remain unresolved.

Two years ago, when Catherine was in sixth grade, she was given a school assignment that would have been unremarkable for most kids: make a timeline for history class in which half the events occurred before she was born and half after. For a while, she worked quietly at the dining room table of her family's rambling Northern California home. Then she looked up.

"Mom?" she asked. "What was the year that you and Dad met our donor?"

Sitting with me in May, Catherine's mother, Marie, a fifty-nine-year-old therapist, smiled wryly, remembering the incident. The crinkling of Marie's eyes gave her a passing resemblance to the actress Anne Bancroft—but not to her own daughter. Marie, who asked me to use only her middle name and a family name for her daughter to protect their privacy, is dark where Catherine is blond, olive-skinned where Catherine is fair, brown-eyed where the girl's are hazel. There is no similarity to their jawlines, their cheekbones, the shapes of their faces. Of course, lots of kids don't look like their mothers; few people would consider that odd, though they might—often incessantly—comment on it in conversation.

"So, what's going to happen with this project?" Marie recalled responding to Catherine at the time, being careful to keep her voice neutral. "Is it going to be put up in the hallway? In the classroom?"

Catherine shrugged. "I don't know," she said. And later, "Mom, this is my timeline."

"I got the message," Marie told me. "But in essence, I was outed on the wall of the middle school. It was there in black and white for everyone to see. They'd all know we used an egg donor. We'd been committed to openness from the beginning, but my first reaction was, 'No!'"

IF MARIE AND CATHERINE ARE UNUSUAL, IT IS ONLY BECAUSE OF Catherine's age. In 1992, the year she was conceived, there were just 1,802 attempts by women to become pregnant using someone else's eggs, according to the Centers for Disease Control. Three years later, there were more than 4,738 such cycles; by 2004, the most recent year for which data has been published, there were 15,175 cycles, resulting in 5,449 babies. By comparison, some 22,911 children were adopted from abroad that year, and although there are no official figures, one survey estimated that at least the same number are conceived annually via donor insemination. Donor eggs are now used in 12 percent of all in vitro fertilization (IVF) attempts, making it among the fastest-growing infertility treatments. Despite the portentous hype around women like Frieda Birnbaum, a sixty-year-old New Jersey resident who in May used donor eggs to become the oldest American to give birth to twins, the bulk of intended mothers are in their forties. The birthrate among women ages forty to forty-four has risen 62 percent since 1990, while the rate among those in their late forties has more than doubled. Among those who used IVF in 2004, about a third of the forty-three-year-olds used someone else's eggs; by forty-seven years old, 91 percent did.

With egg donation, science has succeeded in, if not extending women's fertility, at least making an end run around it, allowing older women who, for a variety of reasons (lack of money, lack of partner, lack of interest, lack of partner's interest) didn't have children in their biological prime—as well as younger women with dysfunctional ovaries—to carry and bear babies themselves. It has given rise to the mind-bending phrase "biogenetic child," meaning a child who is both biologically and genetically related to each of its parents by, for the first time in history, separating those components. In that way, it is fundamentally different from sperm donation, though it also levels a certain playing field: mothers can now do what fathers always could—conceal the truth about their blood relationship to their children. And as with any new reproductive technology, it has provoked a torrent of social, legal, and ethical questions about the entitlement to reproduce, what constitutes parenthood, children's rights to know their origins, and the very nature of family.

I first became interested in the implications of egg donation because I tried it. After five years of repeated miscarriages and invasive, futile infertility treatments, a twenty-one-year-old friend offered to spot me her gametes, the cells containing half the chromosomes necessary for reproduction. It wasn't something I ever imagined I'd consider—it seemed so *Handmaid's Tale*. Then again, with a donor egg, I could feel a baby grow inside me, experience its kicks and flutters. I could control—that sweetest of words—the prenatal environment, guard against the evils of drug and drink. I could give birth to my own child, breast-feed it. After a year of discussion, my husband and I decided to go ahead, only to find that when placed in a petri dish, his sperm and my friend's eggs refused to tango.

Although my husband and I went on, improbably, to conceive our daughter spontaneously, I always wondered what it would have been like had that cycle worked. Would I have felt less authentic as a parent than my husband, or would my gestational contribution have seemed equivalent to his genetic one? Would we tell our child? And when? And how? What about strangers on the street who commented on how little the baby resembled me? What if someone said the baby did look like me and I smiled—would I feel dishonest? How would the experience be different from adoption? What kind of relationship would the child have with our friend, the donor? Would my husband feel awkward about pointing out similarities between our child and himself? What if the child someday turned to me and said, "You're not my real mother?" What if I secretly agreed? What if she wanted to put the date I met our donor on her sixth-grade timeline?

THE WORLD'S FIRST DONOR-EGG-CONCEIVED CHILD WAS BORN IN Long Beach, California, in 1984—just six years after the debut of Louise Brown, the original test-tube baby, in Britain, and three years after Elizabeth Carr, who was America's first. The early recipients were women in their twenties and thirties who had gone into premature menopause or whose ovaries had been surgically removed. The donors were typically older than today's, married with children, often the sisters of recipients or unpaid volunteers.

Back then, doctors extracted women's eggs surgically under general anesthesia. The risks of infection, organ damage, and even death from the procedure may have been justifiable for an infertile woman going through IVF, but not for a donor. So early researchers borrowed a trick from animal husbandry: when the donor ovulated, she was inseminated with the recipient's husband's sperm, the embryo formed in her body and, four to six days later, was flushed out of the uterus and transferred to the intended mother. This adapted procedure "was problematic in many ways," said Dr. Richard Paulson, chief of reproductive endocrinology and infertility at the University of Southern California's Keck School of Medicine in Los Angeles and a pioneer in the development of egg donation. For one thing, if the doctors missed the embryo, the donor could wind up pregnant.

By the late eighties, though, European researchers perfected a new method of retrieving eggs by using a thin needle, guided by ultrasound and inserted through the vaginal wall. The procedure took ten minutes and required only light anesthesia. As Liza Mundy writes in her book *Everything Conceivable*, this technique would revolutionize—or, you could even argue, create—the fertility industry by unhooking clinics from their dependence on hospital operating rooms. Suddenly, any doc with a lab and the right equipment could set up his own shop. Using that advance, Paulson and his team made a breakthrough of their own: some of their patients had aged past forty, which was considered the outer limit for medical intervention, while waiting for donors. Would it be possible, Paulson wondered, to push that threshold? He tried transferring multiple embryos created from a young woman's eggs into the body of a forty-year-old . . . and she became pregnant. In 1990, Paulson published an article in *The New England Journal of Medicine* announcing that as long as the eggs were young, the age of the recipient appeared immaterial. And just like that, the market for donor eggs was born.

ONE DAY THIS SPRING, BECKY, WHO IS THIRTY-EIGHT, MET ME AT the loft where she works in the music industry. She is a tiny woman—just over five feet tall—with dark blond ringlets pulled back in a ponytail, and three earrings ascending one ear. A wedding photo on her desk, taken last summer, showed her tucked beneath the arm of her husband, Russell, a public school teacher who is more than a foot taller than she and who asked that I use only his middle name. Next to the photo was a clutch of supplements and prenatal vitamins that she was downing to prepare her body for pregnancy. Behind those sat a small statue of Ganesha, the pachyderm-faced Hindu deity, lord of both obstacles and beginnings.

Becky, who asked me to use a nickname, sat down and began scrolling through pictures on the Web site of Ova the Rainbow, one of the (regrettably named) agency sites she browsed last fall during her search for an egg donor. "When I first started doing this it was really emotional for me," she said. "I kept thinking about that kids' book, *Are You My Mother?* I'm looking through these pictures of young women and feeling like: 'Oh, my God! Is this the mother of my future child? Is this the mother of my future child?'"

I stood behind her, watching the young women go by. Each was accompanied by an assortment of photos: girls in caps and gowns graduating from high school, sunburned and smiling on family vacations, as preschoolers in princess frocks, sporting supermodel pouts in shopping-mall glamour portraits. Sperm banks rarely provide such visuals, which is just one disparity in the packaging and treatment of male and female donors, according to a study published last month in the *American Sociological Review*. Egg donors are often thanked with presents and notes by recipients for their generous "gift." Sperm donors are reminded that they're "doing a job," providing a "sample," and performing an act they'd presumably do anyway—which may be why many men in the study were rattled when told a pregnancy had actually occurred. And although the men could admit they were in it for the cash, ovum donors were expected to express at least a smidge of altruism.

It was weird to look at these pictures with Becky. I inevitably objectified the young women in them, evaluating their component parts; it made me feel strangely like a guy. Becky clicked on a photo of a twenty-two-year-old brunette with a toothy grin. Each profile listed the donor's age (many agencies consider donors to be over the hill by thirty), hair color (there seemed to be a preponderance of blondes), eye color, weight, ethnicity, marital status, education level, high school or college GPAs, college major, and evidence of "proved" fertility (having children of their own or previous successful cycles). Some agencies include blood type for recipients who don't plan to tell their child about his conception. Others include bust size and favorite movies, foods, and TV shows. One newly pregnant woman told me she picked her donor because the woman liked *The Princess Bride*. "Some donors chose *Pulp Fiction*, and their favorite color was black," she said. "That's just not me. If I have the choice between someone who likes *The Princess Bride* or someone who likes *Pulp Fiction*, everything else being equal, I'm going for *Princess Bride*."

Obviously, a penchant for romantic comedy is not an inherited trait. Nor, for that matter, will appearance or intelligence necessarily be passed along, though they are the first things most prospective parents look for in a donor. It's a curious paradox: couples who conceive a baby this way believe that relationships, not genes, make a family, yet in their search for a donor, they romanticize the potential of DNA. And why not? The culture itself is in conflict over how much genes shape us, even as science and the media claim they determine, or predetermine, more than ever. Consider the schmaltzy news stories of reunions between adopted children and their "real" mothers, or tales of identical twins reared apart who are eerily alike. The notion that blood is thicker than water, that we can pass on our best—or someone else's best—characteristics (but somehow not our worst) is a powerful one, even though anyone who has biogenetic children will tell you that they can be as different from one another, and from their parents, as strangers.

Women using donor eggs know that. But the dream, the hope, of replicating oneself dies hard. "Loss is the first stage of building a family with donor gametes," says Madeline Licker Feingold, a psychologist who works with couples pursuing third-party reproduction. As part of that reckoning, women have to give up not only on using their own eggs but also on the search for the perfect donor, one who is in every way their match. Or, as Becky put it: "It's this tension between letting go and clinging to this ideal of the donor being 'you.'" I understood that. My own potential donor was an aspiring journalist. I knew that didn't mean I'd give birth to a future English major, but I found it reassuring. It felt familiar; more important, it felt familial. And so I, like many potential donor recipients, developed a new mathematical equation. Call it the transitive property of human connection: I liked Charlotte Brontë and she liked Charlotte Brontë, ergo we were the same; I would love our child and it would love me.

Becky's search lasted about two months. Russell participated, too, of course, but since it was her genetic material they were replacing, she had the final say-so. Husbands typically defer to their wives for that reason, according to Feingold.

The reverse, in her experience, is less true: women are usually more involved in choosing sperm donors than men are in choosing egg donors. That may be, she says, because women tend to be more devastated by infertility than men, regardless of whether its source is male or female.

Becky admitted, somewhat sheepishly, to checking her donor's SAT scores, but what clinched the deal for her was a photo of the woman sitting on the floor, smiling, surrounded by camping gear: "I went backpacking through Asia for six months when I was younger," she said. "I know that has nothing to do with her potential as a donor, but . . . it meant something to me. On the other side of the coin, she's athletic and I'm not. I thought that was great. She can give the child that, and I wouldn't be able to."

Becky leaned back in her chair, shaking her head. She never imagined she'd be trolling for ova on the Internet, but really, who could? It came as a shock, shortly after her engagement to Russell, to find out that she was in premature menopause. After an IVF cycle was canceled when she produced just one ovarian follicle, Becky and Russell decided they would use money they had saved for a down payment on a house to pursue egg donation. "That genetic loss takes a lot to overcome," Becky told me. "And I still feel there's a small part of me . . ." She squinted, pinching her thumb and forefinger together. "I'm going into this 90 percent there, but—we went down to spring training this year, and we were sitting behind Barry Bonds's family, and someone asked his daughter, 'Where did you get those cute dimples?' She said, 'From my mommy.'" Becky winced. "Overhearing comments like that, it's like a miniature dagger."

"But I'm really attached to wanting to birth and nurse

a child," she added. "If this doesn't work I might be ready to move on to adoption. But it's not like you can say, 'Okay, I'll adopt.' It's not that easy. And the home visits are so intrusive. And anyway . . . I'm not there yet."

"Why don't you just adopt?" That is the first question most people ask if you say you're considering egg donation. It's the question I asked myself, as had every potential donor recipient I spoke with. Why create a child where none existed? Why spend the money on something that's not a sure bet? Why ask another woman, even (or maybe especially) a friend, to inject herself with drugs—drugs whose side effects, although unlikely, could require hospitalization and even, in extremely rare instances, be fatal? (Recipients of donor eggs are required to buy supplementary health insurance for the donors in case something unexpected occurs.)

The answers among the women I met were both deeply personal and surprisingly consistent. Like Becky, these women longed for the experience of pregnancy, childbirth and breast-feeding. Often they (or, more often, their husbands) resisted adoption, reasoning that egg donation would be psychologically easier on the child, who would be born—rather than relinquished—into his or her family. They wanted the opportunity to handpick a donor's genes rather than gamble on a birth mother's and father's. And they wanted to be able to see at least their husbands, if not themselves, reflected in their children's faces.

Still, many questioned the morality of egg donation. "Taking into your home a baby who needs one is inherently more ethical than pursuing a very intensive route to have a biological child," one potential donor recipient told me. Perhaps that's why public support for and approval of parents who use donor gametes is lower than for those who adopt—the former is presumably perceived by some as a rather selfish act and the latter a selfless one. Yet adoption has often come with its own ethical quandaries, whether it was the girls "in trouble" who were pressured to give up their children in the 1950s or the current State Department caution against adopting from Guatemala in the wake of reports of child smuggling. What's more, the idea of healthy infants who "need" homes, particularly white infants, is a myth: domestically, demand has always far outstripped supply.

Which is not to say that egg donation is without complexity—for either donors or recipients. Looking at the screen, Becky paused at a donor who identified herself as Jewish. I recalled waking up in a middle-of-the-night panic shortly before our cycle was to begin wondering, since my donor friend was gentile, whether our baby would be a Jew. My husband is not, and at any rate, Judaism is traditionally passed down matrilineally. How could the Talmudic scholars of yore have anticipated this conundrum? I called a Conservative rabbi who explained that while there's no general consensus across denominations, his movement's official stance was that the gestational mother determines a child's religion. That mollified me. Sort of.

A gentile donor was a deal-breaker for some Jewish couples I met. "I didn't want to add to any identity conflict the child might already be experiencing," said one potential mother in the Midwest who had found a New York agency that recruits young Israelis. "Certainly not about religion. It's too delicate."

Jewish donors, along with Asians, Ivy Leaguers, and those with proven fertility, are considered "exceptional donors" and can command a hefty premium. A recruitment ad on New York's Craigslist offered up to $10,000 for Asian donors. On some sites I visited, agencies were asking $15,000 for donors with proven fertility. There have been reports of agencies charging more than double that for other highly desirable women.

Yet there is often no way to know whether the information the donor gives, including her medical history and educational background, is accurate. A 2006 study conducted by researchers at New York University found that donors routinely lowballed their weight, and the heavier they were the more they fudged. Agencies, too, which are unregulated and unlicensed, can easily manipulate the truth. Many advertise IQ and psychological testing as part of their services, though there is no independent verification of either the results or the protocols used. Even if there were, jacking up fees for smarts is a dubious prospect. "Fees for donors are based on time and trouble, so I don't see how someone who goes to Brown has more time or trouble doing this than someone who didn't go to college at all," Feingold, the psychologist, told me. "Parents are vulnerable. People would be willing to do a lot to take charge so that they didn't need to feel so sad, bad, fearful, and out of control. They'll pay more money, do testing. But it's impossible to do intelligence testing on an egg."

To discourage both fraud and undue inducement, the ethics committee of the American Society for Reproductive Medicine (ASRM) issued a position paper in 2006 on donor compensation: $5,000, they determined, was a reasonable but not coercive fee. Anything beyond that needed "justification," and sums over $10,000 went "beyond what is appropriate." What's more, the committee denounced paying more for "personal attributes," saying that the practice commodifies human gametes.

Those guidelines, however, are unenforceable among both ASRM physician members and the donor agencies listed on the group's Web site as pledging compliance. A survey published in May of medical clinics with egg-donor programs (which are presumably under greater pressure to act ethically than unlicensed agencies) found that although donors received an average of $4,217 nationally, at least one clinic brokered a $10,000 fee and another $15,000; a recent Craigslist post directing new recruits to Columbia University Medical Center offered $8,000. One in five clinics considered the donor's fertility history or ethnicity in establishing rates.

The word "donor," then, may actually be a misnomer—at least in this country, where the free market prevails. Internationally, when governments say it, they mean it. Canada and France ban payments to egg donors. Britain reimburses expenses up to about $500 after submission of receipts; before deciding to forbid donation, Italy experimented with a partial "mirror" system, a kind of genetic tit-for-tat in which a husband donates sperm to shorten his wife's waiting time for donor eggs. No nation has a pool of donors anywhere near the size of that in the United States.

The agency Becky eventually used charged her a flat $6,500 donor fee (there would've been a comparatively reasonable $500 premium if she had requested a Jewish or Asian donor) along with a $3,800 agency fee. Additionally, there were the costs of the donor's medical screening and health insurance; legal fees; reimbursement for the donor's and possibly a companion's travel expenses if the donor was from out of the area (Becky's wasn't); and reimbursement for lost wages and child care. There were also the costs associated with any IVF cycle: not only the fertility drugs but also physician, clinic, and lab fees. And fees for freezing any unused embryos, in case the transfer failed or the couple wanted to have another child. Becky estimated that she and Russell would eventually be out about $35,000.

Beginning in February, Becky and her donor each took a month's worth of birth-control pills to synchronize their cycles. Then, for about two weeks, the donor injected herself with fertility drugs. Her progress was monitored by a doctor who telephoned Becky after each appointment with a report. "The first call, he said there were twenty-four follicles developing," she told me. "I was over the moon! And he raved about the donor as a person. I don't know if he always does that, but it made me feel good."

Meanwhile, Becky followed a regimen of her own, taking twice-weekly shots of estrogen to ready her uterus for implantation. After the egg retrieval, the donor's job was done. A few days later, the doctor transferred two embryos to Becky's womb. She added nightly shots of progesterone, which, if all went well, would persuade her body to accept them. If it did, she'd continue the injections until the end of the first trimester, when the placenta would take over and the pregnancy, miraculously, would proceed as naturally as any other.

DEBORAH CURLED UP ON THE COZY COUCH IN HER LIVING ROOM, GAZing out at the kind of flat, sprawling Midwestern yard where a child could run himself to exhaustion. Her dark hair hung to her shoulders and she was barefoot, in jeans and a loose, embroidered blouse. Deborah, who asked me to use the name she calls herself in donor-recipient Web groups, had endured multiple abdominal surgeries in her twenties and thirties for ulcerative colitis. Despite that, five years ago, a year after she married her husband, Steven, a lawyer, she conceived her son via IVF using her own eggs. She was forty years old.

"We brought him home from the hospital and I was really . . ." Deborah paused, searching for the right word. "Happy," she finally said, smiling wistfully. When her son was nine months old, though, Deborah began thinking about a second. She knew another pregnancy was a long shot, but the idea took root, blossoming from fantasy to obsession. "I had my sense of self-worth tied up with having a 'normal' family," Deborah explained. "You know, the family with two children. It was always this destination to be counted upon. It was what made tolerable all the losses along the way, the surgeries, the ostomy bags, everything. So when this path felt threatened, all those other losses suddenly took on more substance."

When three more rounds of IVF failed, she asked Steven (his middle name) to consider adoption—she imagined bringing home a daughter from China—but he refused. "Even with one child I wasn't spending as much time with our son as I wanted to," he told me recently. "I wasn't spending as much time with my wife as I wanted to. I wasn't spending as much time on my work as I wanted to. So the combination of all the negatives plus the fact that it wouldn't be mine or her genetic child—it would be kind of a lottery. I know lots of adoption success stories and I know lots of adoption horror stories, and given the overall pluses and minuses, it just wasn't something I wanted to do." Although he'd happily stick with one, Steven told his wife, if she truly wanted two kids, ovum donation—and possibly a gestational surrogate to protect Deborah's health—was the only way he'd agree.

When I met Deborah this spring, she had finally committed to going ahead with a donor egg after several years of flirting with the idea—the donor was chosen, the fees paid, the contracts signed, the appointments planned, the drugs delivered. Yet, days before the process was to begin, she found herself lying awake nights, frantic over whether she was doing the right thing. "What gets to me is that the three of them would be genetically related," she said, "and I would be the one . . . It's not about passing on my genes. It's that I don't want to be an outsider in my own family. I don't want to feel less legitimate in my child's eyes. I'd feel I'd have to prove my status as a mother by not making any mistakes and by being the perfect mother to this child. Otherwise, he or she could . . ." She trailed off, staring out the window again.

"I just don't understand," she went on to say after a moment. "How can one parent tell a child that the genetic connection is irrelevant to their bond—when it clearly means something to the father, or why would they have gone to such lengths to maintain it? How can I tell my son that the special sense of connection he shares with me and with his cousins is irrelevant, even forbidden to mention in front of his sibling, who wouldn't have access to his own genealogy? That's one of the reasons why I preferred adoption. At least it allows the family to maintain a coherent logic."

Most parents expect that clarity, those bright lines in their genetic, biological, and social relationships to their children. Becoming the parent of a donor-conceived offspring means reconciling, even embracing, something murkier. Before starting our donor cycle, my husband and I met once with a social worker, a standard requirement for couples using donor eggs—though, again, not for those using donor sperm. Her job wasn't to screen us (she did, after all, work for the clinic and had little incentive to reject anyone) but to help us imagine how the genetic asymmetry might play out. What would it feel like to see my husband's caterpillar eyebrows or artistic talent in my child but no heritable trait of my own? What about our extended families? My parents had assured me they'd love their grandchild no matter whose genes she carried. I knew they meant it, theoretically, but I wasn't sure they could pull off the particulars. My dad loved to brag, "It's in the genes!" when one of his grandkids excelled in school, sports, or music. I worried over how hearing those comments would affect our child. Or maybe I worried over how they would affect me.

I wasn't alone in my concern. According to a paper published in the March 2005 issue of the journal *Social Science and Medicine*, parents of donor-conceived kids found "resemblance talk"—something most of us consider innocuous—to be "ubiquitous, unavoidable and uncontrollable" and they feared the constant chitchat would stigmatize their child and throw the family's legitimacy into question. This was true irrespective of whether parents had told their children how they had been conceived, and it exacerbated uncertainties about these decisions among both groups. It also made them apprehensive about whether their children could be fully accepted by their extended families.

"People see a child in a supermarket checkout line and almost reflexively make some comment about who he looks like or doesn't look like," said Robert Nachtigall, an adjunct clinical professor of obstetrics, gynecology, and reproductive sciences at the University of California, San Francisco and a coauthor of the paper. "We interpret it as a kind of shorthand by which people validate the child's position in the family, in society, by basically making comments that refer to the blood relationship that must exist between the child and his or her parents. The problem for people who have conceived with donor gametes is that they know it's not true. And the dilemma for them is how to respond, if at all." .

Resemblance talk did something else, too: although emphatic that it didn't change their love for their child, mothers said it was a constant reminder of their own infertility. "Your infertility is always kind of there when you do donor conception," said Marie, the mother of fourteen-year-old Catherine. "It's always there through adoption, too." The difference is that there's widespread cultural support for adoption in a way there isn't for donor conception. Families can access a long-standing network of social workers, psychologists, other parents. Marie knew this from personal experience: she was herself adopted at birth. "Adoptive families are not as isolated," she said. "People have been educated. Although I still think in general the culture is adoption-negative, it's certainly different than thirty years ago."

FOR YEARS THERE HAS BEEN SPECULATION ABOUT HOW HIGH-PROFILE, late-in-life moms got pregnant: Geena Davis had twins at forty-eight; Holly Hunter had hers at forty-seven; Jane Seymour's were born when she was forty-four. Joan Lunden has had two sets of twins, one at fifty-two and one at fifty-four; although she appeared on the cover of *People* with a gestational surrogate, when asked flat-out by reporters if she also used an egg donor she declined to comment. Elizabeth Edwards, who gave birth to a daughter at forty-eight and a son at fifty, has ducked the question as well, demurring that it's not "ladylike" to discuss infertility. Marcia Cross, the actress, is one of the few celebrities to acknowledge, last year in a *USA Today* article, that older women may use donor eggs, "which doesn't make the baby any less beautiful or perfect. One's own eggs only last so long, and sometimes at forty-three or forty-four you can have your own baby, but statistically it's very difficult and expensive. You don't want to wait that long." In a *People* cover story published after her twin girls were born, Cross was described as having "beat the odds" of conceiving via IVF at age forty-four using her own eggs.

Even those in the limelight have a right to privacy, especially where their children are concerned. At the same time, drawing that line at egg donation is troubling. For one thing, the author Liza Mundy says, it perpetuates the fantasy of women's endless fertility, as much a Hollywood illusion as unfurrowed brows, full lips, and perky breasts in middle age. In reality, according to CDC statistics, in 2004, only 5.2 percent of forty-four-year-old women who transferred embryos created through IVF using their own eggs gave birth. Among forty-seven-year-old women, none did. With donor eggs, the odds for both sets of women jump to 51 percent and often far higher. It's also hard to imagine that these same women would be equally circumspect had they adopted. Consider the proudly public stance of the adoptive mothers Angelina Jolie, Sharon Stone, Jamie Lee Curtis, Madonna. By trying to protect their children from stigma, famous egg-donor recipients may inadvertently be creating it.

Most parents of donor-conceived children won't be expected to take a stand in the national press, but they do struggle over who to tell and when to tell, the difference between "secret" and "private" information, and how much of the story is their child's as opposed to their own. "The hardest part about not being willing to disclose until my daughter is old enough to understand is that I feel this responsibility to women my age," said Anne, the mother of a two-and-a-half-year-old girl conceived using a donor egg, who asked me to use only the middle names of her and her husband. "I want them to know they could do this, too—they could carry their baby, give birth to it, and it's wonderful. This girl at work got pregnant. She was forty-three, a year older than I was when I got pregnant. She found out it was a Down baby and terminated."

Anne's eyes welled up, her voice dropping to a whisper. "I was so devastated for her. She came to my office and said, 'You beat the odds.' And I felt so guilty because I didn't beat the odds. And I couldn't say anything about it."

It was a sunny weekend afternoon in Anne's newly renovated kitchen in a San Francisco Bay Area suburb. Anne's husband, David, a forty-year-old contractor, was out back building a new deck. Anne showed me a picture of their daughter, who was taking a nap. Then she showed me a photo of David at the same age: the resemblance was uncanny. "When I was pregnant," Anne said, "I just kept saying to him, 'I hope she looks like you.'"

Anne and David met through an online support group for widows and widowers. Her first husband died seven years ago; David lost his wife not long after. Neither of them had children, though Anne, who describes herself as a "late bloomer," badly wanted them.

By the time the couple married, Anne was forty. "I used to

say, 'I'm willing to adopt but I want the experience of pushing out my own,'" she told me. An enthusiastic advocate of egg donation, she felt truly blessed that technology had so beautifully fulfilled her dreams. She also believed that finding her donor was fated: the young woman was Canadian, as was Anne's first husband. And her favorite flower was the sterling rose, the very same flower he'd sent Anne after their first date. Yet even she had wrestled with loss. "My sisters and I all look so much alike," she said, "and there's part of me that feels ripped off because of that. But not because I want to see my face in my daughter's face. More because . . . there's this feeling of belonging that I have with them. It's always been fun when people have said, 'Oh my God, are you guys twins?' So, I'm sorry my daughter doesn't have that." Anne wondered whether her daughter would feel she was missing out on something. "But then I think, Am I just projecting? Is she ever really going to feel this way? And how can I make sure I don't do something to make her feel this way? Because it might otherwise never even dawn on her."

According to several studies, most donor recipients haven't told their children about their origins, though some researchers argue that this trend is reversing. The women I spoke with, all open enough about their choices to talk with me, said they did expect to tell their children. They talked about integrity and a child's right to know his history. They mentioned the danger and difficulty of keeping family secrets. "If I keep it a secret, then why is it a secret?" Anne said. "Then I create the stigma even if no one else ever does. And I don't want to be responsible for that. I want my daughter to understand that, you know, you were the best egg for the job." Anne laughed. "And she'll learn about perseverance. And that some things are nature: your genetic makeup makes you behave certain ways, or like certain things. That's the way that it is. But I've been nurturing her. I carried her in my body. I pushed her out. She's my child."

The idea that disclosure could be a viable, even preferable, option is relatively new. Taking a cue from donor insemination, which was historically (and often still is) kept secret, fertility doctors initially counseled couples that disclosing to their children would only cause unnecessary confusion. I recall our first appointment to discuss egg donation at the clinic where we had undergone two IVF cycles; a nurse led us to an office in a different part of the building and offered to close the blinds to ensure our privacy. Until then, I hadn't realized we were supposed to feel furtive.

Deborah told me that she heard a clinic counselor speaking on a panel at an infertility conference promoting secrecy as a perk of egg donation. "She said, 'The women who use donors tell me they just forget about it when they're pregnant.' She repeated that. Twice. Isn't that awful?"

In truth, it isn't clear that secrecy is necessarily damaging. In the most extensive longitudinal study to date, Susan Golombok, the director of the Center for Family Research at Cambridge University in England, has compared families who have sperm-donor children with those who have egg-donor children, as well as with those who used conventional IVF and those who conceived naturally. In 2006, when her team last checked in with the donor-conceived children, they were twelve, and most had not been told the nature of their conception. The kids in all of the groups were equally well adjusted. What's more, parents of donor-conceived kids (and those who used conventional IVF) were more involved with their kids' lives than those who had conceived naturally.

Apparently, secrecy has not affected their relationships. But, Golombok wonders, what if those children someday discover the truth? Close to 75 percent of her subjects who were not planning to tell their children had told someone else that they had used a donor. What if the information came out accidentally or was blabbed during the course of a bitter divorce? What if the nongenetic parent contracted a fatal, genetically linked disease? That one hit home: I'd been through treatment for breast cancer five years before our donor cycle; I couldn't imagine allowing a daughter to believe that she, too, would be at risk.

There have been no large-scale studies on how disclosure affects the psychological development of donor-egg-conceived kids or their relationships with their parents. But among teenagers who were told as young children that they had been conceived using donor sperm, there have been no negative repercussions, according to research by Joanna Scheib, a professor of psychology at the University of California, Davis. In 2004, the ASRM switched its official position to support disclosure, though not unequivocally.

According to Robert Nachtigall, who has looked at disclosure decisions as well as "resemblance talk," both those parents who disclose and those who don't have the same motivation: acting in the best interests of their children. "We were struck by how people could use the same argument and come to a different conclusion," he said. "Disclosing parents perceived the danger would come from an internal disruption of the family dynamic: they felt that if the child found out from another person it would destroy the trust and their relationship. Nondisclosing parents were more concerned with threats from outside of the family, with stigma. They didn't want to subject the child or themselves to public scrutiny, to be thought of as different or other. They'd made the decision that that was the greater threat, so they weren't going to disclose. Both types realize that this information is powerful and important; they just have different strategies about how it is to be managed."

Parents who take the leap, though, say they don't regret it. In a study published this March of disclosure strategies among parents who had used donor eggs or sperm, Nachtigall and his coauthors found that many expressed relief at having told their children, as if a weight had been lifted, while most children's responses ranged from neutral to positive. "That's the big take-home message," Nachtigall said. "Nobody regretted telling. Nobody."

ONCE A CHILD KNOWS SHE WAS DONOR-CONCEIVED, WHAT THEN? How far do her rights extend? Should she be able to meet her donor, and who gets to decide? It was clear to Marie, the donor recipient who is also an adoptee, that knowing one's genetic lineage should not just be an option, it should be an entitlement. "There's no way I would have a child of mine go through what I went through in terms of the not knowing and the questioning and the search," she said. Not only did she and her husband, a sixty-five-year-old lawyer, plan from the get-go to be open with Catherine about her conception, they also wanted to ensure that their daughter would, whenever she was ready, have access to the donor.

That was not a popular position in 1992 when Catherine was conceived. The couple had been trying to get pregnant for four years, since Marie was forty. They worked their way through the standard infertility treatments, the pills, the shots, the IVFs. All of it failed. Her husband had never been eager to become a parent in the first place; despite being married to an adoptee, he preferred to remain childless rather than adopt. Marie wasn't ready to give up. So they became among the first couples in their area to use a donor egg.

They have been in phone and email contact with the donor, who at the time of the donation was a college student interning for an acquaintance of Marie's, ever since. Catherine has known about the woman since preschool. "The comments she'd make about it at five were different than at ten," Marie said. "At five, we'd be driving to Safeway, and this little voice in the back of the car would say, 'Now, what's an egg donor again?' At ten there were a lot of questions about who she looked like and 'Why don't I look like you?'"

Then, when Catherine was twelve, came the moment that all of the donor recipients I spoke to told me they dreaded. "She turned to me in this relaxed, *Hey, Mom, isn't this interesting* kind of voice and said, 'You know, technically speaking, you're not actually my mother.'"

This, Marie said, is where it helped to be a trained therapist—and perhaps an adoptee as well, someone who has understood from experience both the salience and limits of genetic relationships, that DNA doesn't make the mom, but children need to figure out what, if anything, it signifies. "It was her way of acknowledging that this means something to her that's completely independent of her relationship to me. And that's inevitable: no amount of being wanted, planned for or loved eliminates that piece of the experience."

Last winter, the donor, who is now thirty-six, single, and childless, began pressing for a closer relationship with

Catherine. She invited the girl and her parents to her house for dinner, the first time they had gotten together in several years. Halfway through the meal, and against Marie's explicit instructions, she pulled out a collection of family photos: her mother, brothers, sisters, nieces, and nephews. Catherine recoiled. "The donor has this great need to make Catherine into family because she doesn't have children of her own," Marie said. "My husband and I had to tell her: 'That's Catherine's decision. It's not yours or even ours.' So now the two continue to email but rarely get together."

When it comes to the question of whether to reveal a donor's identity to a child, at least for now, we leave the decisions to parents. Other nations say that prerogative is trumped by a person's right to know his heritage: Britain, for example, recently banned anonymous donation; any children conceived after 2005 will have access once they turn eighteen to identifying details about their sperm or egg donors. Since 2000, when the debate over this issue began, the number of registered egg donors in Britain has dropped almost 25 percent.

Yet egg donors and recipients may have less to fear from open donations than they imagine, at least if the experience is comparable to sperm donation. According to Joanna Scheib's research, teens who were conceived with "open-identity" sperm—who when they turn eighteen can have access to their donor's name—said that, while more than 80 percent were interested in meeting their donors, fewer than 7 percent wanted to establish a father-child relationship with them.

A few days after my conversation with Marie, I talked to Becky. She had just found out she was pregnant with twins.

"Twins!" she crowed. She had always hoped to have two children: both she and Russell are close to their siblings. Now she was jubilant, if jittery. "When I found out, I walked around in a haze for a week thinking, What have I done?" she said, laughing. "As for the donor piece, I imagine this could make it easier. They won't be alone in their situation. They'll be in the same boat. I'm glad that they'll be together and genetically related to each other."

She paused a moment, thinking about her future. "I'm just happy," she said. Finally, Becky would be a mother, her husband a father, the two of them building a family with all the conflict, joy, and unpredictability that entails—regardless of whose genes are involved.

BRINGING DOWN BABY

It seems bizarre that we are still arguing over whether day care is good for children—don't we have enough healthy, functioning adults who went through it?—as opposed to making absolutely sure that every child in it is getting the highest quality care. That such care can have a profound, even transformative effect is indisputable. The latest in a stack of longterm studies, this one published in 2017, followed children from birth until age thirty-five: it found that quality child care resulted in both mothers and children born into disadvantage leading more successful lives. Yet child care remains punishingly expensive, typically costing one-third of families' income (the Department of Health and Human Services says that figure ought to be more like 7 percent). The study featured in this piece, which ran in April 2001, was seized upon as fodder for the era's Mommy Wars, ratcheting up panic and guilt among working mothers while doing nothing to improve child care.

A 1950s-STYLE ATTACK DEMANDS A 1950s-STYLE RESPONSE, which is why a lot of working moms last week felt the need to duck and cover. The reaction was triggered by news reports that the largest and "most authoritative" study ever conducted on the effect of child care on development found that kids cared for by someone other than their mothers for more than thirty hours a week—that includes grandmothers, aunts, even fathers—are more likely to display behavioral problems in kindergarten. As one headline put it: "Day Care Kids Are Turning out 'Smart and Nasty.'"

It turns out that it was just one researcher—Jay Belsky, a longtime foe of day care—who, to the dismay of many of his coauthors, cast the findings so negatively, even going so far as to suggest women adjust work schedules to avoid leaving their children with others. "If you want to reduce the probability of those outcomes, you reduce the time in care," he advised. Spinning the Mommy Wars angle guaranteed that the study would land smack on the front pages of newspapers across the country. And it did, despite the fact that the findings were well-labeled as preliminary and that the study, funded by the National Institute of Child Health and Human Development, draws no conclusions about whether day care is actually the culprit (or, for instance, whether the problem is stress imposed on parents by inflexible employers) or what the long-term implications might be. Also given short shrift was the news of day care's positive effects, most notably that by age five children in high-quality care have superior language and memory skills compared with those who've stayed home.

But then, where day care is concerned we seem to revel in bad news. If the research had found children in nonmaternal care to be more obedient but less verbal, almost certainly the headlines would have read, "Day Care Kids Are Turning out 'Dumb' and 'Passive.'" Doomsday scenarios, which strike at the heart of Americans' deep anxiety about child care, sell even when they're only based on a press release (the actual report is still unpublished).

A closer look reveals the statistics to be less alarming. Only 17 percent of children in day care showed "explosive," "disobedient," or "aggressive" tendencies, which means the other 83 percent did not. What's more, the differences that do exist are well within the realm of normal—day care hardly breeds school shooters. And since 9 percent of children who stay home with Mom are also seen by their teachers as aggressive by kindergarten, the real differential is only 8 percent. No matter. You can bet that from now on every time a working mother's child defies her or throws a public tantrum or sasses back at a teacher, other adults will shake their heads knowingly: "See, that's what happens when a mother neglects her child."

Of course, infinite variables affect a child's well-being. Behavioral problems have been observed when family income drops or when mothers become depressed, a real vulnerability among those who stay home. According to psychologist Judith Wallerstein, divorce also causes long-term psychological damage to children. But we haven't heard Belsky, himself a divorced dad, advising parents to stay in bad marriages. "I'm not self-serving," he said when asked whether he wasn't pushing mothers to sacrifice themselves in ways he wouldn't personally accept. "I don't read the literature differently because I'm divorced."

Belsky, who volunteered to announce the study's results to the press, infuriated his coauthors who feel he distorted their work. "These are little differences" in behavior, insists Alison Clarke-Stewart of UC Irvine. "If the results showed that

50 percent of children in child care were more aggressive, I would agree that's something we need to be concerned about. But 17 percent is what the test predicts as normal in the general population."

As Clarke-Stewart points out, many factors could account for the disparity. For instance, she says, mothers who stay home may be less aggressive than those who work and so tend to raise more docile kids. Also, their children's measures of aggressiveness rise once they enter kindergarten. Maybe being tossed into an institutional setting with other kids naturally heightens those behaviors—as anyone who went to school recalls, it's a blackboard jungle out there. If that's the case, the differences may diminish or disappear in a year or two as children who've been home acclimate to the classroom. At any rate, Clarke-Stewart and other researchers on the study believe that further research is needed before reliable conclusions can be drawn.

Belsky isn't buying it. "Listen, every one of these authors signed off on the dissemination of these findings," he told me. "Are they saying something else now? People don't like to be unpopular. I don't like to be unpopular either, but I'm not going to say it ain't so. It's clearly so."

So, the authors quibble. The media sensationalizes. Meanwhile, the true impact of all this hype, which places responsibility for children's mental health solely on their mothers' presence in infancy, will be an increase in something far more damaging to families than day care: working mothers' guilt, which undermines parental confidence. It is pathetic, in the year 2001, to have to remind people that two incomes are necessary for basic survival in most families. Or that working fathers are never required to justify why they have to work. Or that even for the few women whose husbands do earn enough to support a family, economic independence protects a woman from divorce, death, downsizing, and depression. Or that earning her own income gives a woman more power and equality within her marriage.

Nor are long-term studies of day care's impact new. Many of the reports stretching back decades, both here and abroad, have found no detrimental effects on children's emotional or intellectual development—in fact, quite the opposite. An ongoing study by the High/Scope Educational Research Foundation, which has followed poor children since they were three (they're now forty), found that those who were enrolled in high-quality preschool were more likely to graduate from high school and earn more money as adults and were less likely to bear children out of wedlock or be arrested. Two other longitudinal studies conducted in Sweden found that early entry into high-quality care correlated with better school performance and positive teacher ratings well into young adulthood. Even the previous findings of Belsky's group, which were released in 1996, showed that if a child is in high-quality care, the key to a healthy bond is a mother's sensitivity to her child, not her employment status.

Still, American parents worry. What if the findings bear out and there is an uptick in children's collective cruelty? Should mothers stay home and, if so, which ones? Should we dismantle the welfare-to-work programs that aim to get poor mothers out of the house, forcing them to place their children in day care? Should young men be granted better educational and employment opportunities than women so that they can support stay-at-home wives? Should the government grant child-care subsidies? Should we extend maternity leaves to five years per child, then allow women to return to their jobs with no penalty in terms of advancement and salary? Or does the buck stop with blaming Mom?

Here's a theory: in a society in which working mothers are still viewed with ambivalence, perhaps their guilt and anxiety—even their resentment—is absorbed by their children and manifested as aggression. If so, it's not mothers' withdrawal from the workforce that's called for, but support, appreciation, and reassurance—by employers, friends, family, and, in particular, husbands. A 1999 survey of one thousand schoolchildren by Ellen Galinsky of the Families and Work Institute found that kids felt fine about the amount of time they spend with Mom whether or not she worked. But children in both camps were more likely to feel they have too little time with their dads. Did that provoke front-page headlines and national soul-searching about how men negotiate work-family balance? Not hardly.

Day care, which now serves thirteen million children, is here to stay. Working mothers are here to stay. In a potentially contracting economy, both will be increasingly indispensable. If anything is harmful to children, it's the false debate over whether mothers should stay home: the real issues are how to ensure the ready, affordable availability of the high-quality child care that researchers know is effective—and all too rare in this country—as well as how to reform the workplace to allow for the healthiest possible family life. Focusing on these things would not only require being truly smart, it would also require being kind. The fact that we haven't risen to that challenge is the real nasty truth.

WHERE I GOT DAISY

My daughter is biracial—Asian Americans often call it "hapa"—which makes her part of one of the fastest-growing populations in this country. As a feminist, I know that issues of race, class, sexuality, disability, gender, and gender identity interplay and overlap. As a parent, I live my life at one of those intersections. This piece, which ran in May 2007, explores a little of what I've learned as the white mother of a child of color.

THE FIRST TIME IT HAPPENED, I WAS ON MY MAIDEN VOYAGE with my four-month-old daughter, Daisy, flying alone with her to Minneapolis to show her off to my parents. I was sure I was prepared for the trip: my carry-on bulged with six changes of clothes, twenty diapers, an industrial-size box of wipes, a stack of baby books, three Whoozits, four puppets, two teddy bears, and her favorite bunny rattle. I'd nursed her on takeoff to ease the pressure in her ears and planned to do the same on descent. For a first-time mom, I thought, I was doing pretty well.

Then, while I was jogging in place in the galley trying to lull Daisy into a nap (and, as a side effect, working off the pregnancy weight), another passenger noticed us. "What a beautiful baby," she cooed and, before I could even smile in acknowledgment, added, "Where did you get her?"

Let me be clear: adoption is a wonderful thing, a great gift to both parents and children. But Daisy is not adopted (though the question would be equally ill worded if she were). She simply inherited the golden skin, dark hair, and eyelid fold of my Japanese American husband, while I have blond ringlets, blue eyes, and a complexion the color of library paste.

"It's a natural question," my father said when I told him about it at the airport luggage carousel. "I mean, look at her. Look at you. People are just curious." Maybe. But why did that curiosity leave me feeling sucker-punched?

Over the next year, what I'd come to call The Question became a regular feature of my life as a mother. It took a variety of forms: "What a beautiful baby. Is she from China or Korea?" "Oh, how cute. Where is she from?" Once even: "How old was she when you adopted her?" I began to anticipate the reaction, tensing up when strangers approached us or prying eyes stared at us too long. I noticed that I was more relaxed, friendlier, when we were out all together as a family and Daisy's provenance was obvious.

I began to wonder: If I found the attention to our racial difference upsetting, how, someday, would she perceive it? And if I didn't know how to respond to it, how would she? After all, she'll probably spend a lifetime hearing, "Where are you from?" or "When were you adopted?" or "What *are* you?"

I'd often contemplated how to raise a daughter with a healthy sense of female identity, but I'd believed matters of race were my husband's job—he, after all, was the person of color. I was wrong. For my child's sake, and my own, I needed to understand what it meant to be a multicultural family in a world that doesn't always see the shades of gray among the shades of brown. I needed to know how to answer The Question.

"Your dad is right, it is a natural question," said Donna Jackson Nakazawa, mother of two multiracial children and author of *Does Anybody Else Look Like Me?* My heart sank. When Daisy was born, a friend sent me Nakazawa's book, considered a kind of bible among parents in racially mixed families. I figured Nakazawa would be the perfect person to call for advice. Now I wasn't so sure. Until she added, "It's natural if you still think of people as only coming in five flavors: Caucasian, African American, Asian, Latino, and Native American. That's what we all learned growing up. But that's not how it is anymore."

In fact, according to the 2000 census—the first to collect multiracial data—more than seven million people identify themselves as mixed race, and, so far, they come in fifty-seven different "flavors" (take that, Baskin-Robbins!). Their ranks include some of our most celebrated movie stars, recording artists, politicians, and sports heroes: Kate Beckinsale, Keanu Reeves, Halle Berry, Norah Jones, Tiger Woods, Apolo Ohno, Derek Jeter, and, of course, Barack Obama. Increasingly visible at universities, they've formed "Hapa Club"s ("hapa" is the Hawaiian term for a person of partial Asian or Pacific Islander heritage) at such schools as Brown, Columbia, UCLA, and Stanford. The upshot: when one includes transracial adoptive families, there is an unprecedented number of white parents of children of color. Parents like me.

I've often thought that there is nothing that makes a man a feminist faster than becoming the father of a daughter. I suspect a similar dynamic is at work here. I'd certainly witnessed the small, corrosive slights my husband, Steven, faced in his daily life, but they didn't cut me as deeply as they did him. Early in my pregnancy, though, a park ranger stopped to chat with him while we were hiking up Mount Tamalpais in Marin County, California. "Where are you from?" he asked. "Berkeley," Steven answered. "No, I mean where are your parents from?" the ranger responded. "Los Angeles," Steven said, less amiably this time. The ranger acted as if Steven were simply being willful. "Okay, so you don't want to tell me." Steven glared at him a moment. "I did tell you," he said, then stalked away.

Imagining my unborn child navigating that exchange hit me right in the belly. "What gets to you is the everyday ignorance," Steven would tell me later. "It's being constantly made to feel like the 'other.'"

That was it. That was exactly what bothered me about The Question. It was a reminder, even when offered under the guise of a compliment, of my daughter's "otherness," of our mutual "otherness."

"Understanding where those comments come from is the first step," Nakazawa advised me. "But next, you have to be clear about your goal. And the goal is: you don't want that track to start in Daisy's head every time there's an incident— the one that says, 'I'm different, I'm different, I'm different, and people don't think she's my mom.' You want to be a buffer for her. You want to make sure that she knows what's wrong is out there in the world, not inside of her."

Great, I thought. So how do I do that? Of course, the process starts at home. We've always talked proudly to Daisy about her joint cultural background and have a tonal rainbow of Groovy Girls as well as a slew of baby face books that feature lots of mixed-race kids. Nakazawa suggested that as Daisy grows older we pull out a map and discuss how people from all over the world migrate to this country; by the time she's eight or nine, we could even talk about the African origin of the human species.

That helped, but it was really *outside* the home that I felt vulnerable, where I feared I was letting Daisy down. I was falling short, both as a buffer and a model. "One way to avoid those comments is to become super interactive with your daughter in public," Nakazawa suggested. "A mom I know reads to her baby and talks to her with such focus that people don't interrupt. It's like being buried in a book on an airplane: it discourages the chitchat that makes people feel they have permission to ask. And there's the bonus that it intensifies your relationship with your child."

But what happens if someone breaks through that force field? I still needed a ready retort to "Where did you get her?" Something so automatic I wouldn't even have to think about it. "You could try deflection," Nakazawa said. "When people start with 'Your children are so beautiful,' I just cut them off and say, 'All children are so beautiful, aren't they?'"

Nice, but not quite what I was after. "Okay," Nakazawa tried, "how about something like 'Yes, she looks like my husband but she has my sense of humor'?"

Still not my style.

"Well," she said, "one woman I know says, 'From my uterus.'"

From my uterus. I loved it. It was insouciant, surprising, and it stopped further conversation in its tracks. Best of all, it works. Every time. Where did you get her? From my uterus. Is she from China or Korea? From my uterus.

I almost look forward to saying it. Each time I do, I smile

brightly and the person pauses, uncertain, long enough for me to make my getaway. The best part is, though Daisy may not know it yet, I'm teaching her an important lesson as a person of mixed race, as a woman—heck, as a human being: Stand up for yourself with grace and wit and then move along.

Daisy will turn four this summer. As she's grown older, I've fielded fewer inquiries about how we fit together. Maybe that's because her hair has lightened to chestnut and the wave in it is more pronounced. Maybe it's because it's a lot easier to objectify a baby than a hyper-verbal preschooler. Or maybe it's because, despite our superficial differences, she really does look like me. There's something indefinable that emanates from her—an attitude, a gesture, a style—that shocks me when I see it, like unexpectedly catching myself in a mirror.

Just because The Question has stopped, though, doesn't mean the teaching should. I want my daughter to understand—I hope all children will someday understand—that the world comes in an infinite variety of flavors. And how much richer we are because of that.

Now, if I could just figure out a snappy comeback for the new round of busybodies who won't stop asking me, "Are you only having one child?"

THE FEMIVORE'S DILEMMA

When this piece was published, in March 2010, a number of readers pointed out that "femivore" actually means someone who eats women. To which I say: whatever. Obviously, I am riffing off of the newly popular, ubiquitous term "locavore" as well as The Omnivore's Dilemma, *the title of Michael Pollan's now-classic book on what and how we eat.*

FOUR WOMEN I KNOW—NONE OF WHOM KNOW ONE ANOTHER—ARE building chicken coops in their backyards. It goes without saying that they already raise organic produce: my town, Berkeley, California, is the Vatican of locavorism, the high church of Alice Waters. Kitchen gardens are as much a given here as indoor plumbing. But chickens? That ups the ante. Apparently it is no longer enough to know the name of the farm your eggs came from; now you need to know the name of the actual bird.

All of these gals—these chicks with chicks—are stay-at-home moms, highly educated women who left the workforce to care for kith and kin. I don't think that's a coincidence: the omnivore's dilemma has provided an unexpected out from the feminist predicament, a way for women to embrace homemaking without becoming Betty Draper. "Prior to this, I felt like my choices were either to break the glass ceiling or to accept the gilded cage," says Shannon Hayes, a farmer of grassfed livestock in upstate New York and author of *Radical Homemakers*, a manifesto for "tomato-canning feminists," which was published last month.

Hayes pointed out that the original "problem that had no name" was as much spiritual as economic: a malaise that overtook middle-class housewives trapped in a life of schlepping and shopping. A generation and many lawsuits later, some women found meaning and power through paid employment. Others merely found a new source of alienation. What to do? The wages of housewifery had not changed—an increased risk of depression, a niggling purposelessness, economic dependence on your husband—only now, bearing them was considered a "choice": if you felt stuck, it was your own fault. What's more, though today's soccer moms may argue, quite rightly, that caretaking is undervalued in a society that measures success by a paycheck, their role is made possible by the size of their husband's. In that way, they've been more of a pendulum swing than true game changers.

Enter the chicken coop.

Femivorism is grounded in the very principles of self-sufficiency, autonomy, and personal fulfillment that drove women into the workforce in the first place. Given how conscious (not to say obsessive) everyone has become about the source of their food—who these days can't wax poetic about compost?—it also confers instant legitimacy. Rather than embodying the limits of one movement, femivores expand those of another: feeding their families clean, flavorful food; reducing their carbon footprints; producing sustainably instead of consuming rampantly. What could be more vital, more gratifying, more morally defensible?

There is even an economic argument for choosing a literal nest egg over a figurative one. Conventional feminist wisdom held that two incomes were necessary to provide for a family's basic needs—not to mention to guard against job loss, catastrophic illness, divorce, or the death of a spouse. Femivores suggest that knowing how to feed and clothe yourself regardless of circumstance, to turn paucity into plenty, is an equal— possibly greater—safety net. After all, who is better equipped to weather this economy, the high-earning woman who loses her job or the frugal homemaker who can count her chickens?

Hayes would consider my friends' efforts admirable if transitional. Her goal is larger: a renunciation of consumer culture, a return (or maybe an advance) to a kind of modern pre-industrialism in which the home is self-sustaining, the center of labor and livelihood for both sexes. She interviewed more than a dozen families who were pursuing this way of life. They earned an average of $40,000 for a family of four. They canned peaches, stuffed sausages, grew kale, made soap. Some eschewed health insurance, and most homeschooled their kids. That, I suspect, is a little further than most of us are willing to go: it sounds a bit like being Amish, except with a car (no more than one, naturally) and a green political agenda.

After talking to Hayes, I rushed to pick up my daughter from school. As I rustled up a quick dinner of whole-wheat quesadillas and frozen organic peas, I found my thoughts drifting back to our conversation, to the questions she raised about the nature of success, satisfaction, sustenance, fulfillment, community. What constitutes "enough"? What is my obligation to others? What do I want for my child? Is my home the engine of materialism or a refuge from it?

I understand the passion for a life that is made, not bought. And who doesn't get the appeal of working the land? That's as integral to this country's character as, in its own way, Walmart. My femivore friends may never do more than dabble in backyard farming—keeping a couple of chickens, some rabbits, maybe a beehive or two—but they're still transforming the definition of homemaker to one that's more about soil than dirt, fresh air than air freshener. Their vehicle for children's enrichment goes well beyond a ride to the next math tutoring session.

I am tempted to call that "precious," but that word has variegations of meaning. Then again, that may be appropriate. Hayes found that without a larger purpose—activism, teaching, creating a business, or otherwise moving outside the home—women's enthusiasm for the domestic arts eventually flagged, especially if their husbands weren't equally involved. "If you don't go into this as a genuinely egalitarian relationship," she warned, "you're creating a dangerous situation. There can be loss of self-esteem, loss of soul and an inability to return to the world and get your bearings. You can start to wonder, What's this all for?" It was an unnervingly familiar litany: if a woman is not careful, it seems, chicken wire can coop her up as surely as any gilded cage.

PART 4

GIRLS! GIRLS! GIRLS!
(AND ONE ABOUT BOYS)

CHILDREN ARE ALONE

In the twenty years since my first book, Schoolgirls, *was published, girls have made important progress: more take higher-level math, more go to college, more feel they can "lean in." Some things, though, have not changed: girls remain less likely than boys to believe they can be leaders, to label themselves as brave, or to pursue most STEM fields. Other issues—especially those relating to body image, sexuality, and sexual violence— seem to have grown more intense. I am still in touch with Becca, now thirty-five, as well as a handful of other girls from the book (I lost track of April after high school). They've told me it's a bit odd to have their thirteenth year immortalized—three were even assigned* Schoolgirls *in college classes—but the portrayals ring true.*

I'm not sure why the editors didn't give this story, an adaptation of the book which ran in July 1994 in the New York Times Magazine, *a title that was specific to its being about girls. Perhaps, in 1994, that notion seemed somehow too limited.*

"ME! ME! ME!" April Welch,* a thirteen-year-old African American girl, leans forward in her seat, waving her hand frantically in an attempt to catch the attention of her math teacher, who has just asked for the proper way to say "two over five."

"Mrs. Sandoval!" she shouts at the teacher. "Me!"

"Okay, April," Mrs. Sandoval says, smiling.

April drops her hand, relieved.

"You can't change it," she announces, indicating the fraction cannot be reduced.

The math teacher's smile tightens almost imperceptibly. "We know that, April," she says. "That wasn't my question."

"Oh," April replies, turning away and rummaging in her backpack for a tube of ChapStick.

As the class proceeds, April volunteers continuously, each time with the same frenetic urgency. When the teacher takes attendance, April, unasked, informs her of the whereabouts of a student who is cutting class. Later, she offers to take a note to the office and then to pass out math books. But most often, April raises her hand in response to a question that Mrs. Sandoval has posed, although whenever the teacher acknowledges her, April's answers are invariably wrong.

When Mrs. Sandoval asks for the difference between the numbers in a series that begins 26, 24, 22, April's hand flies up.

"They're both in the same range," April says when she's called upon, "but one of them is kind of—"

"Listen to my question, April. What is subtracted to get this number?"

April falls silent, more quiet than she has been all period, and darts her eyes desperately.

Someone stage-whispers, "Two."

She raises two fingers, hesitantly, still not speaking.

Michael, a round-cheeked boy who sits next to April, turns to me. "She's loco in the cabeza," he says.

I have been watching April for several days as she moves from English class to math to science to social studies. Today, like the other seventh graders, she rushes from the classroom when the bell rings, and I hurry to catch up. As we fall into step, I tell her she has me a bit confused. Other students raise their hands when they know an answer. She seems to raise her hand simply because a question has been asked.

April spies a paper clip on the floor, picks it up, and begins twisting it open. "I guess," she says, staring at her handiwork, "I guess I raise my hand because I want to be part of the class. I just . . . I just want to talk and feel part of that, you know?"

A friend of April's passes us and April calls out to her, interrupting our conversation. April digs into her backpack again and produces a handwritten invitation to a Halloween party.

"There's going to be music and dancing, and there will be someone to drive everyone home."

The friend studies the invitation. "Is it at your mom's?" she asks.

April shakes her head and fastens her gaze on a spot just to the left of her friend's shoulders. "Uh-uh," she says. "I'm not staying with her right now."

BECCA HOLBROOK TURNS TO ME ABRUPTLY. "DO YOU WANT TO GET into my parents' relationship? My mom and my dad?"

"Sure," I say, caught off guard.

We are sitting on the bleachers at the edge of the P.E. field at Weston Middle School, a bucolic suburb that's a good fifty miles from April Welch's math classroom. A group of boys is playing a rowdy game of after-school football and Becca watches them idly, stopping our conversation when they come too near.

Like April, Becca is thirteen years old. She is a white girl who sits with her shoulders curved and her head hung slightly forward. Today, like the last few times I've seen her, Becca's eyes are red-rimmed. At first, she says the pinkness is caused by her contact lenses, but later admits it's more often from crying.

"A while ago," Becca says, "my mom came into my room and she sat on my bed and said, 'Good night, I love you' and that motherly kind of stuff, but she was in tears. It's not like she was bawling or anything, just these tears on her face, and I don't know what's going on. So I say, 'Okay, good night, Mom,' and she closes the door. The next day, she told me it was 'fear crying.' She told me that she's scared of my dad and that she can't stand sleeping with him anymore. He wants to have sex every night and she doesn't enjoy it at all. She said it's like rape for her every night."

Becca pushes her hair, home-streaked with Sun-In, away from her face, revealing an anxious expression. "She said that if she didn't do it, though, she'd be out of there like the speed of light. So it's like she has to give in to him for, like, an insurance policy or something."

This is not the first time that Becca's mother has confided in her about her embattled marriage. More than once, Becca has told me that she feels older than her friends because of what she knows about "life and relationships and stuff." Given that unique understanding, she believes only she can offer her mother true succor. "When my mom first started telling me these things, I felt suffocated in a way," Becca says now. "But, I realize I'm the only normal thing in her life. I'm the only one who can really comfort her."

She drifts off for a moment as the crowd of football players tromp by us, their game over. "I think sometimes it would be easier for my mom if my parents didn't have kids," she continues when the boys are at a safe distance. "But then, she needs to get things off her chest and so she needs me and I can be there for her. . . . It's like we're two eyes of a hurricane."

I MET APRIL AND BECCA IN THE SPRING OF 1992, AS I BEGAN REPORTing for a book about teenage girls. Beginning the following September, I spent a school year tracking them and seven of their peers in two Northern California middle schools—one in a middle-class, largely white suburb and the other in a low-income, urban community serving mainly children of color. I sat in on the girls' classes, spent time with them on the playground and at home, and talked to parents, teachers, and peers. The girls were a diverse lot, within each community as well as between them. They were from single-parent and dual-parent homes; from affluent, working-class, and poor families. Some excelled in school; some performed poorly.

At first, April and Becca seemed as different as two girls could be. April, who attends John J. Audubon Middle School, was introduced to me as the kind of girl who slips through the cracks of the educational system: although her teachers say she is bright, she attends classes only sporadically, and her mother, who was a teenager when April was born, struggles with an addiction to crack.

Becca is from a two-parent family. Her father is an administrator for the federal government. Her mother, herself a teacher, is well read and deeply concerned about teenage girls' self-esteem. Becca describes herself as a "sensitive" girl. Unlike April, she shies away from participating in class, fearing, she says, that if she makes a mistake, "My self-confidence will be taken away."

In spite of appearances, however, it quickly became clear that Becca and April faced the same predicament: both girls were faltering under the burdens of their mothers' lives and were becoming aware of the limitations of their parents and teachers. Both girls were trying, at home and at school, to make their distress clear. And as the year unfolded, and their attempts to gain attention continued to go unheeded, both girls were ultimately forced to make critical decisions on their own about how—or even whether—to survive.

Initially I was told that April Welch would be entering eighth grade in the fall, but as it turned out, since she had repeated sixth grade, she was entering seventh and was a year behind her peers. At Audubon, repeating students who attain a C average by the end of the first marking period are promoted to their proper grade, but since retained students are often assigned to the same classes with the same teachers and the same curriculum that failed to inspire them the first time around, that goal is seldom realized. At any rate, the students know that at age fifteen, no matter how many times they have been left back—and regardless of whether they can read, write, or add—district policy is to promote them to high school.

"The first time I was in sixth grade, I hardly came to school at all," April tells me early in the year. "I was enrolled, but I'd just cut. I'd walk into school and walk right back out. I was scared, I guess. I'd just graduated from fifth grade and I thought middle school was a big old step." She shakes her head, as if in disgust toward her former self. "My mother didn't say nothin' 'bout it. She just said it was my life and I'd learn in my own time, and I did. I tried to run from it. I wanted to start over at some other school, but I didn't. I knew I had to face what I did. I came back and started sixth grade again. It was kind of embarrassing, but that's how it had to be. I still haven't caught up, neither. I mean, I have a little, but not how I want to. Not like I was in elementary school. Back then, I did good. I used to understand better."

Throughout September and October, April held out hope that she could earn the marks that would advance her to eighth grade. By November, however, her grade point average hovered at D-minus, and by the end of the first semester, her teachers had given up on her.

"She's failing," Mrs. Sandoval tells me flatly when I run into her in the school office. "She doesn't come to class anymore. Maybe she comes three times a week, but math is built on structure, on one thing then the next, so unless you're really bright at it . . . sometimes she tries really hard and seems to get it, but she's just falling behind. I offered her after-school help. But if she doesn't come, I can't make her do it."

I ask her how she thinks she could help April.

She answers quickly and her tone becomes curt. "Hey, I got kids of my own," she says. Then her shoulders droop and she sighs. "Look, I know she's on the 'at-risk' list, that they know about her. But there are so many kids in the class with so many needs . . . someone like April, when she's not there much, it gets to be out of sight, out of mind."

Later that day, when I ask April's science teacher if I can speak to April in the hall for a few minutes, he seems equally frustrated. "Go ahead," he says. "Keep her the whole period if you want to. At this point, she's just a distraction."

April is a distraction, as would be any student who cannot catch up but will not drop out. Toward the beginning of the second semester, when April jokes too loudly and too often in her art class, the teacher sends her to the counselor's office with a discipline referral slip. On it, he writes in capital letters, underlined several times, "It is my opinion that April should have been staffed out last year"; that is, labeled unmanageable and shipped to another school, where she will become someone else's problem—or someone else's to ignore.

"I know I'm not doing good," April says when I find her wandering in the hall one afternoon. "But I'm not tripping or anything, 'cause I'm still gonna graduate after next year and go to high school."

No one at Audubon can explain how a child reaches seventh grade without being able to add or subtract, particularly a vocal child like April who makes her difficulties quite clear. When, toward the end of March, I question April's counselor, Ms. Peck, about this, she lets out a long, slow breath. Ms. Peck is responsible for "counseling" over three hundred students a year. She is a peevish woman with gray skin and sharp features. The first week of school, in an assembly for the entire eighth grade, she announced that the students' fate was already sealed since their high school applications are based on their seventh-grade GPA.

"It's already done and you can't change it," she told them, effectively extinguishing any motivation for improvement. Today, sitting in her cramped box of an office, Ms. Peck leans across her cluttered desk to pull April's file up on her computer screen. She informs me that April has already racked up between twenty-five and thirty unexcused absences in every class.

Ms. Peck leans back in her chair. "She's missing an average of two days a week of school," she says. "There's very little we can do if a child is not here. We contact home, but if she doesn't do the work required and she's not here . . . well, there's very little we can do."

Audubon students who are the most vulnerable to leaving school are placed on a special counseling list. Once a month, the counselors, the social worker, and other appropriate support staff members convene an "at-risk roundtable" to discuss what can be done for these children. They request daily progress reports from the teachers (they are rarely provided), meet with parents when possible, and evaluate whether students require testing for learning disabilities. April was placed on this list in December, and according to Ms. Peck, her case was discussed shortly thereafter.

"I know we talked about her," Ms. Peck says, "but I don't remember what we said and I don't remember what we were going to do."

I ask Ms. Peck how the school will insure that April receives an adequate education. "I don't know if there's anything that we can do to make a difference for April," she says. "I always say that success in school is a three-legged stool: the parent, the school, the child. If you're missing the parent or the child in that stool, you won't have much chance at success. From what I understand, April goes back and forth between her mother and her aunt; I don't have any idea of what goes on there, but she doesn't seem to have any parent backing."

Although there are no comprehensive programs at Audubon designed for girls like April, Ms. Peck insinuates that April's home life is solely responsible for her failure. Yet when one of April's aunts calls Ms. Peck and asks to be kept abreast of her niece's progress, the counselor does not offer to meet with her, nor does she invite her to participate in the at-risk roundtable. Instead, she writes the aunt's phone number on a Post-it that quickly disappears on her desk. She cannot, Ms. Peck explains, be expected to keep track of every relative who calls when her caseload is so overwhelming.

"I don't have the time," she says. "I don't have the time to do much more than discipline."

A few minutes later, as I am about to leave her office, Ms. Peck makes a final remark, which sounds very much like April herself. "It doesn't matter how well or poorly she does, though," she says grimly. "She'll go on to ninth grade in another year anyway."

If, among some of her teachers, there is a tacit understanding that April is doomed by her family's circumstances, it is not an understanding that April shares. Ever since she was a toddler living with her grandmother (who died when April was seven), April has been battling fiercely—and largely unassisted—to keep her mother's addiction from defining her. Sitting in the school's litter-strewn back stairwell on a bleak winter day, she discusses that struggle. As she talks, April squirms, fiddling with the ornately braided ponytail she has woven into her hair. Throughout her story, however, her voice remains steady and she speaks with a level of insight that goes untapped in the classroom.

April explains that after her grandmother died, she became a vagabond, moving back and forth between her mother, who lives in a public housing project with April's ten-year-old brother, and one of her nearby aunts, who seemed more interested in the monthly foster-care check she received from the state than in caring for her niece. Month to month—sometimes night to night—April was unsure of where she'd lay her head. But it wasn't until the summer after her first sixth-grade year, when her aunt moved in with a boyfriend and her mother succumbed to drug addiction, that April decided she had to find a better life.

"I was living with my mom back then," April says. "She was into the fast life, into drugs and all that. She wasn't at first, but then she took up with her boyfriend and he was, so she started doing it, too. She lost her job and she was just doing crack with her boyfriend all day long. I used to call him 'Dope Fiend.'"

She breaks into a small, wry smile. "We didn't get along too good," she continues. "He'd yell at me and hit me sometimes. Once I got so mad at him, I took his drugs and crushed 'em up. He tried to slap me and I kicked him and he said he was going to throw me out of the house. That's when I told my mom, 'You gotta choose between us,' but then, I didn't make her choose. I just left. I called the Child Protection [sic] Services and they took me, and they took my brother, and they put us in a group home for about four weeks.

"I didn't want to go back with my mom after that, but my

brother did. I wouldn't go back to that drug-infested hellhole. I told her that, too, and she cried. So I lived with one of my aunties for a while, until my mom broke up with her boyfriend after he stole some drugs and almost got her killed. My whole family told her to go into rehab then, but ain't nothin' gonna help if you don't want to help yourself. But then, she did.

"I moved back with her now and I stick with her like everything. I watch every move she makes. When she first came back from rehab, she had money and she was going to the store; I followed her where she couldn't see, because I thought she'd buy drugs for sure. But she didn't. So the next time I trusted her, and she came back with food and no drugs, so I think it might be okay now. I pray to God it is."

April has been staring intently at an empty candy wrapper as she talks. Now she abruptly turns to face me.

"I would never do drugs," she says passionately. "I saw what it did to my family and I'd never look at it even. But to this day, I tell my mom: 'I don't hate you, I love you, but I hate what you took me through.' I would never, never, take my children through what she took me through. Never. There was people in that house walking around like zombies; there was people with guns threatening to kill people. Once, my mom's boyfriend owed my cousin a thousand dollars for drugs, and when he didn't pay, my cousin put a gun to his head. I used to go in my room and lock the door and cry, and I'd think I should just kill myself, it was so bad."

She turns away and stares straight ahead, at the gray light that trickles through the stairwell's frosted windows. "But I learned something, too," she says. "I think I learned to be a positive person. And I learned I would not put myself through that and I would not put my children through that. Not never. I learned all that, so that's okay."

UNDER THE WEIGHT OF HER FAMILY BURDENS, BECCA'S ACADEMIC confidence has begun to falter. Like many of the girls I follow at Weston, Becca holds herself to unrealistic standards. (Her mother says Becca's perfectionism sometimes "paralyzes her.") But whereas anxiety drives some of her equally bright peers toward excellence, Becca uses her "sensitivity" as an excuse to shrink from challenge and avoid risk. In sixth grade, Becca was an A student; at the end of seventh grade, she asked to be removed from the advanced math class, and by the middle of eighth grade, her grades in all of her classes were drifting to low C's.

As a quiet girl, Becca has never spoken much in class ("unless I'm really, really sure of an answer and sometimes not even then"), but with her self-esteem flagging, she stops volunteering entirely. She even begins to see her silence as an advantage: as long as she's perceived as shy, her teachers won't notice that she has, in truth, disengaged from school.

At the same time, though, Becca complains that teachers make her feel invisible on the few occasions when she does try to participate. After trying, and failing, to get her English teacher's attention one day, Becca observed sadly: "You know how some people have charisma? I have, like, negative charisma. I feel like I can be talking and people can be looking right at me and they don't even see me."

In a sense, both Becca and April are invisible. April's inappropriate attempts at garnering adult attention are seen as an unmanageable product of her home life, and so she is shunted aside. Meanwhile, Becca's silence allows her to be overlooked as well. She is not seen as someone in need of counseling or special help because, although her grades have dropped, she is never combustible: she never, for instance, yells in class, fights with other children, conspicuously challenges authority. Becca's is a passive resistance. By opting out rather than acting out, Becca is in many ways the classic female student— quiet, compliant, obedient; as such, she is easily overlooked or seen as "making choices" rather than expressing psychological distress.

"Becca is so quiet," her math teacher admits, "she gets lost in the crowd. I don't like that to happen, but it has happened with her. She doesn't disrupt. She always looks like she's paying attention, but maybe she's not. I don't know."

Says her history teacher: "Maybe she thinks she'll be more cool as a C student. But she doesn't even get it together after she gets the bad grade. I'll say, 'Becca, you have a D, you may fail,' then she doesn't turn in the next homework assignment. But I think of her as someone who's responsible for her own grade and I let her be responsible for that."

Becca has indeed let her grades drop, but not out of laziness. Her disengagement is actually an academic strike, a statement of hopelessness that she willingly acknowledges. "Lately I've been thinking I don't care about anything," she tells me in February. "I don't see why I should care about my grades, you know? It's just a letter. What's the difference? Why do I need to learn anything in these classes?" She pauses, weighing the gravity of her statement. "It's not like I really mean that," she says. "I know it's important, but I have to get my anger out."

Ellen Hollbrook is a tall, lanky, forty-four-year-old with sun-roughened skin and, like her daughter, newly blond hair (although hers is professionally tinted). She meets me at the front door of their home, just as Becca did, but where Becca's gaze is circumspect, Ellen's is direct; where Becca draws back, Ellen's handshake is firm. She wears jeans and a black, embroidered blouse; silver earrings coil into lizards just below her lobes, and her red-painted toenails peek out of sling-backed espadrilles.

Ellen teaches special education at a middle school in a neighboring town; she has recently returned to the classroom after fifteen years as a reluctant stay-at-home mom, taking care of Becca and Jason, the Holbrooks' seventeen-year-old, mentally disabled son. She says she took the job in part to try to be a better role model for her daughter.

"Becca and I are kind of on a parallel course," she says, when we've settled into lawn chairs in the Holbrooks' back garden. "We're both learning who we are together. I know the messages I got when I was her age and that's not what I want for her. I want her to be more of an individual, not be defined by her relationship with boys. I try to tell her that responsibility and commitment are important and you have to work on them, but not lose yourself."

Ellen shakes her head and her smile grows rueful. "I said that to her, but I felt like a hypocrite. I mean, I tell you I want her to get the message to be independent, to be strong, but what I tell her is one thing—look at who's the nurturing one in the family, who left off her career to put the family's needs first, who takes care of everything, who's the teacher, who doesn't earn the money."

By making Becca her confidante, Ellen has deepened her

daughter's anxiety. Yet she badly wants Becca to rise above her environment; she wants it so badly that she, too, ignores Becca's retreat from her potential, saying that because of Becca's "sensitivity," she "doesn't want to pressure her in school." So several years back, when Becca decided against enrolling in the district's gifted program, saying she didn't want to be seen as a "schoolgirl," Ellen supported that choice.

Last year, when Becca asked to drop advanced math (although her grade was a B), Ellen agreed again, hoping it would boost her daughter's confidence in the subject; it did, temporarily, but by the third quarter of eighth grade, her math grade had slid to a D. More recently, Becca has begun to express anxiety about college (where she would have "the pressure of midterms and stuff and it would be really hard") and Ellen does not question her timidity; instead, she alleviated her daughter's worry by telling her she could delay the option as long as she wants.

"Becca wants to blend in, be part of the crowd," Ellen explains. "She doesn't want to be smart. She's a very sensitive person and if it's easier for her to be average, then that's okay with me."

With the adults in her life overlooking her pain, Becca's efforts to gain their attention escalate. Several months after our initial meeting, Ellen tells me that Becca, who is twig thin (and is, in fact, sometimes called Twig by her friends), recently asked her what it means to die of starvation.

"I told her people don't actually die of starvation," Ellen says. "Their organs malfunction. I told her that Karen Carpenter died of a heart attack, not actual starvation. And she thought about that and said, 'Well, maybe I can get my appetite back.' I didn't say anything to her. But I've noticed that sometimes her mirror is out of her closet. She brings it out to look at herself, and she does it a lot. And some days she comes down and says, 'I can't go to school today, I'm too fat.' Then a few minutes later, she'll say, 'Okay, I found something to wear that hides it, but I've got to lose weight.'"

Echoing Becca's history teacher, Ellen says that as with academics, developing a body image is Becca's responsibility, so she won't "pick up the rope" and interfere. "I don't say anything," Ellen says. "I see that she doesn't eat for a day or so and then suddenly a whole box of Nutri-Grain bars [is] gone. Or all the leftover Halloween candy. Or a bag of doughnuts. I know she doesn't binge and purge, but she does have this very erratic way of eating.

"Becca doesn't have an eating disorder, but she's messing with the choices, with the possibilities of it. But I'm not going to give her attention on that topic. I don't want food to be a battleground."

Like Becca's teachers, Ellen plays down her daughter's behavior, although she herself once spoke to me of the perils of misreading girls' passivity. "When boys have problems," she said, "they act out and get in trouble. But with girls, they aren't supposed to get in trouble and often they just turn it in. So you don't hear about the problem until they try to commit suicide."

By the time I meet Tom Holbrook, he has become a mythic, frightening figure. I expect a fierce man and am startled to find a mild-mannered, balding fellow with a goatee wearing jeans, a T-shirt, and old deck shoes, who slouches much like his daughter.

Ellen confines her feelings about her husband to a series

of journals that Tom has never read, and he seems unconscious of the depths of her anger. He is aware, however, of his
daughter's increasing moodiness, but he casts about for its
source in vain.

"It doesn't make sense," he says, stroking the family cat,
which has jumped into his lap. "She's got two parents; we're
college-educated; we have all these neat things; she has anything she wants; we don't speak with foreign accents—what's
the problem? I think Becca looks for things to get mad about."

Becca has told me that she thinks her father drinks too
much and that she's alienated from him as a result. When I
mention this to Tom, he seems genuinely shocked. "I don't
drink to excess," Tom insists. "I'm never out of control. But
maybe Becca sees things she doesn't care for. We've never debated the issue; she's never been negative about it to me."

Tom also briskly dismisses a theory of Ellen's, that his
disappointment in his son has placed a wedge in his relationship with Becca. "I didn't expect to live my life through
Jason," he says. "It's not like we called him Tom Jr. or anything. When you have kids, you have to accept that all bets
are off. That 'Father Knows Best' thing is only on TV. I don't
know that Becca understands that. We're not perfect—there
is no perfect family."

Having rejected other alternatives, Tom attributes his
daughter's withdrawal to a natural teenage phase, carried to
an extreme by a pampered child. He considers Becca over-
wrought and hyperbolic in her emotions, but then he blames
himself and Ellen for that: perhaps, he says, their indulgence
of her moods encouraged Becca's hypersensitivity. Since it's
too late for what he calls "behavior modification," Tom feels
the best course of action for him is to steer clear of his daugh-

ter, to communicate through Ellen, and to appreciate the rare moments when Becca and he are at ease in each other's company. In the end, though, he believes that a rift between fathers and daughters is inevitable.

"It's harder to be a father to a daughter than a son," he explains. "I subscribe to that theory that women are from Venus and men are from Mars, and we can't understand certain things about each other because of that."

FOR MONTHS APRIL WELCH TELLS ME ABOUT HER MOTHER, DENISE. I try to meet her: we talk on the phone nearly a dozen times and she seems eager to discuss April's school progress as well as her own attempt to reconstruct her life. But whenever we choose a time and place to meet, she stands me up. Three times we agree to meet at the school, but she never shows; later we agree to meet at a cafe near her apartment and I wait for two hours; twice we agree to meet at the corner of the housing project where she lives, but even when our talk is scheduled just a few hours after a phone conversation, Denise forgets.

In early spring, I ask April if she'll bring me home with her one day for a sneak attack, but she shakes her head. "I can't do that," she says, her voice thick with pain. "I think . . . I think my mom might be on drugs again."

By May, I can no longer reach Denise: the family's phone has been disconnected. As her mother becomes increasingly incapacitated, however, April steps in to fill the void, becoming a kind of junior mother. She takes on full responsibility for caring for herself and her younger brother, begging one of her aunts for a few dollars to buy chicken wings and potatoes for dinner, giving the boy her own small portion when his is inadequate, and insisting that he attend school even when she does not.

In early June, Denise begins stealing from the small stash of money that April has hidden in her room for emergencies, but April says nothing; she just buys a lock for her door. When, a few days later, Denise breaks the lock and rifles through her daughter's possessions again, stealing a VCR that April had bought before her mother's latest decline, the remainder of her money, and some of her clothing, April sits down on her bed and sobs.

"I know my mom," April tells me sadly one afternoon. "I can see what she's doing. She's doing drugs for sure and there's starting to be prostitution, men coming into the house. I don't know what they are doing in there exactly, but I don't want those men coming after me next."

When the year's final grades are reported, April fails every subject except gym. She is still unable to add or to construct a simple sentence, but, as predicted, she is promoted to eighth grade anyway. Yet, although the school system has essentially dismissed her, and her mother all but abandoned her, April perseveres.

On a late June night, she lies awake in bed, listening as the sound of her mother trading sex for crack drifts through the wall. She grabs two socks and jams one against each ear to block out the noise. When that doesn't work, she wraps a pillow around her head, the socks still in place. Lying there crying, she realizes once again that the only way she can save herself is to leave home.

"I was thinking, I have to do something if I want to do something different in my life or I'll end up doing like my mom's doing," she tells me later. "I'll end up doing prostitution for drugs and sleeping with all kinds of different guys and having all kinds of kids maybe. So I prayed to God that night. I decided I'd leave and go with my auntie Lydia. And if she wouldn't have me, I'd go get a job and pay my own rent somewhere. But I couldn't stay there."

The next morning, April called Child Protective Services and was again placed in a group home. After several days, however, she phoned her great-aunt and -uncle, Lydia and George Roberts, who agreed to take her in, at least on a temporary basis. To April, this aunt and uncle are the stuff of fantasy: they both hold stable jobs—Lydia works in the accounting department of a large corporation and George has a job with the city—they go to church every Sunday and the house where they live with their seventeen-year-old son is clean, calm, and safe.

"At first, my husband said this was too much for us, to take April on," Lydia told me when we spoke on the phone shortly after April moved in with her. "We have a child of our own and we're not so young anymore. But somehow, April touched our hearts. The night after she called, my husband woke me up at two in the morning and said, 'I don't know why I'm saying this, but if you want to take April in, I'm with you all the way.' I asked him what happened and he said, 'I don't know, I just know you love her.' Well, I don't know about that, but I know she deserves a break. I know that much.

"April has potential. I believe that. She just needs someone to be there for her when she falls to pick her up, push her back out there, and tell her she can do it. Someone to be there when she's in need. Someone had to get involved, so I did. I did it because I see a future for April; I have hope for her. She's very strong. . . . I still have hope for her mother, too. Denise has come up from the gutter before, gotten a job even. But she's not what concerns me right now. What concerns me is whether April will hold out for the dream, whether she will hold out for all that she hopes for, for all that potential."

THE LAST TIME I SEE APRIL IS DURING A VISIT TO THE ROBERTS' home, a whitewashed row house several miles away from the project where Denise lives. When I ring, April answers the door and immediately apologizes for her appearance. She is wearing purple sweatpants and a ratty T-shirt—what she calls her "kicking around" clothes—and her hair is pulled into a haphazard ponytail.

She leads me to the living room, which is dominated by a large-screen TV, and I sink into an oversize gray sofa. April sits on the floor beside me and leans against a window.

April is noticeably less fidgety than in our previous conversations. And although she says: "I'm hurting. I'm hurting every night about my mom," she is filled with pride in her new life. "With my mother, she let us do what we wanted," she says. "You didn't have to go to school; you could just stay home. You could be out on the street selling drugs—my brother does that. He likes it like that. But I choose not to go down that path. I choose to do good for myself. So I made a change. And it was all me: if I hadn't decided to make that change, there wouldn't never have been no change."

Earlier this year, April told me that she aspired toward a career in cosmetology, but she now says she has a new goal: "I want to help kids in the situation I was in. I want them to see me and say: 'Dang! April got through high school and college and all, and look at all she went through!'

"You know what I want?" She looks down at my notepad. "I want to write my own book someday. I want to write my own book about my experiences so all the kids like me will know they can do better."

As April walks me to the door, I think back to what her counselor said, that there was nothing the school could do for a child who did not want to help herself. If success is, indeed, a three-legged stool, April has, despite profound adult indifference, secured two of those legs on her own. The question is whether she will be provided with the means to shore up the third.

WHEN I FIRST BEGAN TALKING TO THE GIRLS AT THE TWO SCHOOLS, we agreed that—so they would feel free to speak candidly—I would not discuss our conversations with their parents or teachers. To reassure them further, I explained the journalistic notion of protecting your source, an idea that they met with much enthusiasm. But in the spring, Becca asked me to read her journal and I realized that my promise of confidentiality had to be broken.

Early in the second semester, Becca's two closest friends severed their relationships with her. Although the rift began with an inconsequential spat, one of the girls said she realized she was sick of Becca's "putting herself down." The other said: "You have to reassure her fifty times a day that she's not fat, that she's pretty. She's so sensitive; I know I should be more understanding, but it's kind of a relief not to have to worry about that anymore." As girls will in their middle school years, they shifted alliances. But when the new cliques were formed, Becca was left alone.

With few emotional reserves to fall back on, Becca panicked. She began spending her lunch periods in the school library so she wouldn't have to be by herself on the school yard; when her mother would allow it, she took "mental health days," staying at home in bed. As her social isolation increased, she began confiding in her journal (with an eye toward a reader), trying to sort out her anger with her friends from her own culpability.

"I never really felt that I was that good," she writes in one entry. "It felt like no matter what I did, it wasn't good enough. . . . Putting myself down kind of reassured me that I was okay"; later, she muses, "I lack self-esteem and confidence." But when her anxiety doesn't abate (and her friends don't return), Becca begins to conflate her distress over her parents and friends with her dissatisfaction over her weight: "I need therapy and diet pills soon," she writes in March, as if both were needed to effect a true cure.

Then, on March 23, Becca writes: "I downed eight Tylenol P.M. Good. I hope I end up in a coma then die!! . . . Why am I suicidal? . . . I don't even want Peggy to read this entry. She's an adult and would call a drug or suicide hotline."

I considered myself to be an observer of these girls' lives, not a participant in them. Yet I felt I couldn't ignore the significance of Becca's gesture. So on my next visit to Weston, I sat Becca down for a talk. That day, she was feeling better and was more interested in discussing some recent prank phone calls she'd made to boys than her journal entries. I told her that her instincts were right: I did have to talk to an adult about what she'd written and we agreed I would talk to her mother. Becca just asked that I not tell anyone at school.

A WEEK LATER, ELLEN AND I SAT ON THE HOLBROOKS' FRONT STEPS—
she in her gardening gear, sunglasses covering her eyes—
talking about the breach between Becca and her friends. Ellen
had tried to intercede, phoning one of the girls to chat "friend
to friend," but that didn't seem to patch things up for long. In
the meantime, Ellen's own relationship with Becca has grown
strained. "Becca's gotten sullen," she says. "Our relationship
isn't as intimate or consistent as before. She's been pulling
back; sometimes we don't talk at all."

She turns to me confidentially. "A week ago Monday, I
could hardly wake her," she admits. "I came in and her lips
were kind of stiff and I thought: Oh my God, can I do CPR?
How do I revive her? Do I call 911? I was scared she'd done
something. I shook her and she was okay, but she was sort of
stumbling down the stairs, really groggy."

Ellen kept Becca home from school that day and arranged an appointment with the school counselor. She also
broke one of her own rules and snooped around her daughter's room while Becca was out. "All I found was Bayer head-
ache formula and that wouldn't account for it. She's being
deceptive. She's never been deceptive before." Ellen pauses.
"But, she seems okay now, and it hasn't come up again, so I
let it go."

I tell Ellen what I read in her daughter's journal. She rubs
her palms against her thighs; her dark glasses hide her eyes,
but her lips and the muscles in her cheeks tighten. "Well," she
says and lets out a breath, "I'm not surprised." She pauses.
"Oh, dear." Another deep breath. "I guess I'll have to find out
what's in her drawers and talk to her about it."

Ellen continues to rub her legs, looking grim. "I guess

she's been asking for more help than I've been giving," she says. "Maybe I should've paid attention a long time ago.

"I'd decided already to put her in therapy, but I thought we'd do it this summer, because I didn't have time now. So I guess I have that twinge of mother guilt. I know she needs to get her self-image into some perspective. And she needs to get her thoughts on relationships with boys and men in order." Ellen sits for a moment, staring straight ahead, then says, "Becca really needs a boyfriend, it defines her so much."

I ask if she really thinks that's the solution.

"Well, it has so much to do with her self-image right now. But I guess, if they broke up . . ." She trails off; the sentence need not be completed.

"I know that, when she goes into therapy, she may get angry with me as well as Tom," Ellen says. "I'm prepared for that. She may get angry at the role model I've been, tolerating what I've been tolerating. But she's experiencing anger now, obviously. I'd like to see it come out in a more healthy way. I'm not sure I'm prepared for what Tom has to deal with, though. I don't know what he'll do with the issues as they come up. But it will be this summer, so we'll see. I think it's going to be, and I apologize to Mr. Shakespeare for this, the summer of our discontent."

Soon after my last conversation with Ellen, I left these girls' lives, uncertain of how their stories will play out. I think of April as I last saw her, standing at the front door of her aunt's home full of hope, despite the countless challenges she still faces between now and her high school graduation. And I think of Becca, too, looking worried and anxious about the summer, and her transition to ninth grade. Becca's obstacles may be less obvious than April's—less a matter of attaining basic literacy or being assured of a roof over her head—but they are no less daunting. Her future also depends on her ability to transcend the model that her parents, for all their good intentions, have set for her: to, like April, choose "not to go down that path" and instead to chart her own.

Names and identifying details in this story have been changed.

WHAT'S WRONG WITH CINDERELLA?

This story went viral on Christmas Eve Day, 2006; half the readers who commented or emailed called me things like "bad mother," "un-American," or said they felt "sorry for my daughter." The other half were relieved that someone had given words to their own misgivings. Those conflicting, though equally passionate, responses made me realize I was on to something—I wanted to go further. And so, Cinderella Ate My Daughter *was born. Since then, girls' culture has gone in two directions. Princesses may be the number one kids' franchise, topping* Star Wars—*but, thanks to parental pressure (and maybe just a little bit to* Cinderella Ate My Daughter) *Disney, as well as upstart toymakers, are offering a few more alternatives. That makes a difference: archery, for instance, has become the fastest growing sport among American girls, and according to a study by the Geena Davis Institute on Gender and Media, 70 percent of girls cite either Merida from* Brave *or* The Hunger Games' *Katniss Everdeen as inspiration. So forget about princess: start calling your daughter president!*

FINALLY CAME UNHINGED IN THE DENTIST'S OFFICE—ONE OF THOSE ritzy pediatric practices tricked out with comic books, DVDs, and arcade games—where I'd taken my three-year-old daughter for her first exam. Until then, I'd held my tongue. I'd smiled politely every time the supermarket-checkout clerk greeted her with "Hi, Princess"; ignored the waitress at our local breakfast joint who called the funny-face pancakes she ordered her "princess meal"; and made no comment when the lady at Longs Drugs said, "I bet I know your favorite color" handing her a pink balloon rather than letting her choose for herself. Maybe it was the dentist's Betty Boop inflection that got to me, but when she pointed to the exam chair and said, "Would you like to sit in my special princess throne so I can sparkle your teeth?," I lost it.

"Oh, for God's sake," I snapped. "Do you have a princess drill, too?"

She stared at me as if I were an evil stepmother.

"Come on!" I continued, my voice rising. "It's 2006, not 1950. This is Berkeley, California. Does every little girl really have to be a princess?"

My daughter, who was reaching for a Cinderella sticker, looked back and forth between us. "Why are you so mad, Mama?" she asked. "What's wrong with princesses?"

DIANA MAY BE DEAD AND MASAKO DISGRACED, BUT HERE IN AMERica, we are in the midst of a royal moment. To call princesses a "trend" among girls is like calling Harry Potter a book. Sales at Disney Consumer Products, which started the craze six years ago by packaging nine of its female characters under one royal rubric, have shot up to $3 billion globally this year, from $300 million in 2001. There are now more than twenty-five thousand Disney Princess items. "Princess," as some Disney execs call it, is not only the fastest-growing brand the company has ever created; they say it is on its way to becoming the largest girls' franchise on the planet.

Meanwhile in 2001, Mattel brought out its own "world of girl" line of princess Barbie dolls, DVDs, toys, clothing, home décor, and myriad other products. At a time when Barbie sales were declining domestically, they became instant bestsellers. Shortly before that, Mary Drolet, a Chicago-area mother and former Claire's and Montgomery Ward executive, opened Club Libby Lu, now a chain of mall stores based largely in the suburbs in which girls ages four to twelve can shop for "Princess Phones" covered in faux fur and attend "Princess-Makeover Birthday Parties." Saks bought Club Libby Lu in 2003 for $12 million and has since expanded it to eighty-seven outlets; by 2005, with only scant local advertising, revenues hovered around the $46 million mark, a 53 percent jump from the previous year. Pink, it seems, is the new gold.

Even Dora the Explorer, the intrepid, dirty-kneed adventurer, has ascended to the throne: in 2004, after a two-part episode in which she turns into a "true princess," the Nickelodeon and Viacom consumer-products division released a satin-gowned "Magic Hair Fairytale Dora," with hair that grows or shortens when her crown is touched. Among other phrases the bilingual doll utters: "Vámonos! Let's go to fairytale land!" and "Will you brush my hair?"

As a feminist mother—not to mention a nostalgic product of the Garanimals era—I have been taken by surprise by the princess craze and the girlie-girl culture that has risen around it. What happened to William wanting a doll and not dressing your cat in an apron? Whither Marlo Thomas? I watch my fellow mothers, women who once swore they'd never be dependent on a man, smile indulgently at daughters who warble "So This Is Love" or insist on being called Snow White. I wonder if they'd concede so readily to sons who begged for combat fatigues and mock AK-47s.

More to the point, when my own girl makes her daily beeline for the dress-up corner of her preschool classroom—something I'm convinced she does largely to torture me—I worry about what playing Little Mermaid is teaching her. I've spent much of my career writing about experiences that undermine girls' well-being, warning parents that a preoccupation with body and beauty (encouraged by films, TV, magazines, and, yes, toys) is perilous to their daughters' mental and physical health. Am I now supposed to shrug and forget all that? If trafficking in stereotypes doesn't matter at three, when does it matter? At six? Eight? Thirteen?

On the other hand, maybe I'm still surfing a washed-out second wave of feminism in a third-wave world. Maybe princesses are in fact a sign of progress, an indication that girls can embrace their predilection for pink without compromising strength or ambition; that, at long last, they can "have it all." Or maybe it is even less complex than that: to mangle Freud, maybe a princess is sometimes just a princess. And, as my daughter wants to know, what's wrong with that?

THE RISE OF THE DISNEY PRINCESSES READS LIKE A FAIRY TALE ITself, with Andy Mooney, a former Nike executive, playing the part of prince, riding into the company on a metaphoric white horse in January 2000 to save a consumer-products division whose sales were dropping by as much as 30 percent a year. Both overstretched and underfocused, the division had triggered price wars by granting multiple licenses for core products (say, Winnie-the-Pooh undies) while ignoring the potential of new media. What's more, Disney films like *A Bug's Life* in 1998 had yielded few merchandising opportunities—what child wants to snuggle up with an ant?

It was about a month after Mooney's arrival that the magic struck. That's when he flew to Phoenix to check out his first "Disney on Ice" show. "Standing in line in the arena, I was surrounded by little girls dressed head to toe as princesses," he told me last summer in his palatial office, then located in Burbank, and speaking in a rolling Scottish burr. "They weren't even Disney products. They were generic princess products they'd appended to a Halloween costume. And the lightbulb went off. Clearly there was latent demand here. So the next morning I said to my team, 'Okay, let's establish standards and a color palette and talk to licensees and get as much product out there as we possibly can that allows these girls to do what they're doing anyway: projecting themselves into the characters from the classic movies.'"

Mooney picked a mix of old and new heroines to wear the Pantone pink No. 241 corona: Cinderella, Sleeping Beauty, Snow White, Ariel, Belle, Jasmine, Mulan, and Pocahontas. It was the first time Disney marketed characters separately from a film's release, let alone lumped together those from different stories. To ensure the sanctity of what Mooney called their individual "mythologies," the princesses never make eye contact when they're grouped: each stares off in a slightly different direction as if unaware of the others' presence.

It is also worth noting that not all of the ladies are of royal extraction. Part of the genius of "Princess" is that its meaning is so broadly constructed that it actually has no meaning. Even Tinker Bell was originally a Princess, though her reign didn't last. "We'd always debate over whether she was really a part of the Princess mythology," Mooney recalled. "She really wasn't." Likewise, Mulan and Pocahontas, arguably the most resourceful of the bunch, are rarely depicted on Princess merchandise, though for a different reason. Their rustic garb has less bling potential than that of old-school heroines like Sleeping Beauty. (When Mulan does appear, she is typically in the kimono-like *hanfu*, which makes her miserable in the movie, rather than her liberated warrior's gear.)

The first Princess items, released with no marketing plan, no focus groups, no advertising, sold as if blessed by a fairy godmother. To this day, Disney conducts little market research on the Princess line, relying instead on the power of its legacy among mothers as well as the instant-read sales barometer of the theme parks and Disney Stores. "We simply gave girls what they wanted," Mooney said of the line's success, "although I don't think any of us grasped how much they wanted this. I wish I could sit here and take credit for having some grand scheme to develop this, but all we did was envision a little girl's room and think about how she could live out the princess fantasy. The counsel we gave to licensees was: What type of bedding would a princess want to sleep in? What kind of alarm clock would a princess want to wake up to? What type of television would a princess like to see? It's a rare case where you find a girl who has every aspect of her room bedecked in Princess, but if she ends up with three or four of these items, well, then you have a very healthy business."

Every reporter Mooney talks to asks some version of my next question: Aren't the Princesses, who are interested only in clothes, jewelry, and cadging the handsome prince, somewhat retrograde role models?

"Look," he said, "I have friends whose son went through the Power Rangers phase who castigated themselves over what they must've done wrong. Then they talked to other parents whose kids had gone through it. The boy passes through. The girl passes through. I see girls expanding their imagination through visualizing themselves as princesses, and then they pass through that phase and end up becoming lawyers, doctors, mothers, or princesses, whatever the case may be."

Mooney has a point: there are no studies proving that playing princess directly damages girls' self-esteem or dampens other aspirations. On the other hand, there is evidence that young women who hold the most conventionally feminine beliefs—who avoid conflict and think they should be perpetually nice and pretty—are more likely to be depressed than others and less likely to use contraception. What's more, the 23 percent decline in girls' participation in sports and other vigorous activity between middle and high school has been linked to their sense that athletics is unfeminine. And in a survey released last October by Girls Inc., school-age girls overwhelmingly reported a paralyzing pressure to be "perfect": not only to get straight As and be the student-body president, editor of the newspaper, and captain of the swim team but also to be "kind and caring," "please everyone, be very thin and dress right." Give those girls a pumpkin and a glass slipper and they'd be in business.

AT THE GROCERY STORE ONE DAY, MY DAUGHTER NOTICED A LITTLE girl sporting a Cinderella backpack. "There's that princess you don't like, Mama!" she shouted.

"Um, yeah," I said, trying not to meet the other mother's hostile gaze.

"Don't you like her blue dress, Mama?"

I had to admit, I did.

She thought about this. "Then don't you like her face?"

"Her face is all right," I said, noncommittally, though I'm not thrilled to have my Japanese-Jewish child in thrall to those Teutonic features. (And what the heck are those blue things covering her ears?) "It's just, honey, Cinderella doesn't really *do* anything."

Over the next forty-five minutes, we ran through that conversation, verbatim, approximately thirty-seven million times, as my daughter pointed out Disney Princess Band-Aids, Disney Princess paper cups, Disney Princess lip balm, Disney Princess pens, Disney Princess crayons, and Disney Princess notebooks—all cleverly displayed at the eye level of a three-year-old trapped in a shopping cart—as well as a bouquet of Disney Princess balloons bobbing over the checkout line. The repetition was excessive, even for a preschooler. What was it about my answers that confounded her? What if, instead of realizing: Aha! Cinderella is a symbol of the patriarchal oppression of all women, another example of corporate mind control and power-to-the-people!, my three-year-old was thinking, Mommy doesn't want me to be a girl?

According to theories of gender constancy, until they're about six or seven, children don't realize that the sex they were born with is immutable. They believe that they have a choice: they can grow up to be either a mommy or a daddy. Some psychologists say that until permanency sets in, kids embrace whatever stereotypes our culture presents, whether it's piling on the most spangles or attacking one another with lightsabers. What better way to assure that they'll always remain themselves? If that's the case, score one for Mooney. By not buying the Princess Pull-Ups, I may be inadvertently communicating that being female (to the extent that my daughter is able to understand it) is a bad thing.

Anyway, you have to give girls some credit. It's true that according to Mattel, one of the most popular games young girls play is "bride," but Disney found that a groom or prince is incidental to that fantasy, a regrettable necessity at best. Although they keep him around for the climactic kiss, he is otherwise relegated to the bottom of the toy box, which is why you don't see him prominently displayed in stores.

What's more, just because they wear the tulle doesn't mean they've drunk the Kool-Aid. Plenty of girls stray from the script, say, by playing basketball in their finery, or casting themselves as the powerful evil stepsister bossing around the sniveling Cinderella. I recall a headline-grabbing 2005 British study that revealed that girls enjoy torturing, decapitating, and microwaving their Barbies nearly as much as they like to dress them up for dates. There is spice along with that sugar after all, though why this was news is beyond me: anyone who ever played with the doll knows there's nothing more satisfying than hacking off all her hair and holding her underwater in the bathtub. Princesses can even be a boon to exasperated parents: in our house, for instance, royalty never whines and uses the potty every single time.

"Playing princess is not the issue," argues Lyn Mikel Brown, a professor of education and human development at

Colby College and co-author, with Sharon Lamb, of *Packaging Girlhood: Rescuing Our Daughters from Marketers' Schemes*. "The issue is twenty-five thousand Princess products. When one thing is so dominant, then it's no longer a choice: it's a mandate, cannibalizing all other forms of play. There's the illusion of more choices out there for girls, but if you look around, you'll see their choices are steadily narrowing."

It's hard to imagine that girls' options could truly be shrinking when they dominate the honor roll and outnumber boys in college. Then again, have you taken a stroll through a children's store lately? A year ago, when we shopped for "big girl" bedding at Pottery Barn Kids, we found the "girls" side awash in flowers, hearts, and hula dancers; not a soccer player or sailboat in sight. Across the no-fly zone, the "boys" territory was all about sports, trains, planes, and automobiles. Meanwhile, Baby GAP's boys' onesies were emblazoned with BIG MAN ON CAMPUS and the girls' with SOCIAL BUTTERFLY; guess whose matching shoes were decorated on the soles with hearts and whose sported a No. 1 logo? And at Toys"R"Us, aisles of pink baby dolls, kitchens, shopping carts, and princesses unfurl a safe distance from the *Star Wars* figures, GeoTrax, and tool chests. The relentless resegregation of childhood appears to have sneaked up without any further discussion about sex roles, about what it now means to be a boy or to be a girl. Or maybe it has happened in lieu of such discussion because it's easier this way.

Easier, that is, unless you want to buy your daughter something that isn't pink. Girls' obsession with that color may seem like something they're born with, like the ability to breathe or talk on the phone for hours on end. But according to Jo Paoletti, an associate professor of American studies at the University of Maryland, it ain't so. When colors were first introduced to the nursery in the early part of the twentieth century, pink was considered the more masculine hue, a pastel version of red. Blue, with its intimations of the Virgin Mary, constancy, and faithfulness, was thought to be dainty. Why or when that switched is not clear, but as late as the 1930s a significant percentage of adults in one national survey held to that split. Perhaps that's why so many early Disney heroines—Cinderella, Sleeping Beauty, Wendy, Alice in Wonderland—are swathed in varying shades of azure. (Purple, incidentally, may be the next color to swap teams: once the realm of kings and NFL players, it is fast becoming the bolder girl's version of pink.)

It wasn't until the mid-1980s, when amplifying age and sex differences became a key strategy of children's marketing (recall the emergence of "tween"), that pink became seemingly innate to girls, part of what defined them as female, at least for the first few years. That was also the time that the first of the generation raised during the unisex phase of feminism—ah, hither Marlo!—became parents. "The kids who grew up in the 1970s wanted sharp definitions for their own kids," Paoletti told me. "I can understand that, because the unisex thing denied everything—you couldn't be this, you couldn't be that, you had to be a neutral nothing."

The infatuation with the girlie girl certainly could, at least in part, be a reaction against the so-called second wave of the women's movement of the 1960s and '70s (the first wave was the fight for suffrage), which fought for reproductive rights and economic, social, and legal equality. If nothing else, pink and Princess have resuscitated the fantasy of romance that that era of feminism threatened, the privileges that traditional femininity conferred on women despite its costs—

doors magically opened, dinner checks picked up, Manolo Blahniks. Frippery. Fun. Why should we give up the perks of our sex until we're sure of what we'll get in exchange? Why should we give them up at all? Or maybe it's deeper than that: the freedoms feminism bestowed came with an undercurrent of fear among women themselves—flowing through *Ally McBeal*, *Bridget Jones's Diary*, *Sex and the City*—of losing male love, of never marrying, of not having children, of being deprived of something that felt essentially and exclusively female.

I mulled that over while flipping through *The Paper Bag Princess*, a 1980 picture book hailed as an antidote to Disney. The heroine outwits a dragon who has kidnapped her prince, but not before the beast's fiery breath frizzles her hair and destroys her dress, forcing her to don a paper bag. The ungrateful prince rejects her, telling her to come back when she is "dressed like a real princess." She dumps him and skips off into the sunset, happily ever after, alone.

There you have it, *Thelma and Louise* all over again. Step out of line, and you end up solo or, worse, sailing crazily over a cliff to your doom. Alternatives like those might send you skittering right back to the castle. And I get that: the fact is, though I want my daughter to do and be whatever she wants as an adult, I still hope she'll find her Prince (or Princess) Charming and have babies, just as I have. I don't want her to be a fish without a bicycle; I want her to be a fish with another fish. Preferably, one who loves and respects her and also does the dishes and half the child care.

There had to be a middle ground between compliant and defiant, between petticoats and paper bags. I remembered a video on YouTube, an ad for a Nintendo game called *Super Princess Peach*. It showed a pack of girls in tiaras, gowns, and

elbow-length white gloves sliding down a zip line on para-
sols, navigating an obstacle course of tires in their stilettos,
slithering on their bellies under barbed wire, then using their
telekinetic powers to make a climbing wall burst into flames.
"If you can stand up to really mean people," an announcer intoned, "maybe you have what it takes to be a princess."

Now, here were some girls who had grit as well as grace.
I loved Princess Peach even as I recognized that there was
no way she could run in those heels, that her peachiness did
nothing to upset the apple cart of expectation: she may have
been athletic, smart, and strong, but she was also adorable.
Maybe she's what those once-unisex, postfeminist parents
are shooting for: the melding of old and new standards. And
perhaps that's a good thing, the ideal solution. But what to
make, then, of the young women in the Girls Inc. survey? It
doesn't seem to be "having it all" that's getting to them; it's the
pressure to be it all. In telling our girls they can be anything,
we have inadvertently demanded that they be everything. To
everyone. All the time. No wonder the report was titled "The
Supergirl Dilemma."

The princess as superhero is not irrelevant. Some scholars
I spoke with say that given its post-9/11 timing, princess mania
is a response to a newly dangerous world. "Historically, princess worship has emerged during periods of uncertainty and
profound social change," observes Miriam Forman-Brunell, a
historian at the University of Missouri–Kansas City. Francis
Hodgson Burnett's original *A Little Princess* was published at a
time of rapid urbanization, immigration, and poverty; Shirley
Temple's film version was a hit during the Great Depression.
"The original folk tales themselves," Forman-Brunell says,
"spring from medieval and early-modern European culture

that faced all kinds of economic and demographic and social upheaval—famine, war, disease, terror of wolves. Girls
play savior during times of economic crisis and instability."
That's a heavy burden for little shoulders. Perhaps that's why
the magic wand has become an essential part of the princess
getup. In the original stories—even the Disney versions of
them—it's not the girl herself who's magic; it's the fairy godmother. Now, if Forman-Brunell is right, we adults have become the cursed creatures whom girls have the thaumaturgic
power to transform.

IN THE 1990s, THIRD-WAVE FEMINISTS REBELLED AGAINST THEIR
dour big sisters, "reclaiming" sexual objectification as a woman's right—provided, of course, that it was on her own terms,
that she was the one choosing to strip or wear a shirt that said
PORN STAR or make out with her best friend at a frat-house
bash. They embraced words like "bitch" and "slut" as terms of
affection and empowerment. That is, when used by the right
people, with the right dash of playful irony. But how can you
assure that? As Madonna gave way to Britney, whatever self-
determination that message contained was watered down and
commodified until all that was left was a gaggle of six-year-old
girls in belly-baring T-shirts (which I'm guessing they don't
wear as a cultural critique). It is no wonder that parents, faced
with thongs for eight-year-olds and Bratz dolls' "passion for
fashion," fill their daughters' closets with pink sateen; the innocence of the Princess feels like a reprieve.

"But what does that mean?" asks Sharon Lamb, Mikel
Brown's co-author and a psychology professor at Saint Michael's College. "There are other ways to express 'innocence'—

girls could play ladybug or caterpillar. What you're really talking about is sexual purity. And there's a trap at the end of that rainbow, because the natural progression from pale, innocent pink is not to other colors. It's to hot, sexy pink—exactly the kind of sexualization parents are trying to avoid."

Lamb suggested that to see for myself how "Someday My Prince Will Come" morphs into "Oops! . . . I Did It Again," I visit Club Libby Lu, the mall shop dedicated to the "Very Important Princess."

Walking into one of the newest links in the store's chain, in Natick, Massachusetts, last summer, I had to tip my tiara to the founder, Mary Drolet: Libby Lu's design was flawless. Unlike Disney, Drolet depended on focus groups to choose the logo (a crown-topped heart) and the colors (pink, pink, purple, and more pink). The displays were scaled to the size of a ten-year-old, though most of the shoppers I saw were several years younger than that. The decals on the walls and dressing rooms—I LOVE YOUR HAIR, HIP CHICK, SPOILED—were written in "girlfriend language." The young sales clerks at this "special secret club for superfabulous girls" are called "club counselors" and come off like your coolest babysitter, the one who used to let you brush her hair. The malls themselves are chosen based on a company formula called the GPI, or "Girl Power Index," which predicts potential sales revenues. Talk about newspeak: "Girl Power" has gone from a riot grrrl anthem to "I Am Woman, Watch Me Shop."

Inside, the store was divided into several glittery "shopping zones" called "experiences": Libby's Laboratory, now called Sparkle Spa, where girls concoct their own cosmetics and bath products; Libby's Room; Ear Piercing; Pooch Parlor (where divas in training can pamper stuffed poodles, pugs, and Chihuahuas); and the Style Studio, offering "Libby Lu" makeover choices, including 'Tween Idol, Rock Star, Pop Star, and, of course, Priceless Princess. Each look includes hairstyle, makeup, nail polish, and sparkly tattoos.

As I browsed, I noticed a mother standing in the center of the store holding a price list for makeover birthday parties—$22.50 to $35 per child. Her name was Anne McAuliffe; her daughters—Stephanie, four, and seven-year-old twins Rory and Sarah—were dashing giddily up and down the aisles.

"They've been begging to come to this store for three weeks," McAuliffe said. "I'd never heard of it. So I said they could, but they'd have to spend their own money if they bought anything." She looked around. "Some of this stuff is innocuous," she observed, then leaned toward me, eyes wide and stage-whispered: "But . . . a lot of it is horrible. It makes them look like little prostitutes. It's crazy. They're babies!"

As we debated the line between frivolous fun and Jon-Benét, McAuliffe's daughter Rory came dashing up, pigtails haphazard, glasses askew. "They have the best pocketbooks here," she said breathlessly, brandishing a clutch with the words GIRLIE GIRL stamped on it. "Please, can I have one? It has sequins!"

"You see that?" McAuliffe asked, gesturing at the bag. "What am I supposed to say?"

On my way out of the mall, I popped into the tween mecca Hot Topic, where a display of Tinker Bell items caught my eye. Tinker Bell, whose image racks up an annual $400 million in retail sales with no particular effort on Disney's part, is poised to wreak vengeance on the Princess line that once expelled her. Last winter, the first chapter book designed to introduce girls to Tink and her Pixie Hollow pals spent eighteen weeks on the

New York Times children's bestseller list. In a direct-to-DVD now in production, she will speak for the first time, voiced by the actress Brittany Murphy. Next year, Disney Fairies will be rolled out in earnest. Aimed at six- to nine-year-old girls, the line will catch them just as they outgrow the Princess. Their colors will be lavender, green, turquoise—anything but the Princess's soon-to-be-babyish pink.

To appeal to that older child, Disney executives said, the Fairies will have more "attitude" and "sass" than the Princesses. What, I wondered, did that entail? I'd seen some of the Tinker Bell merchandise that Disney sells at its theme parks: T-shirts reading SPOILED TO PERFECTION, MOOD SUBJECT TO CHANGE WITHOUT NOTICE, and TINKER BELL: PRETTIER THAN A PRINCESS. At Hot Topic, that edge was even sharper: magnets, clocks, light-switch plates, and panties featured DARK TINK, described as "the bad-girl side of Miss Bell that Walt never saw."

Girl power, indeed.

A FEW DAYS LATER, I PICKED MY DAUGHTER UP FROM PRESCHOOL. SHE came tearing over in a full-skirted frock with a gold bodice, a beaded crown perched sideways on her head. "Look, Mommy, I'm Ariel!" she crowed, referring to Disney's *The Little Mermaid*. Then she stopped and furrowed her brow. "Mommy, do you like Ariel?"

I considered her for a moment. Maybe the Princess is the first salvo in what will become a lifelong struggle over her body image, a Hundred Years' War of dieting, plucking, painting, and perpetual dissatisfaction with the results. Or maybe it isn't. I'll never really know. In the end, it's not the

Princesses that really bother me anyway. They're just a trigger for the bigger question of how, over the years, can I help my daughter with the contradictions she will inevitably face as a girl, the dissonance that is as endemic as ever to growing up female? Maybe the best I can hope for is that her generation will get a little further with the solutions than we did.

For now, I kneeled down on the floor and gave my daughter a hug.

She smiled happily. "But, Mommy?" she added. "When I grow up, I'm still going to be a fireman."

PLAYING AT SEXY

Cinderella Ate My Daughter explored the ways that even (or maybe especially) in our more "liberated" era, girls learn that how their bodies look to others is more important than how those bodies feel to themselves. It seemed both a natural and crucial next step to question the impact of such lessons on their intimate relationships. That process—which I began in earnest with this piece, published in June 2010—would eventually lead me to write Girls & Sex.

LAST MONTH, OVER THE COURSE OF ONE WORKDAY, SIX FRIENDS sent me a link to the same video along with messages that said, "Have you seen this?" I had, but I clicked it each time anyway. I just couldn't stop myself. The clip showed a troupe of eight- and nine-year-old Los Angeles girls in a national dance contest. Wearing outfits that would make a stripper blush, they pumped it and bumped it to the Beyoncé hit "Single Ladies (Put a Ring on It)." The girls were spectacular dancers, able to twirl on one foot while extending the other into a perfect standing split. But I doubt that two million people had tuned in simply to admire their arabesques. As with TV phenomena like *Toddlers & Tiaras*, the compulsion to watch was like the impulse to rubberneck at an accident, but in this case the scene was a twelve-car pileup of early sexualization.

The girls' routine was debated on CNN, *Good Morning America*, and the *Huffington Post*. For about forty-eight hours it blazed across blogs and filled up inboxes. And then, faster than you can say JonBenét Ramsey, it was gone. Outraged mommy bloggers calmed down. News outlets turned back to the BP oil spill and the Pennsylvania newlyweds who were born on the same day in the same hospital.

Moral panics about pornified girls bubble up regularly these days: Should the self-proclaimed role model Miley Cyrus have stripped for *Vanity Fair* (or given a lap dance to a forty-four-year-old film producer, or pole danced on an ice-cream cart at the Teen Choice Awards)? Is the neckline too low on the new Barbie Basics Model 10 doll—nicknamed, seemingly redundantly, "Busty Barbie"? The next freak-out, mark my words, will explode this summer when Mattel rolls out its Monster High franchise—dolls, apparel, interactive Web site, Halloween costumes, Webisodes, and, eventually, television shows and a movie—which will be the biggest product introduction in the company's history, and its first original line since Hot Wheels in 1968 (back when "hot" had a different connotation, at least to children). Monster High's racy student body is made up of the children of "legendary monsters," including Clawdeen, a fifteen-year-old werewolf who resembles an undead streetwalker, only less demure. But no worries, parents, Clawdeen is not without her wholesome side: although she is a "fierce fashionista" who is "gorgeous" and "intimidating" and hates gym "because they won't let me participate in my platform heels," her Web bio assures us that she is "absolutely loyal to my friends." Well, that's a relief.

I might give the phenomenon a pass if it turned out that once they were older, little girls who playacted at sexy were more comfortable in their skins or more confident in their sexual relationships, if they asked more of their partners or enjoyed greater pleasure. But evidence is to the contrary. In his book *The Triple Bind: Saving Our Teenage Girls from Today's Pressures and Conflicting Expectations*, Stephen Hinshaw, professor in the psychology department at the University of California at Berkeley, explains that sexualizing little girls—whether through images, music, or play—actually undermines healthy sexuality rather than promoting it. Those bootylicious grade-schoolers in the dance troupe presumably don't understand the meaning of their motions (and thank goodness for it), but precisely because of that, they don't connect—and may never learn to connect—sexy attitudes to erotic feelings.

That ongoing confusion between desirability and desire may help explain another trend giving parents agita: the number of teenage girls—22 percent, according to a 2008 survey by The National Campaign to Prevent Teen and Unplanned Pregnancy—who have electronically sent or posted nude or seminude photos of themselves. I have to admit that part of me is impressed by their bravado. Maybe, rather than cause for alarm, this was a sign of progress—indication that girls were taking charge of their sexuality, transcending the double standard. Yet you have to wonder: Does flaunting it mean they're feeling it?

I FIND MYSELF IMPROBABLY NOSTALGIC FOR THE LATE 1970s, WHEN I came of age. In many ways, girls were less free then than they are today: fewer of us competed on the sports field, raised our hands during math class, or graduated from college. No one spoke the word "vagina," whether in a monologue or not. And there was that Farrah flip to contend with. Yet in that oh-so-brief window between the advent of the Pill and the fear of AIDS, when abortion was both legal and accessible to teenagers, there was—at least for some of us—a kind of Our Bodies, Ourselves optimism about sex. Young women felt an imperative, a political duty, to understand their desire and responses, to explore their own pleasure, to recognize sexuality as something rising from within. And young men—at least some of them—seemed eager to take the journey with us, to rewrite the rules of masculinity so they would prize mutuality over conquest.

That notion now seems as quaint as a one-piece swimsuit on a five-year-old. Sexual entitlement, according to Deborah Tolman, a professor at Hunter College and author of *Dilemmas of Desire: Teenage Girls Talk about Sexuality*, has instead become the latest performance, something girls act out rather than experience. "By the time they are teenagers," she said, "the girls I talk to respond to questions about how their bodies feel—questions about sexuality or desire—by talking about how their bodies look. They will say something like, 'I felt like I looked good.' Looking good is *not* a feeling."

Tell that to the zombies at Monster High. Or the girls thrusting their hips at warp speed to Beyoncé (who, incidentally, wears a leotard in *her* video). Better yet, tell it to your daughter: she is going to need to hear it.

THE HILLARY LESSON

Oh how I wish that ten years after May 2008, when this piece was published, I could write that Hillary had triumphed, that sexism and ageism were vanquished in politics. Because if I worried about what our daughters might have learned from the race for president back then . . .

Berkeley's Fourth Street is my town's version of a strip mall: there is little you might need there, but much to want: handcrafted Japanese paper; diaphanous Stevie Nicks–inspired frocks; wooden toys imported from Europe. One recent morning, as my four-year-old daughter and I strolled to our favorite diner, she pointed to a bumper sticker plastered on a mailbox. A yellow, viraginous caricature of Hillary Clinton leered out from a black background. Big block letters proclaimed, THE WICKED WITCH OF THE EAST IS ALIVE AND LIVING IN NEW YORK.

"Look, Mama," she said. "That's Hillary. What does it say?"

Let me state right off that I don't consider Senator Clinton a victim. Her arm is so limber from the mud she has lobbed during her political career that now that the whole president thing is doubtful, she may have a future as the first woman to pitch for the Yankees. So it is not the attacks themselves that give me pause, but the form they consistently have taken, the default position of incessant, even gleeful (and, I admit it, sometimes clever) misogyny. Staring down the sight line of my daughter's index finger, I wondered what to tell her—not only at this moment, but in years to come—about Hillary and about herself. Will the senator be my example of how far we've come as women or how far we have to go? Is she proof to my daughter that "you can do anything" or of the hell that will rain down on you if you try? Voting against Clinton does not make a person sexist—there are other reasons to reject her. But contemplating the LIFE'S A BITCH, DON'T VOTE FOR ONE T-shirts, the stainless-steel-thighed Hillary nutcrackers, the comparison to the bunny-boiling Alex Forrest of *Fatal Attraction*, I struggle over how, when—even whether—to talk to girls truthfully about women and power.

I beamed when my daughter announced her first career choice, firefighter, ridiculously proud (given she was barely two) that she felt no barriers to what was historically a male-only job. Nor did I indicate at the time that there would be any for her. Of course, I didn't really expect her to pursue that dream (she has already moved on to scuba diver) but the truth is, if she did she might face a life of isolation and hostility, much like Rebecca Farris, who, in 2006, after her promotion to engine driver in a firehouse in Austin, Texas, came to work to find her locker smeared with human excrement. At least no one suggested she iron her stationmates' shirts.

In the white-collar realm, I suppose I should celebrate the announcement last month of the first woman named chief executive of a top U.S. accounting firm, but maybe I'm just a

glass-half-empty kind of gal: I mean, the first? In 2008? Are
they kidding? Meanwhile, now that Meg Whitman has stepped
down as CEO of eBay, there are a measly twelve women who
lead Fortune 500 companies; their percentage of female corporate officers has also dropped over the last three years. And
while women make up 48 percent of new lawyers (and have
hovered in that range for around a decade), the percentage of
women who are law partners at major firms remains stuck at a
pitiful eighteen.

Right now, my daughter doesn't know about the obstacles
she may face someday, and I'm not sure of the wisdom of gird-
ing her in advance. Even the supposedly "girl positive" picture
books, designed to address this very issue, pose a dilemma.
Take *Elenita*, a magical-realist tale, given to my daughter by a
family friend, about a girl who wants to be a glassblower. Her
father says she can't do it: she's too little, and besides, the trade
is forbidden to women. The lesson, naturally, is that with a little ingenuity girls can be glassblowers or stevedores or [fill in
the blank]. Nice. Still, I found myself hesitating over the "girls
can't" section. My daughter has never heard that "girls can't
be" or "girls can't do." Why should I plant the idea in her head
only to knock it down?

The same quandary crops up with older girls. They are
sports stars, yearbook editors, valedictorians. We have assured them the world is theirs, and they have no reason to
disbelieve us. Like Clinton, our daughters are no victims.
And yet, all is not quite well. Not when achieving CEO, MD,
or PhD status can still come appended with a second alphabet
of *b*- and *c*-words. Not when a woman who runs for office is
accused of harboring a "testicle lockbox." Clinton, whatever
else she may be, has become a reflection, a freeze frame of

the complications and contradictions of female success. Her bid for the White House has embodied both the possibilities we never imagined for our daughters—shattering not just the glass ceiling but the glass stratosphere—and the vitriol that attaining them can provoke. Both are real; so Godspeed, girls.

Perhaps by the time my daughter is of age, the ambivalence toward powerful women will have dissipated. Judging by the attitudes of today's young adults, however, I'm not optimistic. According to a J. Walter Thompson survey of workplace issues published last month, while many men in their twenties show no preference, a full 40 percent would rather have a male than a female boss.

The bumper sticker my daughter saw on Fourth Street struck me as "viraginous," yet a virago can be defined either as a harpy or as a hero. I have a few years before I have to explain that to her. In the meantime, I did what any good mother would do when confronted with a thorny subject: I pointed to the bakery across the street and said: "Hey, look, honey! Want a cookie?"

THE EMPOWERMENT MYSTIQUE

Since I wrote this piece, in September 2010, Sarah Palin has largely receded from public view: apparently, conservative male politicians no longer need her to camouflage their reactionary policies. The category of "femvertising," however, has ballooned. Some spots rise to the level of innocuously political: the Always #LikeAGirl campaign, for instance, urged customers to join the "epic battle to keep girls' confidence high during puberty and beyond." Most, though, present female empowerment as completely unrelated to the struggle for political, economic, or social equality. Take the ad that Allergan, a pharmaceutical company, released in 2017 for International Women's Day: a heart-swelling montage of inspirational photographs—portraits of Frida Kahlo, Rosa Parks, Amelia Earhart—culminating in a call for "eyepowerment": the feminist stand of using drops to combat chronic dry eye. Seriously: not a joke. Earlier in this collection, I quote Deborah Tolman, who says, "Looking good is not a feeling." Neither, it turns out, is feminism.

TRUE CONFESSION: AT AGE SIXTEEN, I PERFORMED IN A HIGH-school production of the musical *Free to Be . . . You and Me*, dressed in Mork-from-Ork rainbow suspenders and matching toe socks. Our troupe defended William's right to a doll and explained why mommies were people, too, at every elementary school in St. Louis Park, Minnesota; I can still recite "Don't Dress Your Cat in an Apron." So early last month, when I heard the familiar lilt of the New Seekers' voices ("Come with me, take my hand, and we'll liiiiii-IIIIVE . . .") emanating from the TV in my den, I dashed in, already singing along.

What I saw was an irresistible set of triplets walking into a school wearing identical uniforms. Over the course of thirty seconds, the girls evolved—a powder-blue pencil holder, a yellow soccer ball, a pair of pink knockoff UGGs—as each asserted her individuality through brightly colored back-to-school gear from Target.

I don't think that was quite what Marlo Thomas had in mind.

It would be easy to call the ad cynical, an attempt to channel a generation's nostalgia for a time that irony forgot—and it may well be that. Yet other songs could have struck that particular chord. *Free to Be* was foremost about vanquishing gender stereotypes. By choosing *girls* to liberate from the tyranny of antimaterialism, Target implied that buying its wares was part of the victory. That's part of a trend I've noticed across a whole range of sectors over the last several months, from big-box stores to high-end fashion to wireless-phone services to politics: all have discovered the sales potential in female pride.

I am not talking about feminism per se so much as the suggestion, the *feeling*, of "empowerment": an amorphous, untethered huzzah of "Go, Team Woman!" Take the Web site that Thierry Mugler, the couturier, started for Womanity, a perfume extolling "the invisible bond between women." Awash with inspirational quotes ("adventure is worthwhile"), the site asked viewers the world over to join together by submitting what "womanity"—presumably derived from "humanity" rather than "inanity"—means to them.

Then there was last month's Verizon spot, titled "Prejudice," in which a series of earnest everygirls addressed the camera: "Air has no prejudice. It does not carry the opinions of a man faster than those of a woman. . . . So it stands to reason my ideas will be powerful, if they are wise. . . . If my thoughts have flawless delivery"—that is, if her cell phone doesn't punk out—"I can lead the army that will follow."

The girls are the quintessence of sincerity, and their expectation of a bright future can't help but warm a viewer's heart—especially if she is the parent of a daughter. In fact, watching the ad, I realized that daughters have supplanted sons as the repository of hope in tough economic times. To an extent, that has always been the case: Shirley Temple and Little Orphan Annie embodied optimism during the Great Depression. But this time, the symbolism is grounded less in sugar and spice than in cold, hard facts. It's well established that three women now receive bachelor's and master's degrees for every two men, but in 2009, for the first time, they earned more doctorates, as well. Meanwhile, three-quarters of the jobs lost in the current recession were held by men (who were more likely to be in hard-hit industries like construction). Women have not only become (for the first time) the majority of the workforce, but they also hold the lioness's share of managerial jobs and are the primary breadwinners in more than a quarter of dual-income families. According to a recent, ominously titled *The Atlantic* article, "The End of Men," 75 percent of couples who used an experimental sex-selection technology before conception preferred to have girls.

WOMEN'S RELATIVELY RAPID RISE SEEMS TO HAVE BECOME UNEXpectedly entwined with patriotism—the music swelling under the Verizon spots is downright stately—proof of this country's belief in fairness, equality, upward mobility. No wonder another Verizon ad, a freeway billboard I zoomed by, shows an African American woman, eyes gleaming, face tilted upward at the precise angle of Barack Obama's on his ubiquitous campaign poster. We women, not just the air around us, are free.

Of course, there's no actual substance beneath these spots. Nike's 1995 "If You Let Me Play Sports" campaign featured girls in much the same way as Verizon's "Prejudice." But though designed to sell shoes, the Nike ad also presented a compelling case for girls' athletics—and the company donates to programs that promote them. The Verizon ad, by contrast, is cause-related marketing without the cause. Merely buying its service is how you're supposed to strike the blow against inequality. Meanwhile, though the explicit mission of the Free to Be Foundation is to end discrimination, Target was recently forced to apologize for donating $150,000 to an organization supporting the gubernatorial campaign of Tom Emmer, a Minnesota state representative who drafted an amendment to the state's constitution to ban same-sex marriage. That move sparked a boycott (or perhaps I should say a personcott) among the very type of shoppers who were weaned on the song.

Where advertising goes, politics follows. And no one has channeled the power of free-floating female pride better than Sarah Palin. Her "Mama Grizzlies" video—a rallying cry to conservative women—hijacked feminist iconography for the right as effectively as Dan Quayle snagged "family values" back in 1992. In Palin's video, images unspool over music that is nearly indistinguishable from the score of the Verizon spot: women hugging, women marching, women applauding in front of a gigantic flag. There are "a lot of women coming together," Palin observes in a voice-over.

As with the commercial product pitches, simply acknowledging—*celebrating*—that we are female, alluding to the idea that we can make something happen, even though it's never clear what that something is or whether it's in our best interests, is presented as empowerment. Never mind that in addition to being virulently antichoice, Palin opposed legislation to end pay discrimination. But by the time the video was through, I have to admit, I was ready to rear up on my own hind legs and attack those rats in Washington who would dare to provide children with affordable health care.

That's the thing about rhetoric: it can be effective even when it is vacuous. Which is no doubt why I found myself cheerfully humming—"I see a land bright and clear, and the time's coming near"—as my daughter and I browsed under the big red bull's-eye for new notebooks and sharp colored pencils. Despite knowing better, I just couldn't shake the feeling that with the right school supplies, she could rule the world.

THE FAT TRAP

Raising a girl with a healthy body image is challenging for any mother, especially those of us who have struggled ourselves (and, really, who hasn't?). Having a daughter has not necessarily improved my own relationship with body and beauty, but it's certainly taught me to fake it better. This piece ran in April 2010.

FOOD IS NEVER JUST FOOD. FOOD IS LOVE. FOOD IS SOLACE. IT IS politics. It is religion. And if that's not enough to heap on your dinner plate each night, food is also, especially for mothers, the instant-read measure of our parenting. We are not only what we eat, we are what we feed our children. So here in Berkeley—where a preoccupation with locally grown, organic, sustainable agriculture is presumed—the mom who strolls the farmers' markets can feel superior to the one who buys pesticide-free produce trucked in from Mexico, who can, in turn, lord it over the one who stoops to conventionally grown carrots (though the folks who grow their own trump us all). Let it slip that you took the kids to McDonald's, and watch how fast those playdates dry up.

Doing right by our kids means doing right by their health—

body and soul. Yet even as awareness about the family diet has spread across the country (especially among the middle class and the affluent), so, it seems, have youngsters' waistlines. According to the Centers for Disease Control and Prevention, a full third of America's children are overweight, and 17 percent are clinically obese—a rate that has more than tripled since 1976. Those figures may be alarming, yet equally disturbing are the numbers of children, girls in particular, who risk their health in the other direction, in the vain pursuit of thinness. In a 2002 survey of 81,247 Minnesota high school students published in *The Journal of Adolescent Health*, more than half of the girls reported engaging in some form of disordered behavior while trying to lose weight: fasting, popping diet pills, smoking, vomiting, abusing laxatives, binge eating.

Parents, then, are left in a quandary, worrying about both the perils of obesity and those of anorexia. How can you simultaneously encourage your daughter to watch her size and accept her body? My own initial impulse, when I found out I was pregnant with a girl, was to suggest that my husband take responsibility for feeding her. After all, he doesn't see a few extra pounds as a character flaw. Nor does he serve up a heaping helping of internal conflict with every meal. It's not that I'm extreme; it's just that like most—heck, all—of the women I know, my relationship to food, to my weight, to my body is . . . complicated. I did not want to pass that pathology on to my daughter.

At best, weight is delicate territory between mothers and their girls. Michelle Obama found that out firsthand when kicking off her campaign to eliminate childhood obesity. In an attempt to destigmatize the condition, especially for African Americans, she confessed that the family pediatrician warned her that "something was getting off-balance"; she needed to watch her daughters' body-mass indices. So she cut back on portion sizes, switched to low-fat milk, left fruit out on the table, and banned weekday TV viewing.

The news that the First Mom put her daughters on a "diet" set the blogosphere abuzz. She was accused, even by supporters, of subjecting her daughters' bodies to public scrutiny, making their appearance fair game. Some grimly predicted that years of purging awaited the girls. The actual message Mrs. Obama was trying to get across—that minor changes can make a major difference in kids' lives—was, at least temporarily, lost in the uproar.

The president also has overshared about his children's weights, saying in a 2008 interview, "A couple of years ago— you'd never know it by looking at her now—Malia was getting a little chubby." He, too, was criticized, though less harshly, maybe because while fathers' comments sting, nothing cuts deeper than a mother's appraising gaze. Daughters understand that early: according to a study of preschool girls published in the journal *Pediatrics* in 2001, those whose mothers expressed "higher concern" over their daughters' weights not only reported more negative body images than their peers but also perceived themselves as less smart and less physically capable (paternal "concern" was associated only with the latter). The effect was independent of the child's actual size.

A 2003 analysis of the National Health and Nutrition Examination Survey, meanwhile, showed that mothers were three times as likely to notice excess weight in daughters than in sons, even though the boys were more likely to be large. That gave me pause. It is so easy for the concern with "health," however legitimate, to justify a focus on girls' appearances. For organic-eating, right-living parents whose girls are merely on the fleshy side of average, "health" may also mask a discomfort with how a less-than-perfect daughter reflects on them. "'Good' parents today are expected to have normal-weight kids," says Joan Jacobs Brumberg, author of the book *The Body Project* and a professor of history and human development at Cornell University. "Having a fat girl is a failure."

By the time my own daughter was born, I realized that avoiding conversations about food, health, and body image would be impossible: what I didn't say would speak as loudly as anything I did. So rather than opt out, I decided to actively model something different, something saner. I've tried to forget all I once knew about calories, carbs, fat, and protein; I haven't stepped on a scale in seven years. At dinner I pointedly enjoy what I eat, whether it's steamed broccoli or pecan pie. I don't fetishize food or indulge in foodieism. I exercise because it feels good, and I never, ever talk about weight. Honestly? It feels entirely unnatural, this studied unconcern, and it forces me to be more vigilant than ever about what goes in and what comes out of my mouth. Maybe my daughter senses that, but this conscious antidiet is the best I can do.

Still, my daughter lives in the world. She watches Disney movies. She plays with Barbies. So although I was saddened, I was hardly surprised one day when, at six years old, she looked at me, frowned, and said, "Mama, don't get f-a-t, okay?"

At least, I thought, she didn't hear it from me.

THE BATTLE OVER DRESS CODES

Parents of teenagers invariably ask me, "What do we do about what girls wear?" Girls ask me, "What do we do about slut-shaming dress codes?" This piece, published in June 2014, offers no easy answers, but the cross-generational advocacy group Spark Movement suggests the following: Students should have input into forming dress codes; each rule should have a clear explanation; those rules should be the same along gender lines (and evenly enforced within and between them); punishment should not involve humiliation or pulling students out of class; and, most of all, "it's a distraction to boys" is never, ever a viable justification.

IN THE BAY AREA, THE LAST WEEK OF SCHOOL IS A TIME TO DIG OUT cozy jackets and socks, but this year our natural air-conditioning (that's "fog" to you) failed, giving us a few sweltering June days.

On one, my daughter, who is in the final throes of fifth grade, came skipping out of class, her gangly legs poking out of her favorite denim short-shorts. "She won't be able to wear those next year," another mom commented. "They won't pass the dress code." A dress code? In Berkeley? Next they'll be endorsing Darwinism in Kansas.

It turns out that modern middle school parents from San Francisco to New York have been forced to break out the ruler. Are those inseams too short? How wide are those tank top shoulders? In March, middle schoolers in Evanston, Illinois, picketed a policy against leggings. In May, students at a Utah high school opened their yearbooks to discover digitally raised necklines and sleeves added to female classmates' shirts.

Girls, particularly those with ample hips or breasts, are almost exclusively singled out, typically told their outfits will "distract boys." As if young men cannot control themselves in the presence of a spaghetti strap.

The last time classroom attire was this contentious was the late 1960s and early 1970s, when the most high-profile cases centered on boys. According to Jo Paoletti, author of the forthcoming book *Sex and Unisex: Fashion, Feminism and the Sexual Revolution*, young men with long hair were sometimes attacked by their peers. In an all-too-familiar scenario, it was the victims who were blamed for such assaults, accused of provoking classmates with their "distracting" appearance. While girls who violated dress codes were sent home to change, boys were suspended or expelled. Their parents also disproportionately lawyered up: by 1974, there were one hundred fifty court cases involving young men's hairdos.

Boys run afoul of dress codes when they flout authority: "hippies" defying the establishment, "thugs" in saggy pants. For girls, the issue is seductiveness, and that, too, has become politicized, exposing a new generation gap.

Today's canny girls, emboldened by #YesAllWomen Twitter culture, scold their elders, "Don't tell us what to wear; teach the boys not to stare." They are correct: Addressing leering or harassment will challenge young men's assumptions. Imposing purdah on middle school girls does the opposite.

Even so, while women are not responsible for male misbehavior, and while no amount of dress (or undress) will avert catcalls, cultural change can be glacial, and I have a child trying to wend her way safely through our city streets right now. I don't want her to feel shame in her soon-to-be-emerging woman's body, but I also don't want her to be a target. Has maternal concern made me prudent or simply a prude?

More than that, taking on the right to bare arms (and legs, and cleavage, and midriffs) as a feminist rallying cry seems suspiciously Orwellian. Fashions catering to girls emphasize body consciousness at the youngest ages—Gap offers "skinny jeans" for toddlers, Target hawks bikinis for infants. Good luck finding anything but those itty-bitty shorts for your twelve-year-old. So even as I object to the policing of girls' sexuality, I'm concerned about the incessant drumbeat of self-objectification: the pressure young women face to view their bodies as the objects of others' desires.

In its landmark 2007 report on the sexualization of girlhood, the American Psychological Association linked self-objectification to poor self-esteem, depression, body dissatisfaction, and compromised cognitive function. Meanwhile, a study published last year in the journal *Psychological Science* titled "Objects Don't Object," found that when college women were asked to merely think about a time when they'd been objectified, they became subsequently less supportive of equal rights.

Yet, for today's girls, sexy appearance has been firmly

conflated with strong womanhood, and at ever younger (not to mention ever older) ages. Hence the rise of mani-pedi "spa" birthday parties for preschoolers; the heated-up cheers and dance routines of elementary school-age girls; the weeklong "slumber party camp" that promises to teach nine-year-olds "all the tricks of beauty."

In a cruel bait-and-switch, embracing sexualization doesn't even lead to a healthier attitude about sex; quite the opposite. By stressing self-presentation over self-knowledge, girls learn that being desirable is more important than understanding their own desires, needs, and capacities for intimacy and pleasure.

So where does that leave schools? With a mandate to educate—not stigmatize—students. Telling girls to "cover up" just as puberty hits teaches them that their bodies are inappropriate, dangerous, violable, and subject to constant scrutiny and judgment, including by the adults they trust. Nor does it help them understand the culture's role in their wardrobe choices.

After a flurry of parental feedback, my daughter's school is making two changes for next fall. First, the staff is developing lesson plans for students, faculty members, and parents about the impact of sexualization on boys as well as girls. They are also revising the definition of "distracting" apparel. Clothing must allow students a full range of motion—sitting, bending, reaching, running—without requiring perpetual readjustment. It cannot, in other words, pose a "distraction": to the wearer. Beyond that?

It's the families' call, as it should be.

Middle school starts the day after Labor Day, just as Northern California moves into Indian summer, its hottest season. My daughter can hardly wait.

OUR BARBIE VAGINAS, OURSELVES

Young women today are sold the idea that "sexiness" is the same as sexuality, that being desirable is more important than understanding their own desires. Nothing symbolizes that more clearly than the trend toward pubic hair removal, which girls would tell me they did "for myself"—the same girls who told me that they had never masturbated or had an orgasm with a partner. This piece was published in May 2016.

ONE NIGHT NOT LONG AGO WHILE COMING HOME LATE FROM A dinner with friends, I passed frat row near the University of California, Berkeley campus. Groups of girls were clacking along the street in their party uniforms: short skirts, bare midriffs, five-inch heels. One of them stopped and lifted her skirt above her waist, revealing a tiny thong, a flat belly, and some righteously toned glutes. She looked happy and strong, laughing, surrounded by friends, having fun. Then she turned toward a building where two bros, appraising the relative "hotness" of those trying to gain entrée to their party, were posted by the door.

Honestly? I didn't know whether to be impressed or appalled.

I have spent three years interviewing dozens of young women about their attitudes toward and experiences with physical intimacy. On the one hand, girls would enthuse about pop icons like Beyoncé, Gaga, Miley, and Nicki who were actively "taking control" of their sexuality. Whereas earlier generations of feminist-identified women were offended by Kim Kardashian West's "happy #internationalwomensday" tweet and accompanying nude selfie (Instagram caption: "When you're like I have nothing to wear LOL"), many of today's generation talked about it as an expression of her sexuality rather than an exploitation of it—brand promotion done on Kim's own terms.

Young women may not have a million-dollar empire to promote, but they can relate. As one college sophomore told me, she never feels more "liberated" than "when I wear a crop top and my boobs are showing and my legs are showing and I'm wearing super high heels." She added, "I'm proud of my body, and I like to show it off."

But a moment later it became clear that unless, through an accident of genetics or incessant work, you were able to "show off" the right body, the threat of ridicule lurked. The same young woman told me that she wouldn't have worn that outfit a year earlier, when she was twenty-five pounds heavier. It's not that she *couldn't* wear skimpy clothes, but some "asshole-y boys" at the party might call her "a fat girl" and "that would have a very negative impact on my mental state."

Young women talked about feeling simultaneously free to choose a sexualized image—which was nobody's damned business but their own—and having no other choice. "You want to stand out," one college freshman explains. "It's not just about being hot, but who can be the *hottest*."

But as journalist Ariel Levy pointed out in her book *Female Chauvinist Pigs*, "hot" is not the same as "beautiful" or "attractive": it is a narrow, commercialized vision of sexiness that when applied to women, can be reduced to two words: "fuckable" and "sellable." No coincidence, Levy added, that this is "the literal job criteria for stars of the sex industry."

And it may be no coincidence that young people are growing up with far more access to porn than ever before. Which means their early ideas about sex are drawn from fiction that has largely been produced for male masturbation.

Perhaps nowhere is that influence more clear than in the emergence of full-frontal waxing. Once the province of fetishists and, yes, porn stars, the Brazilian moved mainstream in 2000, thanks to *Sex and the City*. ("I feel like one of those freaking hairless dogs!" Carrie complained after visiting an overzealous aesthetician.) In 2003, trendsetter Victoria Beckham declared that Brazilians should be "compulsory" starting at age fifteen. She may get her wish: a study of two universities, published in 2014, found that nearly half of female college students were entirely hairless and just 4 percent went fully *au naturel*.

Most young women I met had been removing their pubic hair—all of it—since they were about fourteen. They cast it as a "personal choice," saying it made them feel "cleaner." Yet, when I pressed further, another darker motivation emerged: avoiding humiliation. "I remember all these boys were telling stories about this girl in high school, how she kind of 'got around,'" one young woman told me. "And people would go down there to finger her, or whatever, and there would be hair, and they were appalled . . . Guys act like they would be *disgusted* by it."

"There's this real sense of shame if you don't have your genitals prepared," agreed Debby Herbenick, an associate professor at Indiana University's School of Public Health. Herbenick studies something called "genital self-image"— how people feel about their private parts. Women's feelings about their genitals have been directly linked to their enjoyment of sex, she told me. In interviews with young women, she found that those who were uncomfortable with their genitalia were not only less sexually satisfied, but also more likely to engage in unprotected sex. Herbenick is concerned that young women's genital self-image is under siege, with more pressure than ever to see their vulvae as unacceptable in their natural state. She recalled a student who started shaving after a boy announced—during one of her class discussions—that he'd never seen pubic hair on a woman in real life, and that if he came across it he'd walk out the door.

There's no question that a bald vulva is baby smooth— some would say disturbingly so. Perhaps in the 1920s, when women first started shaving their legs and armpits, *that* act seemed creepily infantilizing, too, but now depilating those areas is a standard rite of passage. The early wave of hair removal was driven by flapper fashions that displayed a woman's limbs; arms and legs were, for the first time, no longer part of the private realm. Today's pubic hair removal could be seen the same way: we have opened our most intimate parts to unprecedented scrutiny, evaluation, commodification.

Consider: Largely as a result of the Brazilian trend, cosmetic labiaplasty, the clipping of the folds of skin that make up the vulva, has skyrocketed as well. While it's still a small slice of overall cosmetic surgeries, according to the American Society for Aesthetic Plastic Surgery, there was a 16 percent rise in the procedure between 2014 and 2015—following a 49 percent jump the previous year. Labiaplasty is rarely undertaken for sexual function or pleasure; it can actually impede both. Never mind: in 2014, Dr. Michael Edwards, the society's president-elect, hailed the uptick as part of "an ever-evolving concept of beauty and self-confidence." One sought-after look, incidentally, is called—wait for it—the Barbie: a clamshell-type effect, meaning the outer labia appears fused, with no visible labia minora. I trust I don't need to remind the reader that Barbie (a) is made of plastic and (b) has no vagina.

It might be tempting to pass off my concerns as the hand-wringing of an older generation. And if all that sexiness were making for better sex, I might embrace it. Yet while young women talked about dress and depilation as things they did for themselves, when they talked about actual *sex*, that phrase disappeared. Virtually none of the women I met had been told what (or where) a clitoris was. Sex education tends to stick with a woman's internal parts—uteruses, tubes, ovaries. Those classic diagrams of a woman's reproductive system, the ones shaped like the head of a steer, blur into a gray Y between the legs, as if the vulva and the labia, let alone the clitoris, don't exist. Whereas discussion of male puberty includes the emergence of a near-unstoppable sex drive, female puberty is defined by . . . periods and the possibility of unwanted pregnancy. When do we talk to girls about desire and pleasure?

Few of the young women I met had ever had an orgasm with a partner, either, though according to one longitudinal study, the percentage of college women who fake it is on the rise, from less than half in the early 1990s to 69 percent in

2013. Meanwhile, a researcher at the University of Michigan found that when asked to talk about good sex, college men are more likely than women to talk about pleasure while the women are more likely to use their partners' satisfaction to measure their own.

It's not surprising that young women feel powerful when they feel "hot": it's presented to them over and over as a precondition for success. But the truth is that "hot" tells girls that *appearing* sexually confident is more important than actually being confident. And because of that, as often as not the confidence that "hot" confers, comes off with their clothes.

WHEN DID PORN BECOME SEX ED?

The phrase "intimate justice" has become my rallying cry, and I'm so grateful to Dr. Sara McClelland for coining the phrase. Meanwhile, the "glass of water" metaphor actually started out as a latte from Starbucks, but girls would respond, "Well, you have to pay for a latte" so I changed it. Parents tell me both concepts have been of great use in talking with their own daughters about sexual rights, values, and ethics. This piece ran in March 2016, to coincide with the publication of Girls & Sex.

THE OTHER DAY, I GOT AN EMAIL FROM A TWENTY-ONE-YEAR-OLD college senior about sex—or perhaps more correctly, about how ill equipped she was to talk about sex. The abstinence-only curriculum in her middle and high schools had taught her little more than "don't," and she'd told me that although her otherwise liberal parents would have been willing to answer any questions, it was pretty clear the topic made them even more uncomfortable than it made her.

So she had turned to pornography. "There's a lot of problems with porn," she wrote. "But it is kind of nice to be able to use it to gain some knowledge of sex."

I wish I could say her sentiments were unusual, but I heard them repeatedly during the three years I spent interviewing young women in high school and college for a book on girls and sex. In fact, according to a survey of college students in Britain, 60 percent consult pornography, at least in part, as though it were an instruction manual, even as nearly three-quarters say that they know it is as realistic as pro wrestling. (Its depictions of women, meanwhile, are about as accurate as those of the *Real Housewives* franchise.)

The statistics on sexual assault may have forced a national dialogue on consent, but honest conversations between adults and teenagers about what happens *after* yes—discussions about ethics, respect, decision making, sensuality, reciprocity, relationship building, the ability to assert desires and set limits—remain rare. And while we are more often telling children that both parties must agree unequivocally to a sexual encounter, we still tend to avoid the biggest taboo of all: women's capacity for and entitlement to sexual pleasure.

It starts, whether intentionally or not, with parents. When my daughter was a baby, I remember reading somewhere that while labeling infants' body parts ("here's your nose," "here are your toes"), parents often include a boy's genitals but not a girl's. Leaving something unnamed, of course, makes it quite literally unspeakable.

Nor does that silence change much as girls get older. President Obama is trying—finally—in his 2017 budget to remove all federal funding for abstinence education (research has shown repeatedly that the nearly $2 billion spent on it over the past quarter-century may as well have been set on fire). Yet according to the Centers for Disease Control and Prevention, fewer than half of high schools and only a fifth of

middle schools teach all sixteen components the agency rec-
ommends as essential to sex education. Only twenty-three
states mandate sex ed at all; just thirteen require it to be
medically accurate.

Even the most comprehensive classes generally stick with
a woman's internal parts: uteruses, fallopian tubes, ovaries.
When do we explain the miraculous nuances of their anatomy? When do we address exploration, self-knowledge?

No wonder that according to the largest survey on American sexual behavior conducted in decades, published in 2010
in *The Journal of Sexual Medicine*, researchers at Indiana University found only about a third of girls between fourteen and
seventeen reported masturbating regularly and fewer than
half had even tried it once. When I asked about the subject,
girls would tell me, "I have a boyfriend to do that," though, in
addition to placing their pleasure in someone else's hands,
few had ever climaxed with a partner.

Boys, meanwhile, used masturbating on their own as a reason girls should perform oral sex, which was typically not re-
ciprocated. As one of a group of college sophomores informed
me, "Guys will say, 'A hand job is a man job, a blow job is yo'
job.'" The other women nodded their heads in agreement.

Frustrated by such stories, I asked a high school senior
how she would feel if guys expected girls to, say, fetch a glass of
water from the kitchen whenever they were together yet never
(or only grudgingly) offered to do so in return? She burst out
laughing. "Well, I guess when you put it that way," she said.

The rise of oral sex, as well as its demotion to an act less
intimate than intercourse, was among the most significant
transformations in American sexual behavior during the
twentieth century. In the twenty-first, the biggest change

appears to be an increase in anal sex. In 1992, 16 percent of women aged eighteen to twenty-four said they had tried anal sex. Today, according to the Indiana University study, 20 percent of women eighteen to nineteen have, and by ages twenty to twenty-four it's up to 40 percent.

A 2014 study of sixteen- to eighteen-year-old heterosexuals—and can we just pause a moment to consider just how young that is?—published in a British medical journal found that it was mainly boys who pushed for "fifth base," approaching it less as a form of intimacy with a partner (who they assumed would both need to be and could be coerced into it) than a competition with other boys. They expected girls to endure the act, which young women in the study consistently reported as painful. Both sexes blamed the girls themselves for the discomfort, calling them "naive" or "flawed," unable to "relax."

According to Debby Herbenick, director of the Center for Sexual Health Promotion at Indiana University and one of the researchers on its sexual behavior survey, when anal sex is included, 70 percent of women report pain in their sexual encounters. Even when it's not, about a third of young women experience pain, as opposed to about 5 percent of men. What's more, according to Sara McClelland, a psychologist at the University of Michigan, college women are more likely than men to use their partner's physical pleasure as the yardstick for their satisfaction, saying things like "If he's sexually satisfied, then I'm sexually satisfied." Men are more likely to measure satisfaction by their own orgasm.

Professor McClelland writes about sexuality as a matter of "intimate justice." It touches on fundamental issues of gender inequality, economic disparity, violence, bodily integrity, physical and mental health, self-efficacy, and power dynamics in our most personal relationships, whether they last two hours or twenty years. She asks us to consider: Who has the right to engage in sexual behavior? Who has the right to enjoy it? Who is the primary beneficiary of the experience? Who feels deserving? How does each partner define "good enough"? Those are thorny questions when looking at female sexuality at any age, but particularly when considering girls' formative experiences.

We are learning to support girls as they "lean in" educationally and professionally, yet in this most personal of realms, we allow them to topple. It is almost as if parents believe that if they don't tell their daughters that sex should feel good, they won't find out. And perhaps that's correct: they don't, not easily anyway. But the outcome is hardly what adults could have hoped.

What if we went the other way? What if we spoke to kids about sex more instead of less, what if we could normalize it, integrate it into everyday life and shift our thinking in the ways that we (mostly) have about women's public roles? Because the truth is, the more frankly and fully teachers, parents, and doctors talk to young people about sexuality, the more likely kids are both to delay sexual activity and to behave responsibly and ethically when they do engage in it.

Consider a 2010 study published in *The International Journal of Sexual Health* comparing the early experiences of nearly three hundred randomly chosen American and Dutch women at two similar colleges—mostly white, middle class, with similar religious backgrounds. So, apples to apples. The Americans had become sexually active at a younger age than the Dutch, had had more encounters with more partners and were less likely to use birth control. They were also more likely to say that they'd first had intercourse because of pressure from friends or partners.

In subsequent interviews with some of the participants, the Americans, much like the ones I met, described interactions that were "driven by hormones," in which the guys determined relationships, both sexes prioritized male pleasure, and reciprocity was rare. As for the Dutch? Their early sexual activity took place in caring, respectful relationships in which they communicated openly with their partners (whom they said they knew "very well") about what felt good and what didn't, about how far they wanted to go, and about what kind of protection they would need along the way. They reported more comfort with their bodies and their desires than the Americans and were more in touch with their own pleasure.

What's their secret? The Dutch said that teachers and doctors had talked candidly to them about sex, pleasure, and the importance of a mutual trust, even love. More than that, though, there was a stark difference in how their parents approached those topics.

While the survey did not reveal a significant difference in how comfortable parents were talking about sex, the subsequent interviews showed that the American moms had focused on the potential risks and dangers, while their dads, if they said anything at all, stuck to lame jokes.

Dutch parents, by contrast, had talked to their daughters from an early age about both joy and responsibility. As a result, one Dutch woman said she told her mother immediately after she first had intercourse, and that "my friend's mother also asked me how it was, if I had an orgasm, and if he had one."

Meanwhile, according to Amy T. Schalet, an associate

professor of sociology at the University of Massachusetts, Amherst, and the author of *Not under My Roof: Parents, Teens, and the Culture of Sex*, young Dutch men expect to combine sex and love. In interviews, they generally credited their fathers with teaching them that their partners must be equally up for any sexual activity, that the women could (and should) enjoy themselves as much as men, and that as one respondent said, he would be stupid to have sex "with a drunken head." Although Schalet found that young Dutch and American men both often yearned for love, only the Americans considered that a personal quirk.

I thought about all of that recently when, driving home with my daughter, who is now in middle school, we passed a billboard whose giant letters on a neon-orange background read, PORN KILLS LOVE. I asked her if she knew what pornography was. She rolled her eyes and said in that jaded tone that parents of preteenagers know so well, "Yes, Mom, but I've never seen it."

I could've let the matter drop, feeling relieved that she might yet make it to her first kiss unencumbered by those images.

Goodness knows, that would've been easier. Instead I took a deep breath and started the conversation: "I know, honey, but you will, and there are a few things you need to know."

HOW TO BE A MAN IN THE AGE OF TRUMP

The first question I get from audiences after giving a talk about Girls & Sex, *is nearly always, "Would you please write a similar book about boys?" So, after decades of focusing on young women, I am now doing just that: my next project is on boys' attitudes, expectations, and experiences of sex and masculinity. I began well before the 2016 election, before the "grab them by the pussy" tape, and the allegations that Donald Trump had sexually harassed or assaulted multiple women—clearly, when this story ran in October of that year, it was beyond my imagination that he would triumph—but now the work feels more urgent than ever.*

ONE AFTERNOON, WHILE REPORTING FOR A BOOK ON GIRLS' SEXual experience, I sat in on a health class at a progressive Bay Area high school. Toward the end of the session, a blond boy wearing a school athletic jersey raised his hand. "You know that baseball metaphor for sex?" he asked. "Well, in baseball there's a winner and a loser. So who is supposed to be the 'loser' in sex?"

That question has floated back to me over the past ten days as the stream of revelations about Donald J. Trump surfaced: the vile comments he fobbed off as boys will be fifty-nine-year-old boys bluster; the allegations that he jammed his tongue down the throat of a *People* magazine reporter; grabbed the rear of a woman who was visiting his home in Palm Beach; came at a stranger on an airplane "like an octopus"; groped and kissed a former *Apprentice* contestant during a meeting in his office; and barged into the dressing room of the Miss Teen USA pageant on seminude contestants, some of whom were underage.

The reports have sparked unprecedented discussions in the news media of "rape culture" and sexual consent. Except that the discussions aren't really unprecedented. They are part of a cycle of soul-searching that is repeated whenever news of a high-profile incident of alleged harassment or assault breaks—Robert Chambers; the Spur Posse in Lakewood, California; Glen Ridge, New Jersey; Clarence Thomas; William Kennedy Smith; Mike Tyson; Steubenville, Ohio; Bill Cosby; Ray Rice; St. Paul's; Roger Ailes; Brock Turner. In each case, by the time it's over, we turn away from the broader implications toward a more comforting narrative: the perpetrators are exceptions, monsters whom we can isolate, eliminate, and occasionally even prosecute.

Certainly, such behavior is not representative of men, not by a long shot. Yet neither is it entirely atypical. Sexual coercion, in one form or another, is as American as that baseball metaphor—a metaphor that sees girls' limits as a challenge boys should overcome.

For many high school and college women I met, enduring a certain level of manhandling was the ticket to a social life. It started at their first middle school dance, when male classmates would sidle up behind them on the dance floor, grab them by the waist, and, without asking, begin to "grind" against their rears. Sometimes the girls were fine with that, even excited by it. Still, all had, over time, been forced to develop strategies to disengage without offending an unwanted partner—they were, to a girl, deeply concerned with preserving boys' feelings and dignity, even when the reverse was not true.

By college, young women told me, drunken party boys felt free to kiss, touch, and rub up against them at will. "You're supposed to swat them away like flies," a junior at a school in the Northeast explained, adding that the behavior is "just accepted as the way of the world."

I've listened to girls try to make sense of feeling like objects: Was it empowering or the opposite, and under which circumstances? I've also realized—known all along, really—that they were neither the only ones struggling, nor solely responsible for solutions.

Lately, I have begun interviewing young men about their attitudes toward sexuality. Most are not mini-Trumps in the making. Instead, they, too, express confusion, uncertainty: eager to fit in, yet troubled by assumptions and expectations of masculinity. Many are girls' staunchest allies—or would like to be. One nineteen-year-old in Northern California, for instance, told me he'd spent the summer working at a bicycle shop. The all-guy staff whiled away their days talking in what he described as "incredibly degrading ways" about girls. At the printable end of the spectrum, they referred to the cafe down the street, which was entirely staffed by young women, as "the Bitches." As in, "Hey, you want to go grab coffee from the Bitches?"

He didn't participate in such "locker room talk," but neither did he challenge it. "I was just there for the summer," he said. "So I put my head down and did my job." Yet, according to Michael Kimmel, the author of *Guyland* and a sociologist at Stony Brook University, silence in the face of cruelty or sexism "is one of the ways boys *become* men."

I wonder if any of those snickering male staffers on the *Access Hollywood* bus were actually thinking, "Jesus, God, get me out of here." How many reassured themselves, as Billy Bush would later claim, that they were just "playing along" with Mr. Trump? How many more remained mum, believing that made them good guys rather than complicit?

Sometimes coercion is actually part of the script. Mr. Bush's responses to Mr. Trump ("Donald is good! Whoa, my man!" and "Yes, the Donald has scored!") were repugnant, but also reminiscent of the sports narration accompanying the old Meatloaf hit "Paradise by the Dashboard Light": "Holy cow, stolen base."

Recently, when Fox broadcast a live production of the musical *Grease*, a favorite of high school drama clubs, I was struck by the lyrics to "Summer Nights." A chorus of girls, enthralled by Sandy's account of her school break romance, sings: "Tell me more! Tell me more! Was it love at first sight?" A parallel chorus of boys, listening to Danny tell his version, comes back with: "Tell me more! Tell me more! Did she put up a fight?" Despite the progress women have made since the 1950s, when that show was set, or even 1971, when the original musical was written, some things have not changed.

Michelle Obama was right when she said that were Mr. Trump to win the election, we would be "telling our sons that it's okay to humiliate women." While the warning that assault will cost you the presidency may be the beginning of a conversation, it should not be the end. "Don't sexually assault women" (or, for that matter, "Don't get a girl pregnant") is an awfully low bar for acceptable behavior. It does little to address the complexity of boys' lives, the presumption of their always-down-for-it sexuality, the threat of being called a "pussy" if you won't grab one, or the collusion that comes with keeping quiet. Boys need continuing, serious guidance about sexual ethics, reciprocity, and respect. Rather than silence or swagger, they need models of masculinity that are not grounded in domination or aggression.

Last year, California became the first state to make lessons on sexual consent mandatory for high school students. Meanwhile, the Our Whole Lives program—a model for positive, comprehensive sex education that was developed by the Unitarian Universalist Association and the United Church of Christ—encourages students to dismantle stereotypes from a young age. The Population Council's *It's All One Curriculum* offers adolescents lessons about gender, power, and rights within intimate relationships (not for nothing: including those discussions in sex ed has been proven to reduce rates of pregnancy and sexually transmitted infections). And, of course, we can meet kids on their own turf, with clever Internet resources such as the viral video comparing sexual consent to a cup of tea (just because a person wanted tea last week doesn't mean she wants it now; unconscious people never want tea) or "The Sexually Enlightened R&B Song."

Republican leaders and big donors are now distancing themselves from Mr. Trump, piously proclaiming that no one with daughters can in good conscience support him. Who would have guessed that Donald Trump, of all people, would inspire a bipartisan feminist movement? Despite that tasty irony, though, if we see this moment as exclusively about girls' and women's rights, we are bound to repeat the cycle.

Donald Trump (and, for that matter, Billy Bush) have unwittingly provided grist for a more radical, challenging discussion: about what it means—what it should mean, what it could mean—to be a man, a discussion that must continue in public and in our homes long after the candidate himself is told it's game over.

ACKNOWLEDGMENTS

A WRITER IS ONLY AS GOOD AS HER EDITOR AND I'VE BEEN LUCKY enough to work with the best. Thank you to Laurie Abraham, Jane Amsterdam, Bruce Anderson, Lisa Bain, Gillian Blake, Katherine Bouton, Betsy Carter, Sewell Chan, Susan Chumsky, Judith Coyne, Will Dana, Lucy Danziger, Paula Derrow, Lee Eisenberg, the late Clay Felker, Douglas Foster, Deb Futter, Penelope Green, David Hirshey, Sue Horton, the late Nora Kerr, Laura Marmor, Douglas McGray, Mike Mechanic, Chris Miles, Robbie Myers, Peggy Northrop, Karen Rinaldi, Hanna Rosin, the late Duncan Stalker, Ila Stanger, Maria Streshinsky, Vera Titunik, Deborah Way, Doreen Weisenhaus, Anna Wintour, and Patti Wolter. And special love and gratitude to Jennifer Barth, Adam Moss, Aaron Retica, and Ilena Silverman.

I dedicate this book to my husband, Steven Okazaki. Early in our relationship he hosted a champagne brunch to toast my first *New York Times Magazine* cover story. In the twenty-seven years since then, we have celebrated all our successes and weathered all of our losses together. SP, your true partnership has made my work possible and my life a joy.

CREDITS

"A Graphic Life," "The Good Girl," "Thirty-five and Mortal: A Breast Cancer Diary," "The Problem with Pink," "Mourning My Miscarriage," "Baby Lust," "Your Gamete, Myself," "The Femivore's Dilemma," "Children Are Alone," "What's Wrong with Cinderella?," "The Hillary Lesson," "The Fat Trap," "The Battle over Dress Codes," "When Did Porn Become Sex Ed?," and "How to Be a Man in the Age of Trump" all first appeared in the *New York Times*. "*Ms.* Fights for its Life," and "Our Barbie Vaginas, Ourselves" first appeared in *Mother Jones*. "Put to the Test" and "Call of the Wild" first appeared in *MORE*. "The Nonconformist" first appeared in *New York Woman*, "The Story of My Life" in *O: The Oprah Magazine*, "Breast Friends" in *Elle*, "They Don't Make Feminists This Outrageous Anymore" on *Slate*, "The Perfect Mother Trap" in *Redbook*, "Does Father Know Best?" in *Vogue*, "Why Science Must Adapt to Women" in *Discover*, "Bringing Down Baby" in the *Los Angeles Times*, and "Where I Got Daisy" in *Parenting*.

ABOUT THE AUTHOR

PEGGY ORENSTEIN IS THE *NEW YORK TIMES* BESTSELLING AUTHOR OF *Girls & Sex, Cinderella Ate My Daughter, Waiting for Daisy, Flux,* and *Schoolgirls*. A contributing writer for the *New York Times Magazine*, she has been published in *USA Today, Parenting, Salon, The New Yorker*, and other publications, and has contributed commentary to NPR's *All Things Considered* and *PBS NewsHour*. She lives in Northern California with her husband and daughter.